Cover illustrations (from right to left):
Medieval earthworks in Chilton Trinity, Brent Knoll,
Stone Allerton, Montacute House, Newbury Hill

Aspects of

THE MEDIÆVAL LANDSCAPE
of SOMERSET

&

Contributions to the landscape history of the county

Edited by MICHAEL ASTON

Published by Somerset County Council 1988
Design & artwork by Peter Webb
Text set in 9/10pt Times Roman by Bigwood & Staple Ltd.
Display Headings Garamond and Garamond Italic
Printed by Bigwood & Staple Ltd., Bridgwater, Somerset
© Somerset County Council 1988

ISBN 0 86183 129 2

Frontispiece:
Carved benchends from North Cadbury Church dated 1538

FOREWORD

Many of the traditional features of the landscape which characterise the Somerset countryside today have their origins in the medieval period. The scatter of farms and small villages in the west, the larger and 'typically English' villages of the south and east typify the rural nature of the county. Within the physical constraints of its geology, soils, vegetation and climate, the landscape of Somerset has been adapted, managed and farmed to suit man's own particular local requirements.

Our county contains many memorable and beautiful landscapes. There are the broad flat wetlands of the Levels and Moors, on the one hand, and the open moorlands of Exmoor on the other. The upland landscapes of the Quantocks and Mendip Hills have unique environments, each with its own particular history. The broad open areas, the field systems, the woods and parks form the essential characteristics of the Somerset scene, but with today's demands for further development, coupled with the lessening agricultural requirements upon the land, there needs to be constant vigilance if the essential character of the landscapes are to be retained.

It is in order to set out new initiatives for the protection of our landscape that this book is so valuable. It gives us an insight and understanding into the richness of our historic countryside, one which the County Council, along with many others, is anxious to preserve and conserve for future generations.

It is the County Council's intention to publish information which will draw the attention of both residents and an increasing number of visitors to Somerset's heritage. This book is an attempt to help in that educational process by concentrating on certain aspects of the medieval landscape. A notable gap in this collection of essays is a chapter on historic buildings but this is a deliberate omission since this will be a subject covered in a detailed publication at a future date.

The publication of this book follows the successful format of **Christianity in Somerset** (1976) edited by Robert Dunning and **The Archaeology of Somerset** edited by Michael Aston and Ian Burrow which appeared in 1982.

Like **The Archaeology of Somerset**, this volume arose from a conference organised by Michael Aston of the Extra-Mural Department of Bristol University which was held at Dillington House in 1983. I am most grateful for the collaboration of the University in the preparation of this volume and hope co-operation of this kind can continue to the benefit of the people of Somerset and the environment in which they live.

Ralph Clark

Chairman of the County Council

7

EDITOR'S PREFACE

This book grew out of a conference held at Dillington College on 18–20 March 1983. Originally it was intended to develop themes first outlined in Michael Havinden's book **The Somerset Landscape** published in 1981 by Hodder and Stoughton in The Making of the English Landscape Series edited by W G Hoskins. Thus it was intended to include chapters on prehistoric and Roman themes as well as the on the post-medieval period. In the end it has only proved possible to put together the medieval section and so, rather than delay further, the Libraries Department with the assistance of the Planning Department of Somerset County Council decided to go ahead and publish what was to hand.

Unlike archaeology there are only a few people working on the archaeology and history of the landscape in Somerset, although in closely related areas, such as the compilation of parish surveys and the preparation of the topographical volumes of the Victoria County History of Somerset, a great deal of research is progressing.

At present much of the work on the county's landscape is being conducted by members of the Extra-Mural Department of Bristol University, as will be seen from the list of contributors, although newcomers to the county, such as James Bond, Robert Croft and Christopher Gerrard, will no doubt add much in future years.

This present volume follows very closely the format and layout of several volumes recently published by the County Council—**Christianity in Somerset** (1976) edited by Robert Dunning and **The Archaeology of Somerset** (1982) edited by Michael Aston and Ian Burrow. In the latter it was stated in the editors' preface that *'landscape archaeology'* would form another useful volume and it was hoped that this would be produced later: this volume I hope will form a modest contribution to the study of landscape archaeology in the county.

Inevitably the contents of such a volume will vary a great deal and other chapters could have been included. There is, for example, little on castles, monasteries or domestic buildings and nothing on communications or industrial activities. It is to be hoped, however, that much of use and interest will be found here. Although the central theme is the middle ages no contributor has felt restricted to that period alone. Thus there is much of relevance to those interested in the prehistoric, Roman and indeed post-medieval periods in this book as well.

The chapters included here show that most of the major themes of the landscape archaeology of post-Roman Somerset are being considered at the moment. The disposition of the wildwood and forests and their relationship to settlements is considered by Oliver Rackham while Michael Costen shows the well-developed state of the landscape by the time of the compilation of Domesday Book in 1086. In the middle ages there is no doubt that the presence of the Church, as an institution, would have been felt everywhere and Joe Bettey clearly demonstrates this. Nevertheless, the lives of most medieval people were dominated by the major elements of the landscape, the settlements where people lived, and the land around them; their horizons were probably limited to an extent which we find difficult to appreciate today.

After the medieval period, but beginning during it, the landscape was changed in many ways. In a largely non-industrial county like Somerset, at least not industrialised like the Black Country or the West Riding of Yorkshire, the development of parks and gardens was merely one of these changes, here described by John Harvey. Somerset proves to have been in the forefront of many national developments in gardens and landscaping.

Consistent themes emerge in all the aspects covered in this volume. The influence of major landowners and institutions in shaping the development of the landscape in all its aspects is evident all through this period. The influence of the Church as an institution is particularly important in the Middle Ages.

At lower levels in society continuity is the order of the day. Changes are gradual while all the time the activities of the farming year persist as a perpetual background.

Readers will appreciate that there are still matters of great debate about many aspects of the Somerset landscape. Differing interpretations can be seen particularly in the chapters by John Harvey, Michael Costen and Oliver Rackham. The editor felt that differing viewpoints and conclusions showed a healthy state of debate in the subject.

The local government changes of 1974 pose a slight problem for a work of this kind. Some of the authors found it difficult to ignore examples formerly in north Somerset but now lying in south Avon. The editor has not been too vigorous or insistent about this and hence much of interest will be found here for those people living in south Avon.

A work of this kind involves many people. I am grateful to my fellow contributors for writing interim reports on what is generally ongoing research. This volume would never have been prepared without the encouragement of the Publication Liaison Group of Somerset County Council and in particular David Bromwich and Robert Dunning. David Bromwich helped with references and bibliographical details with his customary efficiency and good cheer; Robert Dunning suggested the shortened version of the intended original, thereby ensuring the completion of this book. It is a pleasure also to acknowledge the help of Professor Edward Thomas, Director, and Frank Walthew, Assistant Director, of the Extra-Mural Department, Bristol University and to Eric Barnett, County Planning Officer, and Tony Haskell, Deputy County Planning Officer, for their support in many ways.

Officers of the County Planning Department undertook the preparation of the text, illustrations and the design of the publication. I am particularly grateful to Peter Webb and Bob Winn.

Bob Croft, Ken Brown, Russell Lillford and Robert Dunning all assisted with editorial help and advice for which I am most grateful.

Acknowledgement of other help and assistance to individual authors is given where appropriate at the end of each chapter. I would like to extend my thanks to those who assisted the individual authors.

Once a volume like this is completed all sorts of new and exciting possibilities are shown up for consideration as future projects. The pre-medieval landscape, Somerset's Industrial history, Somerset's rich heritage of domestic buildings and so on would all make admirable future volumes complementing those produced so far. It is to be hoped that the County Council will continue to see their role of interesting and enlightening the inhabitants of the county and its visitors as an important one in the future and that some of these other titles will eventually see the light of day.

Notes are given at the end of each chapter.

References, given in the text in the Harvard system (author and date), are gathered together in the Bibliography at the end.

The lightly shaded area on the county maps was north Somerset but is now in the county of Avon.

Michael Aston

CONTRIBUTORS

Michael Aston BA FSA MIFA
Staff Tutor In Archaeology,
Extra-Mural Department, University of Bristol

Joseph Bettey MA PhD FSA
Staff Tutor In Local History,
Senior Lecturer in Adult Education,
Extra-Mural Department, University of Bristol

Kenneth Brown BA, DipLA, AILA
Principal Planning Officer (Countryside),
County Planning Department, Somerset County Council

Michael Costen MA DMS
Resident Tutor for Somerset,
Extra-Mural Department, University of Bristol

Robert Croft BA MIFA
Field Archaeologist,
County Planning Department, Somerset County Council

John Harvey D.Univ(York) FSA FRSL FSG
formerly Hon Archivist, Winchester College,
and past President of the Garden History Society

Russell Lillford DipTP ARICS MRTPI FRSA
Principal Planning Officer (Conservation),
County Planning Department, Somerset County Council

Oliver Rackham PhD
Fellow of Corpus Christ College, Cambridge and
School of Botany, University of Cambridge

ACKNOWLEDGEMENTS

Somerset County Council 1.1, 1.6, 2.1, 3.1, 3.2, 3.3, 3.5,
3.7, 3.8, 3.11, 3.13, 3.14, 3.15, 3.16, 4.3d, 5.1, 6.6, 7.1,
7.3, 7.4, 7.5, 7.11, 7.13, 7.14, 7.15, frontispiece
Michael Aston 1.5, 1.9, 1.10, 2.3, 4.2, 4.7, 4.8, 5.2, 6.4,
6.5, 7.7, 7.8, Cover photographs
Corpus Christi College, Oxford 1.11, 2.7
Joseph Bettey 3.9
Christopher Gerrard 3.12, 4.4, 4.5
Peter Webb 3.10, 7.12
County Records Office 4.1, 6.1
John Hardwick 5.3
Bodleian Library, Oxford 6.3
Alan Wilson 7.6
Cambridge University Collection 7.9

CONTENTS

FOREWORD 7

EDITOR'S PREFACE 8

CONTRIBUTORS 10

ACKNOWLEDGEMENTS 10

Chapter 1 WOODS, HEDGES *and* FORESTS   *Oliver Rackham* 13

Chapter 2 THE LATE SAXON LANDSCAPE   *The evidence from charters and placenames   Michael Costen* 33

Chapter 3 THE CHURCH *in the* LANDSCAPE   *Part 1 The Anglo-Saxon period   Michael Costen* 49

Part 2 From the Norman Conquest to the Reformation   Joseph Bettey 55

Chapter 4 SETTLEMENT PATTERNS *and* FORMS   *Michael Aston* 67

Chapter 5 LAND USE *and* FIELD SYSTEMS   *Michael Aston* 83

Chapter 6 PARKS, GARDENS *and* LANDSCAPING   *John Harvey* 99

Chapter 7 CONSERVING *the* HISTORIC LANDSCAPE   *Kenneth Brown, Robert Croft and Russell Lillford* 109

BIBLIOGRAPHY 128

INDEX 133

Chapter 1
WOODS, HEDGES *and* FORESTS
Oliver Rackham

*I*n the millennia following the last Ice Age, trees
returned to Britain and came to form a series of
wholly natural forests known as **wildwood.** Wildwoods
covered virtually the whole of Somerset, except the wettest
parts of the Levels, from roughly 12,000 to 4500 BC
(Note 1).

With the coming of civilization in the Neolithic period,
the wildwood began to be transformed into the cultural
landscape of farmland, moorland, woods, and hedges that
we now have. Apart from such obvious artefacts as avenues,
forestry plantations, and orchards, trees form part of the
cultural landscape in three separate ways *(Rackham 1976).*

Woods

Woodland is managed by the tradition of **woodmanship,**
making use of the property that most British trees have of
growing again when cut down. Woods are normally
coppices. The majority of the trees, called **underwood,** are
cut to near the ground every four to twenty years to yield a
crop of **wood** in the form of rods or poles, used for fuel
and for many more specialized purposes. After felling,
most species sprout from the stump, which becomes a
stool, yielding an indefinite succession of further crops of
underwood (Fig. 1.2). Some trees, such as aspen and some
elms, instead sprout by **suckers** from the roots. Scattered
among the stools there may be **timber** trees, which are left
standing for several rotations of the underwood and are
then felled to make beams and planks; usually oak is
selected for this purpose, though it can be treated as
underwood as well.

Woods are self-renewing and permanent: planting trees

1.1 *Adcombe Wood in 1988, a scenically important
ancient oak wood*

1.2   Ways of managing trees

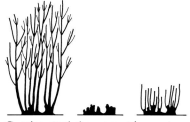
Coppice, stool above ground

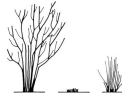
Coppice, stool below ground

Suckers

bolling

Pollard

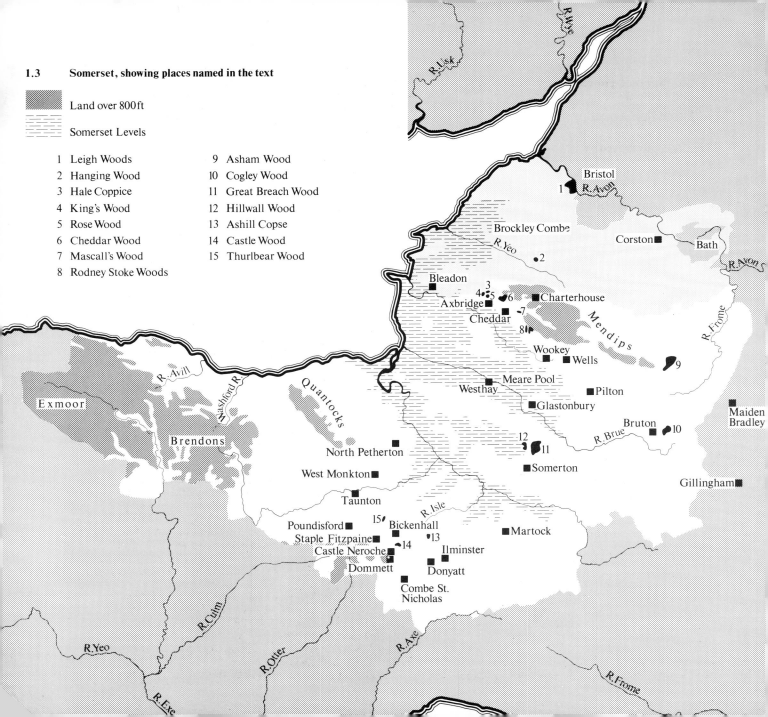

1.3 **Somerset, showing places named in the text**

Land over 800 ft

Somerset Levels

1 Leigh Woods
2 Hanging Wood
3 Hale Coppice
4 King's Wood
5 Rose Wood
6 Cheddar Wood
7 Mascall's Wood
8 Rodney Stoke Woods
9 Asham Wood
10 Cogley Wood
11 Great Breach Wood
12 Hillwall Wood
13 Ashill Copse
14 Castle Wood
15 Thurlbear Wood

is not a usual (nor indeed a practical) part of woodmanship. They need protection from cattle, sheep, and deer which would eat the young shoots: much attention has always been paid to defining and fencing wood boundaries, which are often delimited by an earthwork called a **woodbank**.

Woodland is not destroyed by cutting down or using up the trees, but by some action to prevent the trees from growing again: by grubbing out the stumps to make farmland, or by long-continued grazing destroying successive generations of saplings and regrowth. (British trees, except perhaps pine, cannot be destroyed by fire.)

Any piece of land which is not periodically tilled, grazed, or burnt is invaded by trees and turns into **secondary woodland**. This is a common process in modern Somerset, especially the Levels and Mendips, and has probably happened in past periods of agricultural neglect.

Wood-pastures and Forests

Use of the same land for trees and for grazing animals is self-contradictory, unless we keep monkeys. The shade of the trees is bad for the pasture, and the livestock eat the regrowth of the trees. When they have to be reconciled, there exist definite techniques of **wood-pasture** management: for instance by not coppicing trees but **pollarding** them, cutting at 8–10 ft above ground so that the livestock cannot reach the young shoots.

Wood-pasture goes back, as a separate tradition from woodmanship, at least to Anglo-Saxon times. The earliest wood-pastures were **wooded commons**, land on which there were common-rights of pasture and sometimes also of cutting wood (rarely timber).

After the Norman Conquest there developed two special forms of wood-pasture connected with the husbandry of deer. A **park** was a piece of private land, usually wood-pasture, on which the owner kept deer, confined by a deer-proof wall or a special fence called a **park pale**. A **Forest** was a common on which, in addition to the rights of landowners and commoners, the king (or some other magnate) had the right to keep deer and to make by-laws and to set up a bureaucracy, ostensibly for protecting the deer. A Forest had no perimeter fence, and the deer stayed by force of habit. To the medievals **a Forest was a place of deer, not necessarily of trees**. Some Somerset Forests were wooded and others not.

Hedges and farmland trees

The third tradition, of hedges, hedgerow trees, and trees in fields and around farmsteads, also goes back at least to Anglo-Saxon times. These might seem to be highly artificial features of the landscape, in contrast to the balance of natural processes and human activities which is displayed in woods and wood-pastures. The tradition of planting hedges and non-woodland trees is much older than that of planting in woods *(Rackham 1986 p 224)*, but is not the whole story. Any fence or field-boundary will turn into a hedge by natural invasion unless carefully prevented from doing so. (The United States has little tradition of hedge-planting, yet has at least a million miles of hedge.) Hedges may reflect past neglect as well as action.

Somerset and the Three Landscapes *(Rackham 1986 Chapter 1)*

Somerset lies across the boundary between the Highland and Lowland Zones. The Quantock and Brendon Hills and Exmoor, with their moorland, oakwoods, and mountain way of life, are sharply set off from the rest of the county. Somerset is bisected also by a more subtle but no less important frontier, that between the Planned Countryside of the Midlands and the Ancient Countryside of the outer parts of Lowland England. Much of Somerset is the latter—an intricate land of hamlets, scattered farms, small woods, winding lanes, and ancient hedges. But particularly in the north and south-east, there are also open, Midland-like landscapes of big villages, few roads, flimsy modern hedges, and straight lines—their present form is the result of abolishing open-field strip-cultivation in the eighteenth and nineteenth centuries.

WILDWOOD

After the last glaciation, birch, pine, and hazel migrated into the British Isles and were followed by other trees to create various kinds of wildwood. There was a long period of stability, ending with the coming of Neolithic men. What wildwoods were there in Somerset just before civilization took a hand? Direct evidence comes from five pollen analyses, all from the Levels *(Note 2)*.

The Levels themselves, where not too wet, were covered with fen woods of birch and alder, whose stumps are found in the peat. The peat contains the pollens of these trees, and also of others which evidently grew on the surrounding upland and islands. In Fig. 1.4 I have extracted the figures relating to 'dry-land' trees, and have adjusted them for the fact that some trees produce more pollen than others *(Note 3)*.

The most abundant dry-land tree was small-leaved lime,

1.4 *Comparison of dry-land tree species in Somerset wildwood, in Neolithic woodwork, and in ancient woods as now extant. (Figures are percentages.[a])*

	Wildwood just before Elm Decline[b]			Wildwood just after Elm Decline[b]			Sweet Track[c]	Surviving ancient woods[d]
	Westhay	Glastonbury	Mean of 5 sites	Westhay	Glastonbury	Mean of 5 sites		
Hazel	5	16	19	5	36	34	34	30
Ash	—	—	2	—	—	4	12	25
Lime	26	53	35	28	31	25	5	35
Oak	34	12	17	50	26	24	25	7
Elm	34	16	26	18	5	12	8	1[e]
Pine	1	2	2	0.2	2	1	—	planted only
Beech	—	—	—[f]	—	—	0.1	—	planted only
Holly	—	—	—	—	—	—[f]	10	local
Aspen[g]	—	—	—	—	—	—	2	rare
Hornbeam	—	—	—	—	—	—[f]	1	—
Dogwood[h]	—	—	—	—	—	—	1	local
Ivy	—	—	—[f]	—	—	—[f]	1	locally abundant
Yew	—	—	—	—	—	—	rare	not native
Crab[h]	—	—	—	—	—	—	0.6	rare
Maple[h]	—	—	—	—	—	—	—	2

[a] Alder, willow (or sallow), and birch are omitted throughout because, at least in part, they represent wetland woods.
[b] Mean of: Westhay (Clapham and Godwin 1948), Tollgate House (Godwin 1960), Meare Pool (Godwin 1956), Glastonbury Lake Village (Godwin 1956), Drake's Drove (Godwin 1956).
[c] Estimate of mean abundance (in terms of number of pieces) at ten major points of excavation (Orme and Coles 1985).
[d] Mean of: Hale Coppice, Rose Wood, King's Wood, Mascall's Wood, Cheddar Wood.
[e] Before the present Dutch Elm Disease.
[f] Probably occurred elsewhere in Somerset.
[g] Pollen is not easily preserved.
[h] Produces little pollen.

Tilia cordata, which was the commonest tree at three sites and the third commonest at the other two. The next was some species of elm, followed by hazel and oak. In general the dry-land wildwood around the Levels was about one-third lime, one-quarter elm, one-fifth each of hazel and oak, with occasional ash. Pine may have been a fen tree or may represent pollen blown from distant pinewoods.

Somerset wildwood cannot have been a simple mixture of trees, as witness the difference between the Westhay and Glastonbury samples. It will have shown regional and local variation, depending on differences of soil and climate (*Rackham 1986a*). Hazel does not produce pollen if shaded by taller species; although it could grow into a biggish tree (it still does in Hillwall Wood, Compton Dundon), it could not have kept up with the very tall, densely-shading lime. Abundant hazel pollen therefore implies areas of hazelwood without lime.

From this evidence, eked out by analogy with other parts of Great Britain, I reconstruct at least three wildwood regions in Somerset:
1—The Levels, with fen birchwoods and alderwoods.
2—The upland, a mosaic of limewoods and hazelwoods (probably with a scatter of oaks), elmwoods on the most fertile soils, and patches of ashwood. This was

part of the Lime Province of Lowland England
(Rackham 1986 p 70).

3—The western highlands, which would be expected to
have belonged to the Oak–Hazel Province of Highland
England, with oakwoods on the less fertile and
hazelwoods on the more fertile soils and probably also
some elm.

Little is known of the structure of wildwood. Unlike the
managed woods of historic times, it included old
upstanding trees and fallen logs. Excavations in the Levels
have revealed a rich beetle fauna, including many species
now confined to those wood-pastures that still have
ancient trees, and some now extinct in Britain *(Girling 1985).*

THE NEOLITHIC AND THE BEGINNINGS OF WOODMANSHIP

The beginnings of agriculture, in about 4500 BC, are
recognized in pollen diagrams by a sudden decline of elm.
Around the Levels (Fig. 1.4) elm fell to less than half its
previous abundance; there was a less abrupt decline in
lime, leaving hazel as the most abundant tree. The Elm
Decline may have been due to the inadvertent letting-loose
of Elm Disease *(Rackham 1980 p 265–6).* The result was an
upland wildwood about one-third of hazel, a quarter each
of oak and lime, one-tenth of elm, and 4 per cent of ash,
with traces of beech.

The Somerset Levels contain the earliest evidence in
Britain, and perhaps in the world, of the systematic
management of woodland, which was an integral part of
our earliest settled civilization. Products of woodmanship
are preserved in trackways and similar structures now
buried in the peat. At present 36 of these are known,
dating from the Neolithic onwards *(Orme and Coles 1985).*

Simple trackways (e.g. the Bronze Age 'Tinney's
Ground') are made merely of birch and alder branchwood,
presumably the boughs of trees growing on or near the
spot, their trunks used for some other purpose. Others are
made of split logs of timber size; these may be alder billets
(e.g. the Neolithic 'Abbot's Way'), or else planks cleft
from oak trunks brought from the upland (the Bronze Age
'Meare Heath Track'). More elaborate trackways show a
definite understanding of the growth and selection of
underwood.

The earliest of all, the 'Sweet Track' (c.4000 BC), is the
most elaborate as regards both carpentry and
woodmanship. It is a mile long, made of oak, ash, and lime
planks and of rods and poles of various sizes and species
(Fig. 1.4). Alder and birch poles could have grown locally,

1.5 *The 'Abbot's Way' trackway*

17

but most of the wood is of dry-land trees and must have been brought from at least as far as the upland at either end of the trackway. The rods and poles are of many species and suggest a mixed coppice-wood. Planks (mainly oak) could have come either from wildwood or from timber trees within the coppice. Compared with the post-Elm-Decline pollen record, oak and hazel occur in about the proportions to be expected; ash is a little over-represented; there is vastly less lime and a little less elm than there should be. There is also abundant holly, of which only the occasional pollen grain has been found, and several other trees such as *Populus* (probably aspen) which are not in the pollen record at all. Some of the discrepancies may be due to chance variations in the local wildwood: the composition of the track varies along its length. But the over-representation of holly—which, although a poor producer of pollen, appears in many diagrams elsewhere—implies that it was preferred for the specific purpose of making pegs. The scarcity of lime and maybe of elm suggests that these trees were selected against, perhaps because they were more highly valued for some other use.

Hurdle-ways begin in the Middle Neolithic (e.g. 'Walton Heath' and 'Rowland's' Tracks, 3100 BC). They are of hurdles laid down to form walkways, constructed of interwoven rods much as in a medieval or modern wattle hurdle, save for such differences as result from using stone tools *(Coles and Orme 1977)*. The rods are nearly all hazel, with occasional ash, alder, birch, and willow. They are of very even size—without metal tools the thicker ones could not have been split—and hence vary in age (4 to 10 years' growth). They were apparently grown in a hazel-wood with occasional ash and other species (like Hale Coppice, Winscombe, today) and managed mainly by coppicing, though I have found occasional indications of pollarding *(Rackham 1977)*. The technique was more elaborate than modern coppicing. Some rods were cut and others left to grow on; many had had their tops cut off, and allowed to grow again, part-way through the coppice cycle; much of the cutting was done in summer. A main purpose of the coppices may have been to grow leaves for feeding livestock (as is still done in the Alps), wood being something of a by-product.

LATER PREHISTORY
Down the millennia men continued to grub out trees and to extend fields and pastures. They continued also to manage woods: the marks of bronze and iron axes are found on the wood of later trackways.

The pollen record shows a continuing gradual decline of lime, doubtless because it grew on soils which were more worth cultivating. The apparent increase of hazel, compared with the original wildwood, may be a consequence of coppicing. Hazel starts to produce pollen only two years after felling, whereas most other trees take at least eight years. In the longer term, coppicing may also encourage hazel actually to increase, by freeing it from the competition of taller trees.

By the Iron Age at latest, settlement had penetrated to every part of Somerset and there cannot have been much wildwood remaining. As the woods shrank, demands on them increased; conservation, which could hardly have been a motive for Neolithic woodmanship, would have become a consideration. By Roman times, Somerset had a

1.6 *Cheddar Gorge in 1971*

dense, partly urban population. Lake villages, timber-framed villas, 'wattle huts', hypocausts, ironworks, lead-smelting, potting, and many less obvious uses suggest that whatever woodland still remained must have been highly organized to yield a continuous supply of wood and timber. Whether the distinction between woodland and wood-pasture yet existed I cannot say.

It is not known when hedges first appear. They may well have been a feature of all permanent field boundaries, right back to the Neolithic, unless farmers spent time in preventing them from growing. Hedges were planted by the Romans in Italy, and evidence is occasionally found that they existed around Iron Age and Roman fields in Britain *(Robinson 1978; Boyd 1984)*. We should probably assume that prehistoric Somerset was a hedged landscape until the contrary is proved.

ANGLO-SAXON SOMERSET
The charters
Somerset is rich in Old English charters, title-deeds of land which define estates by perambulating their boundaries. There exist 74 perambulations, scattered over the whole county including the Levels, and mentioning a total of 1362 boundary features—one-eleventh of all the charter evidence in England. They portray the landscape mainly of the ninth and tenth centuries AD.

Somerset was not a very wooded county. Woods are mentioned 41 times, making 3.0 per cent of all boundary features, and there are a further 12 places named after woods. These figures are close to the average for England as a whole *(Rackham 1986 p 80)*. The terms for woodland include *wudu* 'wood', *graf* 'grove', *hangra* 'hanger', and less familiar ones such as *bearu, scaga*, and *hyrst*; I shall not try to guess what different sorts of wood were meant. Many of the woods have their own proper names, such as *Catschaga* 'Cat-shaw' in the Ilminster bounds dated 725 *(Bates 1899)* and *Duddincg Bearuðu* in the Taunton bounds of 854 *(Birch 1885–93 no. 476)*. The word *wyrtruma*, which appears to mean a woodbank *(Rackham 1986 p 82)*, is specially common in Somerset, occurring 20 times (e.g. 'the *wyrtruma* of Loxan Wood') at Bleadon in 956 *(Birch 1885–93 no. 959)*.

Hedges are mentioned under such terms as *haga* and *hege* 'hedge' and *hegerœwe*. In all they occur 29 times, 2.1 per cent of all boundary features (for example an 'old hedgerow' at Pilton, apparently early eighth century *(Birch 1885–93 no. 112)*. There are also three places named after hedges. The proportion is close to the average for England

(Rackham 1986 p 185–6); little above average in the Mendips and a little below average in the Levels, where watercourses provided many boundaries. Field-walls are rarely mentioned in Old English charters and are a speciality of the Mendips, where there are nine references, such as the 'old stone wall' at Corston in 941 *(Birch 1885–93 no. 767)*.

There are 81 mentions of trees (5.9 per cent of all boundary features), plus 42 places named after trees. A few were remarkable, such as *'the ash which the ignorant call sacred'* (Taunton, 854 *(Birch 1885–93 no. 476)*), but most seem to have been ordinary hedgerow and farmland trees. About a quarter of all the trees chosen for boundary points were thorns, the next commonest being 'apple' (probably crab), then ash, oak, elm *(wice)*, followed by alder, elder, and maple. In general this is close to the average for England, except that thorn is less abundantly named than usual, and elm and ash more abundantly (especially elm in the Mendips) *(Rackham 1986 p 209–15)*.

The words *furlang* 'furlong', *œcer* 'acre', *gar* 'triangle', *heafod* 'head(land)', *hlinc* 'baulk', and *foryrþ* appear to indicate open-field cultivation *(Rackham 1986 p 173–5)*. They form 3.9 per cent of all boundary features in the Mendips, which is below the average for England; in the rest of Somerset they are rare (0.9 per cent).

Somerset in c.900 may have looked not unlike Hampshire a thousand years later. Perhaps one-eighth was woodland: there was more woodland (especially in the Mendips) than in contemporary Wiltshire or Devon. Hedges were common, though less common than in north-west Dorset at the time. There were many hedgerow and downland trees, though not as many as in the Cotswolds. The making of open-fields (the 'De-Enclosure Movement') had reached the Mendips, but was not as advanced as in Berkshire or south Wiltshire; in the rest of Somerset it is doubtful whether strip-cultivation as yet existed at all.

The hunt of King Edmund the Magnificent
How much of the landscape of the charters has survived into our own time remains to be explored. As in other parts of England, a large minority of the woods and at least a few hedges ought still to be extant. An instance is the earliest wood named in Somerset, *'the famous wood which is called Cantacuudu'*, in the apparently seventh-century charter of West Monkton *(Birch 1885–93 no. 62)*. Quantockwood was still a great wood until overrun by twentieth-century forestry plantations.

A fragment of tenth-century topography is preserved in the **Life of St Dunstan**. Following a meet of hounds at Cheddar Palace

> *The King and his men . . . came to the woods to hunt, and took various footpaths through byways in the groves. And now, because of the multifarious din of hornblowers and baying of hounds, a number of harts began to run nimbly away. The King alone, with the pack of hounds, chose one of them to hunt by himself; and he eventually tired it out by the agility of his horse by pursuing it with the hounds through various byways. Now there is, in a place very near Cheddar, a certain precipice, one among many others on a steep mountain, of marvellous and immense height; to which this hart . . . came in its flight; and it plunged headlong from the top of this precipice together with the hounds following it, and they rushed together to death and were ground to particles. . . . The King following, seeing the precipice, tried as hard as his strength allowed to stop the gathering speed of his horse. But because he was contumacious in the neck and stiff-necked he could not.*

(He repented of his previous rudeness to St Dunstan and miraculously)

> *stopped the horse . . . on a tussock on the brink of the precipice, when the forefeet of the horse were almost rushing to the bottom of the gulf. . . . (Stubbs 1874).*

The king's repentance took the form of making the young Dunstan abbot of Glastonbury, which took place c.944. This Life was written c.1000.

A local writer, Eadmer, recounting the incident a century after this, says more about the topography:

> *Now this wood occupies a mountain of great height: this mountain is divided at its summit and displays to the spectator a huge precipice and dreadful abyss (Stubbs 1874).*

The better-known but much later version of the story, in the **Axbridge Chronicle**, quotes from Eadmer; the reviser says that the chasm is called Cedderclyff—the old name for the Gorge—and adds that the place was a Forest, forgetting that Anglo-Saxon kings had no Forests (Smirke 1866). Although presented by pious biographers as a punitive miracle on behalf of St Dunstan, the story is not improbable: another hart fell into Cheddar Gorge in 1240 (Cox and Greswell 1911) and the same disaster befel the Wells Harriers in 1895 (Athill 1976).

The existence of a big wood on both sides of Cheddar Gorge is confirmed by Domesday Book, which assigns $2 \times \frac{1}{2}$ leagues (3 by $\frac{3}{4}$ miles) of woodland to Cheddar. The Compton Bishop boundary, attached to a grant just post-Conquest, has a separate little perambulation for a detached 'wood' on the east side of Cheddar cumbe- (Grundy 1927–34). The present Mascall's, Cheddar, and possibly Rose Woods are therefore parts of what was a continuous great wood covering all the heights of Cheddar and Axbridge; although by the tenth century it was, in part, reduced to such a wood as a king could ride through at speed.

DOMESDAY BOOK

The great survey of 1086 records 538 woods in Somerset, either by acreage or in the form '*x* leagues long and *y* leagues wide'—a league being $1\frac{1}{2}$ miles. These add up to 11 per cent of the county, compared with 15 per cent for England as a whole (Note 4). Somerset had a multitude of small woods, half of them smaller than 35 acres. The biggest wood assigned to a single place is 5×1 leagues at Bruton—probably the Somerset share of Selwood.

Woods were generally distributed through Somerset, but there were few in the Levels and on Exmoor (Fig. 1.7). They were not always located in the places to which they belonged; as we have seen, Compton Bishop's wood was five miles away.

The Neroche area was a classic example of detached woodland. Around Castle Neroche, south of Taunton, the Domesday record has a curious lacuna—a blank area with only a few small settlements. A few miles to the east, there is an excess of recording around Ilminster, with big settlements whose farmland and woodland totals are too much for the space available. The excess and the deficiency cancel each other out. As we know from later records and parish boundaries, seven of the eastward places had detached portions in the Neroche area. Most of the woodland appears to have been in the exclaves and nearly all the farmland around the parent settlements. Some woodland exclaves later grew into settlements of their own: for instance, Westcombland began as a detached portion of Martock, 14 miles away. We do not know how far they had developed by 1086. All the woodland belonging to places within the Neroche area or on its edge or having exclaves adds up to some 17,600 acreas—about three-quarters the extent of the modern Forest of Dean (Rackham 1980 p 115). This was the biggest tract of woodland between Salisbury and Land's End.

Domesday does not systematically record the uses of woodland. Frequent mentions of underwood, *silua minuta*, imply coppicing. A fuel-using industry is implied by five places where rents were paid in blooms of iron (including Bickenhall in Neroche).

By the eleventh century, woodland was quite a scarce resource in Somerset: some 30 per cent of settlements did not have any. All but the biggest woods are likely to have been highly valued, clearly defined, and intensively used. This state of affairs was probably not recent: the arrangements for apportioning Neroche among distant townships appear to have been devised by the Anglo-Saxons to deal with an inconvenient distribution of woodland left them by their predecessors.

FORESTS

The six and a half royal Forests of medieval Somerset are an excellent example of the purpose, meaning, and operation of Forests, and a counter-example to many pseudo-historical myths. Forests were not necessarily wooded: of those in Somerset, only Neroche and the half-Forest of Selwood can clearly be shown to have had more woodland than the rest of the county, whereas Exmoor and Somerton were not wooded. Nor were they hunting preserves of the king. The only place in Somerset where a king could stay was Cheddar Palace; after it fell into disuse, c.1300, kings seldom if ever set foot in the county.

Forests were a Norman introduction. A few are mentioned in Domesday Book. Their numbers were added

1.7 Woodland in and around Somerset in 1086
The size of each black circle represents, at the scale of the map, the total area of woodland recorded by Domesday Book for places located within the 10km square. Woodland recorded for places in the square marked N (the Neroche anomaly) has been mapped in the next square to the west.

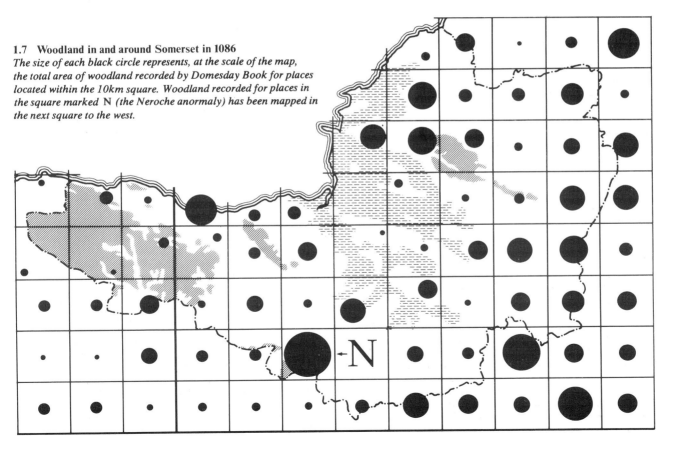

1.8 The Distribution of Forests and Crown Lands compared

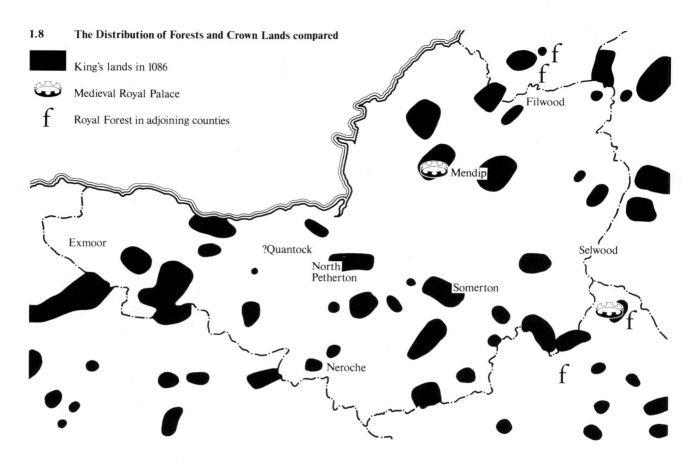

■ King's lands in 1086

♜ Medieval Royal Palace

f Royal Forest in adjoining counties

Filwood

Mendip

Exmoor

?Quantock

North Petherton

Somerton

Selwood

Neroche

to until the early thirteenth century. They were set up in a poorly-documented period, and no record of their beginnings is known to survive. Establishing a Forest ought to have involved defining the bounds by a perambulation, setting up the bureaucracy, and (where necessary) introducing deer. Except in moorland, the legal bounds of a Forest always included a much wider area than the actual wood-pasture or other roughland where the deer lived; hence the pseudo-historical belief that Forests were of vast extent.

The Somerset Forests came late: the first reference is to Exmoor Forest in 1204 *(McDermott 1911)*. They must have been somewhat earlier than this, for they were seldom disputed as being an unauthorized extension of royal

power, and by the end of the century were accepted as *antiqua foresta*. They may be due to Richard I (1189–99).

The sites of Forests seem to us to be arbitrary, but they are connected with places where the king had lands or palaces. Each Somerset Forest is close to some concentration of Crown lands (Fig. 1.8). Not that the king necessarily owned the land on which he kept his deer: Forests symbolized the king's status rather than his property.

Exmoor

This is a typical moorland Forest. Its bounds, like those of Dartmoor Forest, included only the central part of the actual moor, which had been moorland since the Bronze or Iron Age; at times the legal boundary was extended to include lower, more hospitable terrain on which the deer would have spent more of their time.

The Forest is well documented *(McDermott 1911)*. The only deer were red deer, which may have been native. Medieval kings were great eaters of deer, and sent professional huntsmen to catch them for the table royal. For example:

> The king sends Richard de Candevr' and William de Candevr' to take 30 harts for the king's use in the forest of Exmor'. And the keeper of the same forest is ordered . . . to help them to take the same harts *(Calendar of Close Rolls 1259)*.

Such orders were rare. Henry III ate about two harts or hinds a year out of Exmoor, which was a smaller producer of them than many other moorland or even woodland Forests *(Rackham 1980 p 181–4)*. He also licensed others to kill them. Poachers gave him an income through paying fines in the Forest courts. Small sums came from fining neighbouring landowners who allowed their moor-burning to spread into the Forest, and from licences to dig peat. A minor return came from the *lawing* of dogs living in the legal Forest—cutting off part of one of the animal's feet lest it run after the deer, or rather (since lawing was a negotiable asset worth £1 a year) being paid by the dog's owner for not doing so.

The king's deer can hardly have been a major land-use of Exmoor. Long before it became a Forest there had been common-rights. The lower parts of the moor are full of deserted medieval settlements *(Aston 1983 p 122–33)*. Commoners, who have left few records, continued to graze cattle, sheep, pigs, and horses down the centuries.

After the Middle Ages the Crown leased out its interest in the deer *(McDermott 1911)*. In 1815 the Forest was abolished, and the site made private, by an Enclosure Act. It thus became legally possible to destroy the moor; this was begun soon after by John Knight, and is still a matter of controversy today.

Mendip

This was a mainly moorland Forest, extending down the scarps to include some woodland. Its chief qualification for being a Forest was its nearness to Cheddar Palace. King John sold Cheddar to the Bishop of Bath and Wells but retained the Forestal rights—the right to keep deer and to pocket fines levied in Forest courts—and part of the woodland.

Mendip Forest had indigenous red deer and also fallow deer, an exotic species which must have been put there. The **Close Rolls** and other official correspondence show that between 1220 and 1272 Henry III consumed, or gave as presents, 158 harts and 73 hinds, and 15 bucks and 18 does from here (plus occasional orders for unspecified numbers of animals). Usually the source is given as the Forest of Mendip or of Cheddar, but occasionally 'the king's *brullii* of Cheddar' are specified. This is a Latinization of the uncertain word *brail* (as in Wilton Brail, still the name of a wood in Great Bedwyn, Wilts). Lexicographers usually render it 'deer-park' but give no English examples to support that meaning. A more likely meaning is 'covert', a wood within a Forest where deer were in the habit of congregating and where the king, as owner of the Forestal rights, was entitled to take them.

Henry III owned some timber trees at Cheddar, and occasionally made grants of timber. He gave away 15 oaks (*quercus*) in 1229, three 'suitable for timber' in 1266, and three in 1267. In 1225 he presented the Bishop with 30 oaks from the king's wood at Cheddar for a limekiln (an exceptional use of timber as fuel). In 1224 he sent 10 *fusta* (probably timber trees other than oaks) to Wookey, and 50 in 1235 to Glastonbury Abbey *(Calendar of Close Rolls)*. A grant of twelve oaks in 1234 was partly revoked on the ground that the king had forgotten that the wood in which he had given them was the Bishop's and not his own *(Calendar of Patent Rolls)*.

Wood is occasionally mentioned. In 1233 the king ordered 3000 hurdles from the wood at Cheddar: evidently coppicing was well established there *(Calendar of Close Rolls)*. In 1220 he gave 60 great **robora** (probably the bollings of pollards) to Wells Cathedral for a limekiln *(Calendar of Liberate Rolls)*. In 1223 officials were appointed to sell the king's *cablicium*—trees blown down *(Calendar of Patent Rolls)*.

In an average year Henry III took about five red and two-thirds of a fallow deer from the Forest, and gave away $3\frac{1}{2}$ trees. Mendip was not intensively used as a Forest; compared to other Forests it was a small producer of deer, though bigger than Exmoor *(Rackham 1980)*. Numerous poaching cases, in which the Carthusian Brothers of Charterhouse commonly appear, suggest that the king's deer were of more benefit to the local inhabitants.

The king retained a small wood in Cheddar; this may be King's Wood which still exists in Axbridge. Other woods within the legal Forest belonged to private landowners, who were supposed to get the king's licence (doubtless against some consideration) if they wanted to grub them

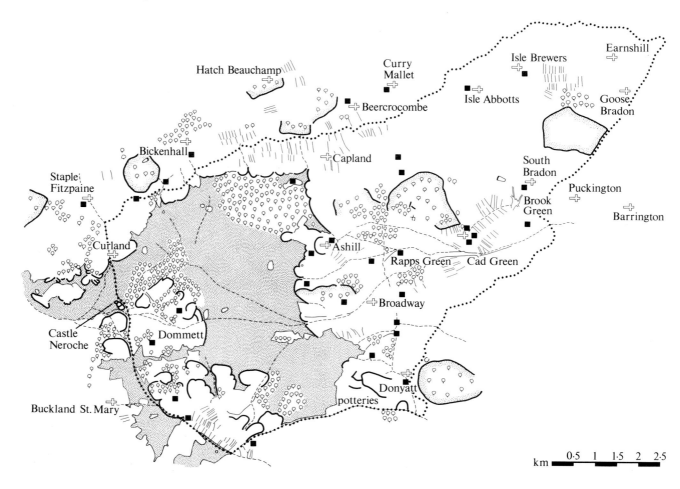

1.9   The Forest of Neroche, the late medieval landscape

Probable extent of woodland at the end of the medieval period

Probable extent of common-land and wood-pasture at the end of the medieval period

Park

Intake from the physical Forest

Evidence of strip-cultivation

Parish church

Settlement

Approximate maximum extent of legal Forest

Earnshill

Curry
Mallet

Isle Brewers

Hatch Beauchamp

Beercrocombe

Isle Abbotts

Goose
Bradon

Bickenhall

Capland

South
Bradon

Puckington

Staple
Fitzpaine

Brook
Green

Barrington

Curland

Ashill

Rapps Green   Cad Green

Castle
Neroche

Broadway

Dommett

Buckland St. Mary

Donyatt

potteries

km   0·5   1   1·5   2   2·5

24

out. Licenses should have been needed for any non-routine tree-felling within a legal Forest, although in practice the requirement seems usually to have been ignored. The Bishop of Bath and Wells had the still extensive woods in Cheddar and Axbridge; in 1234–5 and 1277 he was given licences to assart a total of 160 modern acres and to cultivate the sites *(Calendar of Close Rolls)*. Presumably these woods were on the lower or middle slopes, otherwise they would have become common land. One of the licences had the unusual clause that the Bishop was allowed to use the trees (*vestitura*—the word apparently includes timber and wood) arising from the assarting in a mine that he was going to dig at Charterhouse.

The Forest was effectively abolished in 1338 *(Neale 1976)*, and reverted to being common moorland and private woodland. Most of the moorland was enclosed and destroyed in the nineteenth century and since.

Neroche
Two accounts of this Forest had been written *(Sixsmith 1958; Rackham forthcoming)*. It was originally wooded, representing about half of the 'Neroche Anomaly' woodland in Domesday Book. The legal boundary was arbitrary; it extended far into the plain to the north-east, but excluded the western half of the Neroche massif itself.

The deer in Neroche Forest were fallow and must have been introduced. Between 1232 and 1279 Henry III ate 32 bucks from Neroche; he gave away the carcases of 28 bucks and 15 does; he presented favoured subjects with 30 live bucks and 65 live does for starting parks. The total, 170 deer in 47 years, is fewer than the yield from an average deer-park.

The king owned very little of the land or trees. There are two references to his timber and none to his underwood. Occasionally he granted licenses for unusual fellings, or transport of their own trees, to other landowners within the Forest. Neroche, like other Forests, was a common, and common-rights interfered with coppicing. For instance, in 1397 the king licensed the Provost of Wells Cathedral to cut down 100 acres of wood, providing that it be fenced afterwards *'according to the assize of the forest'*—that is, to protect the regrowth. In 1398 the Provost was released from that condition *'because he cannot rightly do so, as the ground is . . . common of pasture' (Calendar of Patent Rolls)*.

Forestal rights sat lightly on Neroche, which differed little from any other large wooded common. The king

derived from it chiefly revenue from poaching fines etc., and rights of patronage and perquisites going with the Forest administration. Most of the practical activity was by landowners and commoners.

Down the centuries the Forest suffered encroachments, and what remained changed from wood-pasture mainly into grassland. It was formally abolished by Charles I in 1633 by a deal which was to have enriched the Crown and the landowners at the expense of the commoners. Although the scheme was upset by the Civil War, there was a big encroachment on the Forest, and the deer apparently disappeared *(Sixsmith 1958)*. The rest of the Forest remained in existence as a common until it was enclosed by Act of Parliament in 1830; it was then destroyed so thoroughly that even its site is not now correctly remembered.

Selwood
This lay half in Wiltshire. It was a wooded Forest—the Anglo-Saxons remembered the district as having been called by the Welsh *Coit Maur*, 'Great Wood' *(Asser p 155)*. Its qualification for being a Forest was probably its nearness to the king's palace at Gillingham (Dorset).

When Selwood became a Forest, fallow deer were put into it, and it became one of the chief producers of them among English Forests; for example 67 bucks and does were taken in the one year 1258. Although the king can have owned little of the land or woods, there are occasional references to underwood and grants of felling or transport licenses. In 1232 he gave a general dispensation to the leperesses of Maiden Bradley Hospital to take their horses and carts to fetch any wood, charcoal or timber that they might be given or buy in the Forest *(Calendar of Patent Rolls)*.

North Petherton
This densely-settled part of Somerset is an unlikely place for a Forest. Maybe there was a fenland Forest somewhere in the Levels (like Kesteven Forest in the Lincolnshire Fens). Alternatively the Quantock Hills may once have been a Forest like Mendip, linked with North Petherton by detached rights of the Neroche kind; this is suggested by the phrase *'when Canntock was a forest'* in the **Hundred Rolls** of 1279 *(Rotuli Hundredorum 11 p 12)*.

The Forest was short-lived, and by the thirteenth century its administration had been transferred to looking after the royal park at North Petherton. This park yielded occasional harts and timber; its underwood included thorn,

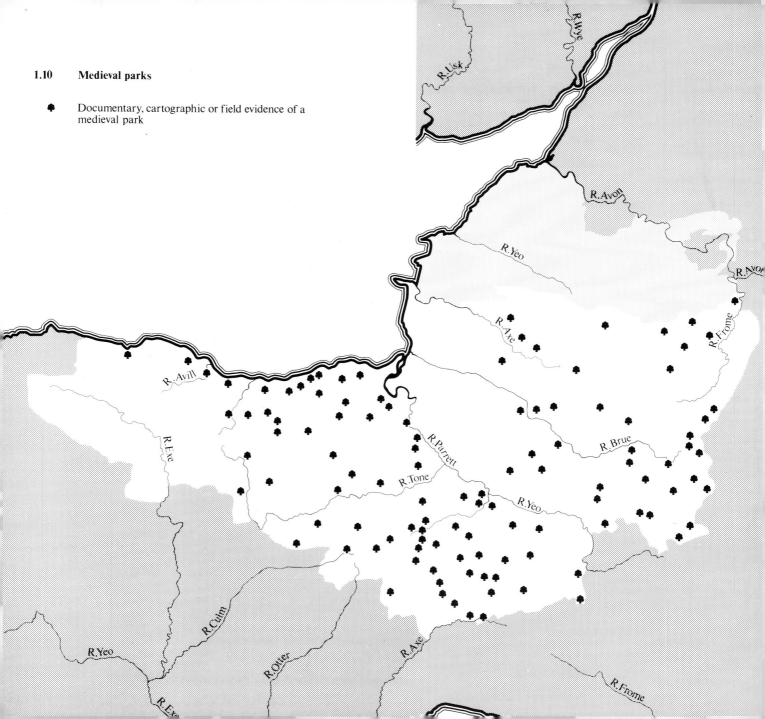

1.10   Medieval parks

♣   Documentary, cartographic or field evidence of a medieval park

alder, and maple *(Cox and Greswell 1911).*

North Petherton Forest became famous long after it was obsolete, for in 1390 Chaucer the poet was made under-Forester of it. Forests were a source of patronage; they enabled poor kings, like Richard II, to reward their busy and faithful servants, like Chaucer, with honorific sinecures in the Forest hierarchy.

Filwood
This was a shadowy Forest; I cannot find that it consisted of anything except administrators.

Somerton
In Somerton, uniquely, the hare was deemed to be a deer, and she supported all the apparatus of Forest Law. This was the king's chief manor in Somerset, and etiquette evidently required that it should have a Forest. In a highly-agricultural countryside there was no room except for a mini-Forest of mini-deer. This was not wholly a joke. In 1256 a hare was found dead, and a jury of good men and true duly sat on the body—as if it had been a deer or a man—and solemnly found that it had died of the murrain *(Cox and Greswell 1911).*

OTHER WOOD-PASTURES
Forests played no large part in Somerset woodland history. Only a very few surviving woods can be shown to have had any connection with a Forest (e.g. Cheddar Wood in Mendip, Castle Wood in Neroche), and even that was probably only a legal technicality; they are now indistinguishable from woods that were not attached to Forests.

Parks
Medieval Somerset had a moderate density of deer-parks. Professor L. Cantor lists 72 places known to have had them *(Cantor 1983),* and others are known or suspected. They were mainly in the south and east, having (as throughout England) a much stronger connection with woodland than Forests had. There were none in the Levels and few around Exmoor. Most parks seem to be of the thirteenth and fourteenth centuries; at Donyatt there was one of the very few as old as Domesday Book. Poundisford Park in Pitminster has been claimed as a medieval park still extant *(Fowler 1979).* The perimeters of several others can be traced (e.g. Robert the Bruce's park at Staple Fitzpaine *(Note 5))*; other remains may lurk in woods called Park Wood.

Wooded commons
Somerset probably had many wood-pasture commons. One such still remains, with many ancient pollard trees, at Leigh Woods in the Avon Gorge. It is an instructive survival, because there also exists an adjacent coppice-wood with which to compare it. I have discussed the details elsewhere *(Rackham 1982; Rackham 1986 p 141–4)* and summarize the story thus:

1—The site was originally a mixed coppice with abundant lime.
2—In the middle ages it was divided into a woodland and a wood-pasture part.
3—Where exposed to grazing, lime and other edible trees disappeared (except for a few limes perched on rocks and cliff ledges) and were replaced by oak, which is a distasteful and browsing-resistant tree. The oaks were managed by pollarding.
4—In the nineteenth century the common-rights were suppressed and the wood-pasture allowed to revert to ordinary woodland. What grew up was not oak (unsuited to these limestone soils unless competing species are browsed) nor lime (which does not recover lost territory), but ash and wych-elm (very palatable species which grow fast on limestone).
5—The former wood-pasture now consists of a few huge lime stools in inaccessible places; old pollard oaks; and century-old ashes and elms (the last now coppiced as a result of Elm Disease). The coppice-wood, where not destroyed by replanting, still has the original mixed composition with much lime.

WOODS DOWN THE CENTURIES
The thirteenth-century destruction of woods reduced what was left to something like its modern distribution. There were minor alterations in the next 600 years. Occasional woods were grubbed out or were allowed to disappear through grazing. For example, a survey of Donyatt in 1567 records

> *one Coppice called Stybeare wood, set with very small underwood and containing by estimate 16 acres (Straton 1909).*

The grazing of the wood was let for the trifling sum of 2s 3d per annum. Evidently the owner did not trouble to protect the underwood, although there was a big pottery nearby to which he might have sold wood as fuel. Not surprisingly, the wood is not heard of again. Against this we must set the occasional, usually unrecorded, appearance of new woods through lack of grazing on farmland or common.

Woodmanship altered little down the centuries. For example, in 1794 it was claimed of the northern Mendip woods that

> *These woods are very romantic and picturesque, and being secured from the south-west breezes, the growth is very rapid, and the profits . . . more certain than any other produce. You have only to divide a coppice of 48 acres into 12 parts, that is 4 acres per year, 12 years growth. The more ashes in these coppices the more valuable, as the poles are very saleable at the coal pits, and I have known many instances of an acre producing in value £16 net after the expenses of cutting, carriage, etc. have been deducted . . . besides the accumulating value of timber trees. . . . On the southern declivity of Mendip hills, there are also some coppice woods, Stoke wood the principal, but these being exposed to the western breezes, are not so productive (Billingsley 1794).*

The great Asham Wood in Downhead was the subject of regular woodsale auctions, advertised in such terms as these:

> *. . . the 8th of February 1817 . . .*
> *the following CAPITAL COPPICE WOOD, POLES, HURDLE RODS & THORNS . . .*
> *felled and lying in lots as follows:*
> *Lot 1—82 Lug of Wood, 2 Loads of Hurdle Rods, and 1 Load of Thorns . . .*
> *[and 26 other lots] . . . (Note 6.)*

> *8th of December 1817 . . .*
> *Eleven Acres of very Prime Wood, containing Hurdle Rods, Spar Gads &c growing and standing in Asham Wood aforesaid, divided into seven lots and numbered with red paint (Note 7).*

In the nineteenth century there was some renewed destruction of woods; e.g. part of Rodney-Stoke Wood in order to grow strawberries on the south-facing slopes *(NCC 1977).*

Woods have been less managed in the twentieth century than at any time in the last thousand years. Coppicing began to decline in the 1880s and died out usually before World War II, though Mascall's Wood (Cheddar) was felled as late as 1953 (judged from the annual rings).

The hand of modern forestry has been heavy on Somerset woods. In Selwood coniferization began early,

and two or more rounds of replanting have by now effaced almost all trace of the original character of many of the woods (save for earthworks). Most big woods have been lost to forestry, as in the Neroche area, Quantockwood, and Cogley Wood (Bruton). In smaller woods replanting is less univeral and often unsuccessful (e.g. Hanging Wood (Butcombe), Ashill Copse (Ashill)). There have been smaller losses to agriculture and quarrying: much of Asham Wood has disappeared into a large quarry. A Nature Conservancy Council study found that 46 per cent by area of ancient woodland in Somerset disappeared between 1930 and 1983 *(Grove 1983).* Most of this destruction was in only thirty years (1945–1975), and is almost certainly greater than all the losses in the previous 400 years.

Since 1973 the conservation of woods has prospered. The Nature Conservancy Council has had a National Nature Reserve in Rodney-Stoke Woods since 1957. Somerset Naturalists' Trust has been very energetic in acquiring woodland nature reserves, and has revived coppicing in several of them for the benefits which result to plant and animal life.

ANCIENT WOODS NOW

Many Somerset woods can be shown to be ancient on documentary evidence alone. For example, the coppiced part of Leigh Woods (Abbot's Leigh) can be traced back in Abbey records to the thirteenth century *(Rackham 1982).* Thurlbear Wood can be equated, in part, with Priors Wood belonging to Taunton Priory before the Dissolution *(Sixsmith 1957).* Such evidence has not been as fully explored for Somerset as for some other parts of England, and the history of many woods rests on field evidence.

By no means all Somerset woods are ancient. Rose Wood (Axbridge) is much larger than it was in 1910; the original wood is embedded in secondary woodland which has sprung up on all sides, except the north, through lack of grazing on the surrounding commons. Most Mendip woods have thus grown bigger. This can be a conservation problem: Brockley Coombe has lost most of its limestone grassland to secondary woodland, and Cheddar Gorge will suffer the same fate unless prevented. Great Breach Wood in Butleigh, though a big wood, has mostly arisen through neglect of a nineteenth-century plantation on former farmland.

Woodbanks, though seldom very massive in Somerset, are present round most ancient woods. Much of the history of a wood is embodied in the varying character of the banks, their profiles, and the extent to which they have been revetted or replaced by drystone or mortared walls (for an example just outside Somerset see *Hendry et al. 1984*). The original Rose Wood is clearly defined by its banks. King's Wood nearby is bisected by a great bank set with old pollard limes, evidently an important, though now forgotten, boundary. Hanging Wood in Butcombe has a complex set of different kinds of boundary bank, the result of centuries of piecemeal alterations.

Coppice stools may live for many centuries (longer than the uncut tree), and are a record of management as well as continuity. For example, the one wych-elm stool, 12 ft in diameter, in Baucombe Coppice (adjacent to Asham Wood) is proof of several centuries of coppicing. A lime stool 10 ft in diameter in Rose Wood resolves any doubt as to that wood's antiquity; stools at least 6 ft across occur in most woods that have lime. Giant stools are also produced by ash, maple, and occasionally oak.

Some plants are characteristic of woods having particular histories *(Peterken 1974)*. Small-leaved lime appears to occur in Somerset only in ancient woodland: in the Great Breach group of woods it is confined to the one small area that is not recent woodland. Service, herb Paris, lily-of-the-valley, and columbine are other plants in this category. Many others will doubtless be discovered; the first step is to consider species that grow in known ancient woods but not in ancient hedges.

Kinds of ancient woodland
The woods of Somerset, even now, are very diverse: as the maps of Dr G. F. Peterken indicate, they contain at least half of all the types of woodland recognized in England *(Peterken 1981)*. This account gives an impression of the variation but is by no means exhaustive.

The main division, which certainly goes back to Mesolithic times, is between the Highland part of the county, with predominant oakwoods (of sessile oak), and the Lowland part, where there is a mosaic of woodland types in which every ancient wood is uniquely different from every other.

Lime, although generally reduced from its prehistoric predominance, is more abundant in Somerset than in any other southern county. It occurs in 15 out of 24 woods known to me. It is a gregarious tree and tends to form patches of lime-dominated woodland, usually with ancient stools or ancient boundary pollards. Its historic importance in Somerset is attested by the common thirteenth-century surname De la Lynde *(Rotuli Hundredorum)*. (This must refer to native lime, as the now familiar 'common' lime, much planted since 1700, did not then exist).

Hazelwoods are another kind of ancient woodland with obvious prehistoric antecedents. In Thurlbear and Asham Woods, for instance, large areas of underwood are dominated by hazel. Many hazelwoods contain more or less ash; indeed those on the Mendips are known among ecologists as 'Mendip ashwoods' *(Moss 1907)*, apparently from the notion that hazel, however abundant, is not a tree and does not count. Although ancient stools of ash occur (e.g. in Cheddar and Rodney Stoke Woods) the majority of ashes have been felled only once or not at all; the Mendips are a good example of the widespread, but unexplained, increase of ash at the expense of hazel in the last hundred years *(Rackham 1986 p 106)*.

Elm is much less common in woods even than in the Neolithic: doubtless the soils on which it grew are now nearly all farmland. Occasional wych-elm stools are scattered in many woods, sometimes sufficiently to bring them within Peterken's 'ash-wych elm' tree community. Rarely, as in Thurlbear Wood, there are patches of more definite wych-elm woodland indicating unusually fertile soils for woodland. A suckering elm species has invaded Ashill Copse.

Oaks are scattered through most Lowland Somerset woods, but only as timber trees; several south Mendip woods lack them. Oakwood (in which the underwood also is of oak) is uncommon in Somerset except the west. There are patches of it on more acidic soils within Castle Wood (Neroche) and Thurlbear Wood.

Alderwood is usually not ancient; but on Combe St Nicholas Common there is a tiny patch of it, surviving from the destruction of a wood-pasture common which adjoined Neroche Forest. Giant stools of alder stand on black ooze of unknown depth in a swamp fed by powerful springs.

Maplewoods lack a prehistoric record. They are local in Somerset and near their western limit. Maple is co-dominant with ash in the more clayey parts of some woods, such as Hanging Wood (Butcombe) and Thurlbear Wood.

In Fig. 1.4 I compare the proportions of dry-land trees around the Levels after the Elm Decline with that of ancient woods near the Levels now. The agreement is unexpectedly close: mid Somerset is one of the few parts of England where lime has not much declined relative to other trees since the Neolithic. But there have been some changes. Elm is now mainly a non-woodland tree. Ash has much increased, especially in recent decades; a little maple has appeared. Oak is probably more prominent than in the Neolithic, but this is partly due to its being encouraged as a timber tree. Beech and hornbeam, uncommon in the Neolithic, are now probably extinct as native trees in Somerset. Of the additional trees used in trackways, holly is now widespread in Somerset woods, but among those near the Levels it is abundant only in Mascall's Wood (Cheddar); crab is very thinly scattered.

An example—Cheddar Wood

This is probably the grandest ancient wood in Somerset. It is a big wood of about 134 acres (on the flat), climbing the tremendous south-facing slopes above Axbridge. It is very inaccessible, which is doubtless why it survives. It is now a reserve of Somerset Naturalists' Trust and coppicing has been resumed.

Cheddar Wood, and the smaller Mascall's Wood near the Gorge, are what remains of the wood of the Bishops of Bath and Wells in the thirteenth century and of King Edmund the Magnificent's wood in the tenth. Cheddar Wood was bigger in 1801, as shown on the Cheddar enclosure map; its lower fringes were grubbed out in the mid-nineteenth century to make a series of tiny strawberry fields, most of which are abandoned and now woodland again. Since 1801 the wood has extended itself by secondary woodland invading the plateau above.

The wood is on Carboniferous Limestone. The lower slopes are almost precipitous, with much rock showing through. Here lime is dominant, sometimes by itself as overgrown stools of towering height, sometimes mixed with ash, hazel, and coppiced oak. The place-name Lynhold, said to be attached to the adjacent plateau, shows that there was already a limewood in Anglo-Saxon times (Old English *linde* 'lime-tree'+*holt*, one of the words for 'wood'). Lime occurs over the greater part of the wood, often as giant stools. At the top the slope lessens and the soil becomes deeper, red, and probably acidic. Here lime peters out, being represented only by single huge stools; it is replaced by low-growing hazel-ashwood in which ash is increasing, with privet thickets and scattered oak stools.

Despite the steep slopes, Cheddar Wood was fully coppiced up to 1917 (judged from counting annual rings). Vertical gullies are said to have been used as slides for getting logs to the bottom of the wood. In places growth is slow, doubtless because of drought.

The wood has a rich flora. Lime and service indicate ancient woodland, as may also uncommon species such as autumn crocus and tutsan. A notable and beautiful rare plant, a speciality of ancient Mendip woods, is *Lithospermum purpureocaeruleum* ('Blue Gromwell'), whose glorious blue flowers carpet the wood and its former edges in late May.

The history of Cheddar Wood is recorded in its boundaries. It was once surrounded by a strong woodbank, possibly made after the bishop's grubbings of the thirteenth century. This is best preserved on the north side, where it has been partly revetted with a dry-stone wall; the work was left unfinished in such a way as to prove that the bank came first and the wall was added. Elsewhere the bank has been altered by having a lane made on top of it for access to adjoining fields, but is still discernible, especially on the south-east side. Even where it no longer forms the edge of the wood, the stools of the hedge which it once bore have grown over the centuries into a massive, continuous 'wall of lime', such as sometimes marks the ancient boundaries of limewoods.

At the top of the wood, the woodbank has been left behind by the wood's gradual advance. The oldest fringe of secondary wood, about a century old, is of hazel and some hawthorn. Beyond this is a zone of hawthorn-wood with some ash and hazel. The outmost, youngest fringe consists of furze-thickets invaded by oak with much birch and sallow. These differences reflect the changing ability of different trees to encroach on moorland. Hazel has lost the invasive power that it had a century ago. Lime is a very poor invader and is not represented at all *(Rackham 1980 p 210)*.

HEDGES

Hedges and farmland trees have been a feature of Somerset down the centuries. The perambulation of Neroche Forest in 1298 begins at Donyatt Poplar: *Incipit ad popelerum de Dungate (Turner 1899)*. At the time a poplar was a *black* poplar, a non-woodland tree *(Rackham 1976 p 37–8)*, a few examples of which still linger in the Taunton area.

Charcoal finds from the excavation of the Donyatt pottery have a balance of species, including elm and willow, which suggests that they came from hedges and farmland trees rather than woods. I have estimated that in 1567 hedges are likely to have covered about 3 per cent of the area of the farmland of Donyatt *(Rackham forthcoming)*.

The elm hedges, which are still a distinctive feature of Somerset, impressed the traveller John Leland, who in

1542 remarked on the

> *elme wood, wherewith most part of al*
> *Somersetshire ys yn hegge rowys enclosid*
> *(Toulmin Smith 1906).*

In general, the Somerset hedgerow scene was set by the close of the Middle Ages. In detail, hedges tell a very long and complex story, whose study has as yet hardly begun. Many individual hedges are probably older than Leland's time; some of those in Anglo-Saxon perambulations are likely to be still extant; and sometimes, as in Dommett on the edge of Neroche Forest, a labyrinthine system of tiny irregular fields and massive hedges suggests even Celtic antiquity. Conversely, the east of Somerset, with an open-field tradition, has quite wide areas of Enclosure-Act hedging; there are big tracts of modern, straight-edged fields on Exmoor and the Mendip plateau; and here and there, in many parts of the county, groups of straight hedges, standing out among the curving and irregular hedges of pre-1700 fields, proclaim either the enclosure of a small common or the reorganization of an existing field system.

The rule of thumb, that the number of tree and shrub species in a 30-yard length of hedge equals the age of the hedge in centuries *(Pollard et al 1974),* must be used with caution in Somerset. It works for the modern hedges of pure beech on Exmoor; but elm hedges, though ancient, can consist of elm alone, for suckering elm is a very competitive tree and may eliminate all others *(Rackham 1986 p 199).* On the site of Neroche Forest I have been able to compare the hedges resulting from the enclosure of the Forest in 1833 with those of seventeenth-century encroachments on the Forest and those of fields just outside the Forest, which are known to be older than 1567 *(Rackham 1986 p 202; Billingsley 1794).* The three groups of hedges have, on average, 6.0, 6.7, and 6.3 species in a 30-yard length, and are indistinguishable on statistical grounds. But the species are not the same. Elm and hazel are characteristic of the medieval hedges; furze of the Caroline ones; sallow, privet, and oak of the post-1833 hedges.

Somerset was remote from the large-scale Enclosure-Act hedging of the Midlands and from the nurserymen who supplied the hawthorns. Even recent hedges are likely to have been made by people digging up whatever plants they could get in the wild, or by allowing fences to turn into hedges by neglect. Somerset hedges are a rich historical source, but to read them we must study not merely the number of species but what those species are, the course and structure of the hedge, and how mixed hedges behave and develop.

Note 1 *All dates are in calendar years*
Note 2 *I omit others, which do not distinguish between the pollens of hazel and bog-myrtle*
Note 3 *Method of Anderson 1970 adapted as in Rackham 1980 page 101*
Note 4 *For method of calculation see Rackham 1980 pages 113–7*
Note 5 *Kindly told to me by M Aston*
Note 6 *Lug—synonym for a (square) perch; 82 lug would be about ½ acre*
Note 7 *Kindly sent to me by L Cram*

1.11 *Man pruning trees, from document c.1280. Pruning was characteristic of orchards and hedgerow trees but is rarely recorded in woodland*

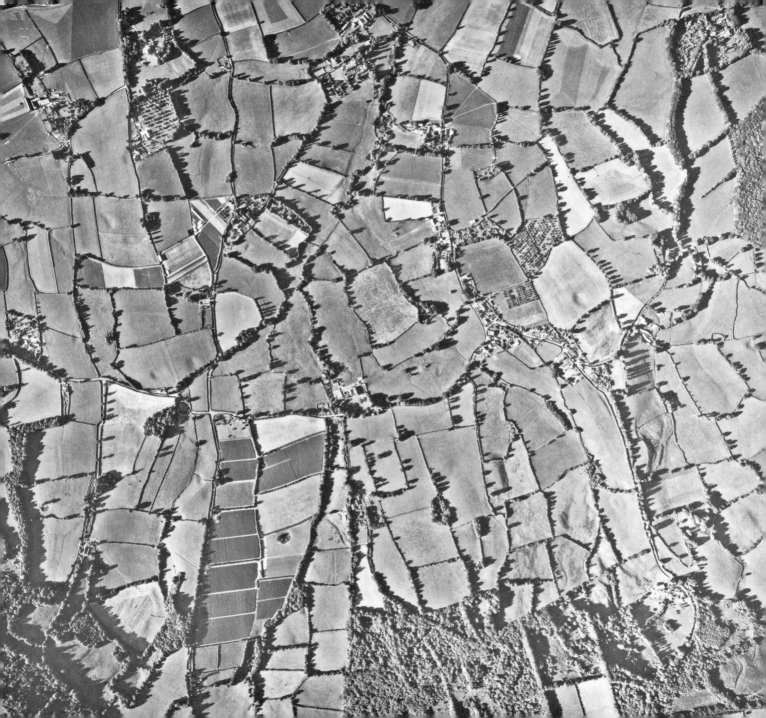

Chapter 2
THE LATE SAXON LANDSCAPE
The evidence from charters and placenames
Michael Costen

The written evidence which survives from the pre-Conquest period and which is reliable is inevitably very limited in quantity and in variety. The comparative rarity of documents which carry landscape information, combined with the chance nature of survival, leaves us dependent upon sources which are often in grave need of critical examination before they can be accepted for the evidence they contain. However the charters and place-names are so fruitful as a source of information that they must be used despite their dangers. Other potential sources of evidence such as archaeological and topographical material will not be considered in detail here.

The major source of information available is in the charters of the pre-Conquest period. These are records of grants of land, often made by kings, usually to churches and monasteries, but also, towards the end of this period, to secular individuals. The total number with a text surviving amounts to about ninety-five for the old county of Somerset *(Finberg 1964)*. Seventy-seven *(Note 1)* sets of boundary descriptions occur in these charters and 65 discrete areas are covered, some more than once. An example of a perambulation, with details of the landscape, is given at the end of the chapter. Unfortunately, the survival of a charter in its original form is almost unknown in Somerset. Of all the charters for the county only three exist as single sheet charters penned before the end of the

Anglo-Saxon period. These are the charters for Pennard, S236, East Pennard, S563, and Withiel, S697 *(Note 2)*. All other charters survive as copies in the cartularies of monastic houses compiled later in the Middle-Ages *(Note 3)*.

The problem of the authenticity of the charters is immediate, since some appear to be contemporary with the date they carry, while others purport to date from the seventh and eighth centuries. The two genuine pre-Conquest survivals in the Longleat archives both covering Pennard, (Longleat 10564 (S236) and 10565 (S563)) are extremely valuable, helping us to assess the worth of other charters in the Glastonbury cartulary. It is apparent immediately that 10564 cannot be contemporary with its nominal date of 681 and neither can it be a copy of an original of that period. The handwriting alone shows that it is of the tenth century, while the form of the bounds in Old-English suggests that they too were written in the tenth century, and should be taken as such. Longleat 10565, on the other hand probably is more or less contemporary with the date it contains, 955. The charter for Withiel (S697) is almost certainly also contemporary with its tenth century date.

Even where they survive only in the form of later copies, some charters show authentic early features suggesting that they do contain some evidence of the period to which they claim to belong. The charter for Brent (S238) probably does have late seventh century boundaries, while the two Muchelney charters for 'Ile' *(Bates 1899, p 46 and p 47)* are also probably of eighth century date *(Whitelock 1955, p 498)*. Other charters for 'Poelt' (S253), Baltonsborough (S1410), Hamp *(Bates 1899 p 144)*, and Wellow (S262), may all be considered as having bounds of the dates claimed for them in the seventh and eighth centuries.

2.1 *The landscape to the south of Wellington and north of the Blackdown Hills escarpment. Area of small, irregular fields probably cleared from woodland and waste in late Saxon and early medieval times*

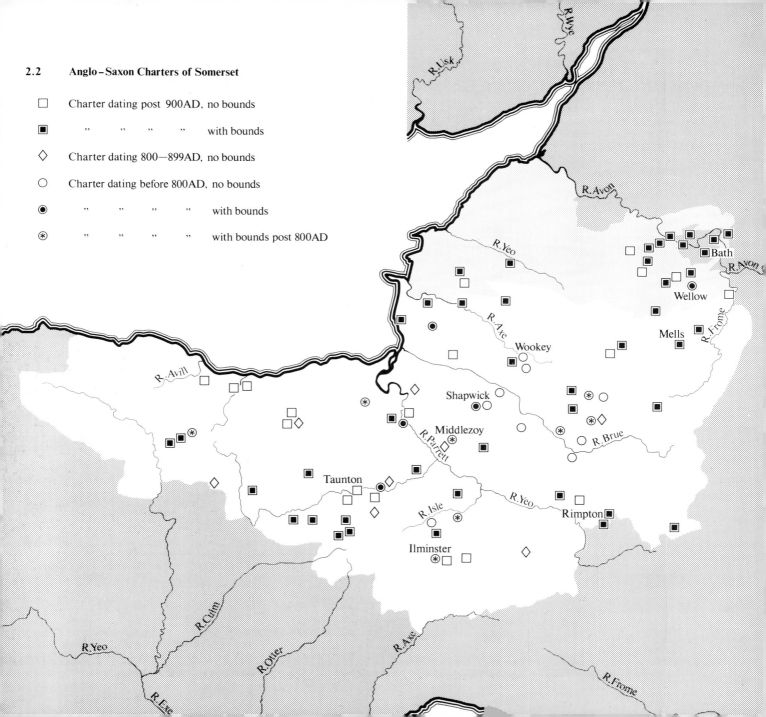

2.2   Anglo–Saxon Charters of Somerset

□   Charter dating post 900AD, no bounds

■   ˮ   ˮ   ˮ   ˮ   with bounds

◇   Charter dating 800—899AD, no bounds

○   Charter dating before 800AD, no bounds

◉   ˮ   ˮ   ˮ   ˮ   with bounds

⊛   ˮ   ˮ   ˮ   ˮ   with bounds post 800AD

Rivers labelled on map: R.Wye, R.Usk, R.Avon, R.Yeo, R.Avon, R.Axe, R.Frome, R.Avill, R.Parrett, R.Brue, R.Isle, R.Yeo, R.Cum, R.Otter, R.Axe, R.Yeo, R.Exe, R.Frome

Place names: Bath, Wellow, Mells, Wookey, Shapwick, Middlezoy, Taunton, Rimpton, Ilminster

However the charter for Ham was condemned by Stevenson *(Bates 1899 p 95, note 4)* and must be dismissed as probably much later than its claimed date.

Another whole group of charters would be most easily accepted as containing tenth century surveys to which spurious dates have been attached. This group includes S236, for Pennard, S247 for Pilton, S270a for Butleigh, S249 for Ilminster, S254 for Withiel Florey, S251 for Middlezoy and S265 for North Stoke. Here all the charters show well-developed Old-English boundary clauses and yet all date from before any known originals with Old-English bounds (S37 of 846) and are contemporary with authenticated Latin bounds (S89 of 736).

The rest of the examples of charter bounds date from the tenth century with a very few exceptions of the ninth century. What information can be gleaned must therefore be regarded as essentially tenth century with occasional material of the late seventh and early eighth centuries (Fig. 2.2).

Other charters which have no boundary clauses, and also those charters which are known to have existed but are now lost, provide valuable information about the existence of estates in the Anglo-Saxon period, as well as providing early place-name material. Sources such as the Chronicle of John of Glastonbury also preserve information of pre-Conquest date although incorporated in a post-Conquest source *(Carley 1978)*.

The Domesday Book provides the most valuable source for the end of the Anglo-Saxon period and it would be difficult to exaggerate the importance of this document *(Thorn and Thorn 1980)*.

Finally the field names of the county provide a vast reservoir of information on many aspects of Anglo-Saxon landscape history which has scarcely been touched.

PLACE-NAMES AND CENTRALISED ESTATES

In the past it has been customary to deal with the place-names of an area as if the landscape in which they are found did not differ significantly in its social and political organisation from the period of the Domesday Book. This view of the local organisation of an area suggests an underlying pattern of ownership and of social organisation which was based upon the direct relationship between a landowner and the individual estate. This view no longer seems tenable *(Jones 1979)*. The social and political organisation of the very first Anglo-Saxon estates in Somerset was probably based upon large centralised estates, in which a central authority was served by a variety of smaller sub-units, each of which might be recognised as a hamlet or farmstead in its own right, but which was economically and socially subservient to the central authority. In 1979 Professor Sawyer argued that the fragmentation of the large estate was the main development in the settlement of Anglo-Saxon England. Such sub-units would have been integrated into the economy of the whole in such a way that they may not have been self-supporting in everything, but needed to exchange specialist goods within the estate. Such an estate has been demonstrated for Sherborne (Dorset) and its district *(Barker 1984)*. In Somerset it seems likely that the great royal estates were organised on just such lines and that the outline of those units persisted throughout the Anglo-Saxon period because they stayed in the hands of rather conservative landowners, such as the Anglo-Saxon kings and the bishops.

2.3 *Anglo-Saxon boundary bank and hedge at Rimpton*

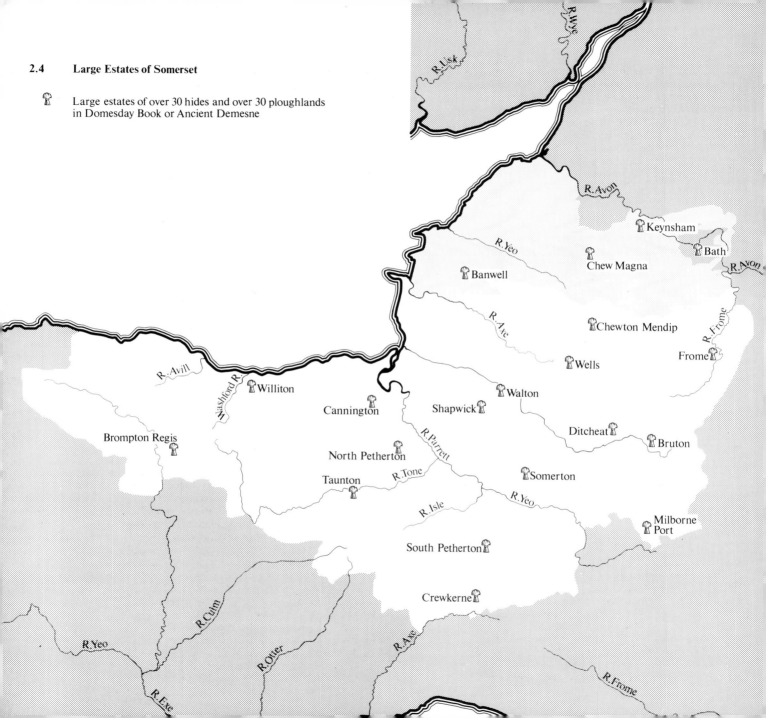

2.4   Large Estates of Somerset

♟ Large estates of over 30 hides and over 30 ploughlands
in Domesday Book or Ancient Demesne

Crewkerne, Cannington, Williton, Bruton, Somerton, North Petherton, Frome and Milborne Port stand out as possible examples of centralised estates under Royal control. All these places were marked by being very large, even in 1066 (Fig. 2.4). Crewkerne had forty ploughlands. Cannington was linked to Williton and Carhampton to form three units with 100 ploughlands between them. Frome had fifty ploughlands, as had Bruton, Somerton and Milborne Port, while North Petherton had 30 ploughlands *(Thorn and Thorn 1980)*. Because these places had always been royal estates, probably since the time when the kings of Wessex first exercised authority in the region, they had never been hidated. This was the method of assessment which made it possible for the Anglo-Saxon kings to impose a uniform land tax on all estates. Since the kings took all the income from their own estates there was clearly no need for such an exercise. Many of these early royal estates also share common features in the way in which they are named. Typically they have been named by taking the name of a prominent local topographical feature and adding to it the Anglo-Saxon *'tun'*. Thus Taunton, the two Pethertons (North and South) and Bruton, Chewton (Mendip), and Williton all fit this type, being the 'tun' on the rivers Tone, Parret, Brue, Chew and Willet respectively. Others add the 'tun' to a topographical feature such as a range of hills. Brompton is *'brunan'+'tun'*, the first element being the Old Welsh name from which the Brendon Hills take their name. Cannington also contains a somewhat similar element, though here it is possible that both hills and settlement take their names from an Old Welsh element which describes an estate here rather than the hills. (The element is *'cantuc'*, from which comes the later Quantock, which with its 'uc' suffix is very like the names of other known places with Old Welsh estate names, i.e., Fideok, Chideock (Dorset)).

Other names in this same group of estates, such as Frome, simply take the Old Welsh river names upon which the estates stand. The same criterion, extended to other large estates outside the King's ancient desmesne, points to Chew (Magna), Bath and Wells as being estates of the same type. They were all very large in 1086, and their possession by the Church over long periods helps to explain how they survived as single units for so long.

Inside the multiple estate units many place-names probably indicate the uses to which the individual units were put. Thus the many Sheptons in Somerset probably represent specialist sheep keeping units. Shepton

Montague may have performed such a function for the estate at Milborne Port, while Honeywick, a settlement near Bruton, probably supplied the central estate with its sweetening agent. This same explanation may also serve for some of the settlements with woodland names, such as 'Barrow', near Bruton, which is probably Old English *'bearu'*, a wood or *'baer'*, a wood-pasture, normally used for grazing pigs *(Note 5)*. The more specialist and unusual name, Hornblotton, meaning *"the tun of the horn blower"* *(Ekwall 1960)* may refer to the use of the estate as the benefice of a man who performed an important honorific service for the lord of the estate, once more perhaps the estate at Bruton. Raddington near Wiveliscombe, may be an estate with a similar history, since the name means "councillors' tun".

LAND HOLDINGS
The major division in the late Anglo-Saxon countryside in the control of property was between the lands in the control of the "State apparatus": the royal family, the major church institutions such as the bishop and the monasteries, plus the holdings of the great earls where they were in alliance with the king; and, on the other hand, the rest of the aristocracy, however rich or important they may have been. The lands of the Church need to be included with the king's holding because the bishop and the abbots were all royal appointees and had little freedom of manoeuvre on their own account. The evidence of the Domesday Book is very clear on this point since it records the ownership of land as it was at the moment of collapse in 1066.

The differences between the two types of holding are quite clear in 1066. The King's estates averaged just over 72 ploughlands each in size, while the average for the whole of the "state apparatus" was 23.36 ploughlands. Seventy-four per cent of all the ploughlands in the hands of this group were in estates of twenty ploughlands and over. Among the rest of the landowning class the situation was almost exactly reversed. The average number of ploughlands in each estate was only 3.36 while 73 per cent of all estates were of five ploughlands or under. Estates with this assessment and smaller formed 48 per cent of all the land-holding of this class, while no less than 159 estates were of one ploughland or smaller. Another significant feature of these estates was that 20 of less than one ploughland were in multiple ownership.

Within the landowning class there were clearly wide disparities of ownership which have nothing to do with

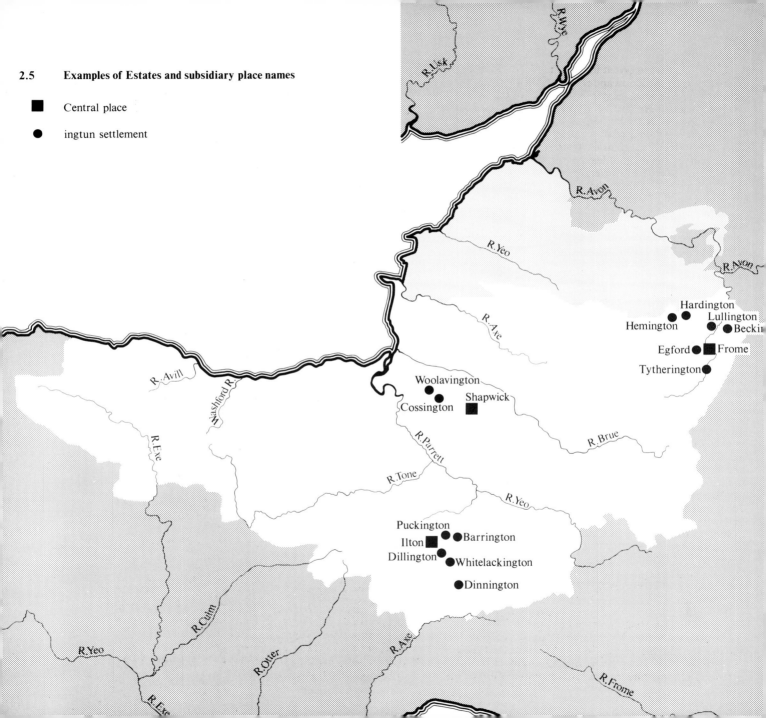

2.5   Examples of Estates and subsidiary place names

■   Central place

●   ingtun settlement

Somerset. What is important in assessing the effect of land ownership upon the landscape is the existence of this pattern of large estates, mostly in the hands of the "state apparatus" on the one hand, and the much smaller estates of those outside this small group. It seems likely that the reason for the existence of so many small units has to do with the inheritance customs of the Anglo-Saxon nobility which included the habit of leaving land by will and division among heirs. However, the beginnings of this state of affairs must be sought in the period when land was first alienated from the "state apparatus" to outside family groups on a permanent basis. This period was marked by a growth of a distinction between **bookland,** that land which was really owned and might be let, sold, or left in a will, and **folkland** which had remained in the king's hand and could be let by him for life, but not permanently alienated. At first in the mid to late seventh century the device of bookland was used only to grant land to the new church institutions which were appearing, but quite soon the device became a way of transferring land outside royal control on a permanent basis *(John 1966)*. It seems likely that we should regard the numerous examples of small estates with names formed from a **personal name+tun** as examples of this process. Groups of names of the form **personal name+ingtun** *(Note 6)* occur from time to time suggesting that sometimes whole blocks of land were granted away into smaller private estates at the same time. One such group lies close to Ilminster (Fig. 2.5), where Barrington, Puckington, Whitelackington, Dillington and Dinnington are all within a distance of six kilometres of one another. A somewhat similar group occurs on the Polden Hills where Woolavington and Cossington lie close to one another, on the northern side of the hill. They may have formed part of the earlier estate of "Poelt" (S948 of 705), which later became the Glastonbury estate of Shapwick, and which at the time of the Domesday Book included within its bounds Catcott, Ashcott, Chilton and Shapwick itself *(Watkin 1947–56)*. Another group of a similar kind is to be found in the Frome area, where Beckington, Hardington, Hemington, Lullington, Tytherington and Egford (Egferdingtun) all cluster around the royal manor.

With estates in the hands of the nobility and with the development of both a market in land and division by inheritance the tendency would be for estates to become smaller over the centuries. The greatest number of these small units occurs in the far west of the county. The extension of more intensive cultivation into this area in the latter part of the Anglo-Saxon period, when estates were already becoming smaller, combined with the local geography, would go some way to explain the particular pattern found there.

WOODLAND

In any landscape the presence or absence of woodland is the most important factor in deciding the general appearance of the land and it is an important indicator of the type of farming being practised. By 1086 Somerset had only about 11 per cent of its area wooded *(Rackham 1980)*. However Rackham makes the very important point that some 70 per cent of all Somerset manors actually had some recorded woodland in the Domesday survey and that the median size of this woodland was about thirty-five acres. This is an extremely important finding, since it shows that if there had been a time when woodland was more extensive, then it must have been widely dispersed throughout the county and not just concentrated in great blocks of woodland with much open land between. Though as a cautionary note, possession of woodland by a Domesday vill does not necessarily mean that it was physically located there—in many other parts of the country woodland recorded under the name of the vill to which it belonged was actually located in a heavily wooded district 15–20 miles away.

It seems reasonable to assume that part of the pattern of development of the county landscape was a gradual reduction in the amount of woodland and in its distribution as the Anglo-Saxon period progressed. Some major place-names are useful indicators of the early distribution of woodland. *Leah* names associated with woodland clearing, place-name elements such as *bearu*, *wudu, graf, holt,* and *hangra*, wood-names as well as *bær,* a woodland pasture and *feld,* an open space in woodland all point to areas of active colonisation of woodland in the early part of the Anglo-Saxon period *(Note 2)*. The distribution of such names taken from the Domesday Book (Fig. 2.6) shows that the most important concentration is in the area between the River Parret and the edge of the Brendon Hills. However, it is as well to remember that this is an area which was particularly rich in small Domesday manors, many of which have "woodland" names. It may be, therefore, that names of this type are disproportionately represented and the activity exaggerated. Nevertheless, the evidence does seem to point to this district as especially well wooded in the early Anglo-Saxon period.

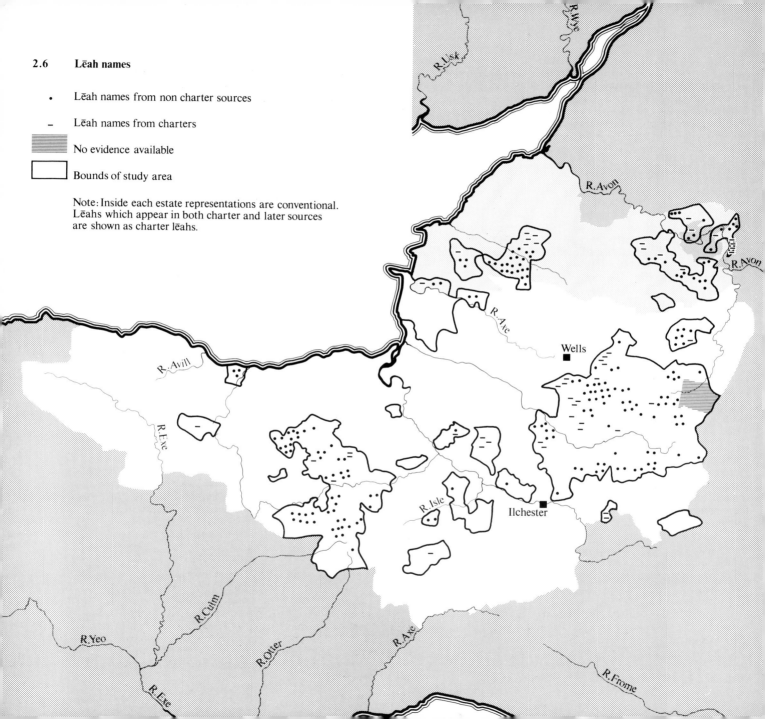

2.6 Lēah names

- •   Lēah names from non charter sources

- –   Lēah names from charters

No evidence available

Bounds of study area

Note: Inside each estate representations are conventional.
Lēahs which appear in both charter and later sources
are shown as charter lēahs.

R.Wye

R.Usk

R.Avon

R.Avon

R.Axe

Wells

R.Avill

R.Exe

R.Isle

Ilchester

R.Yeo

R.Culm

R.Otter

R.Axe

R.Exe

R.Frome

A more extensive survey of *leah* names helps to fill out the picture. All the surviving *leah* names in a block of land covering about 65,000 acres (26,300 hectares) were collected (Fig. 2.6). Seventy-four examples survived in an area with a wide variety of woodland cover in the Domesday Survey. West Lydford for example had 1108 acres of woodland in its 1900 acres, a woodland cover of 58 per cent. Milton Clevedon had 770 acres out 1243 acres wooded, some 61 per cent. On the other hand, North Cadbury, with an area of 2810 acres had only 53 acres of woodland—a cover of about 2 per cent. The spread of *leah* names does not correspond directly with the pattern of Domesday woodland. Instead it presents a distribution of names in a regular pattern which suggests that Selwood once spread nearly to Wells while further south the area around Ilchester was wood-free. The *leah* names can only be explained by assuming that an initially extensive area of woodland was cleared after *leah* names became fixed in the landscape. However, inevitably, different estates would have had different internal histories leading to a diversity of woodland cover by the mid-eleventh century. On that basis, we might imagine that by the tenth century, at the latest, woodland clearance had been extensive and that the considerable disparities in woodland cover already apparent in Domesday Book had been long established.

Information for the rest of the county is not so readily available, but similar patterns to the Selwood area exist on estates where charters detail the bounds. Some estates with charters had no woodland in 1086 and had no *leah* in charters, or in modern material. On others, *leah* names appear even where woodland cover was sparse in 1086. In general the existence of *leah* names in charters is a guide to their survival at a later date, and the distribution of these names is not different as between "charter estates" and "non-charter estates". The concentration of surviving *leah* names in the modern landscape, even when no early material survives, can be linked to early woodland cover. Consequently it is no surprise to find a concentration of such names around the Quantocks and the Brendon Hills and along the south-western boundary of the county (Fig. 2.6). The survival of a large number of such names in the north-west of the county (the modern Woodspring District in south Avon), which is now open country, suggests that there was once extensive woodland.

So far the pattern conforms with the distribution of settlement names connected with woodland. The direct evidence of woodland as it occurs in the charters of Somerset estates confirms this view and also supports the thesis that by the late Anglo-Saxon period the extent of woodland had sharply declined and the remaining woodland was being conserved. Woodlands occur in charters of the tenth century for Weston, near Bath (S508, S661), Marksbury (S431), East Pennard (S563), Batcombe (S462), Compton Bishop *(Liber Albus 2—no S number)*, Taunton (S311), Pitminster (S475), Curry Rivel (S455), Rimpton (S441), Wellington (S380) and Lyng (S432). In each case the boundary clauses suggest that the woods concerned were not large. In some cases, as at Adber and Weathergrove, both mentioned in the Rimpton charters *(Costen 1985)*, it is likely that the references were to settlements with woodland names rather than to woodland areas, since both these places were settlements in 1086.

Only around the edges of the county were there large tracts of continuous or near-continuous, woodland. The forest of Neroche has an English name meaning *"the nearer place of the hunting dogs" (Ekwall 1960)*. This suggests one of the prime uses of the forest area and the Domesday evidence shows that this forest had already been apportioned for the use of surrounding estates in the mid-eleventh century and it is likely that communal use of Neroche goes back to the earliest period in settlement history.

Selwood was mentioned obliquely in 709 when Bishop Aldhelm died and was described as having been *"bishop west of the wood" (Garmonsway 1953)*. It was again mentioned by Asser in his Life of Alfred *(Keynes and Lapidge 1983)*, when he gave the then current Old Welsh version of the name *'Coit Maur'*, 'the great wood', probably using the name which had been in use among the British speakers of the area since Roman times at least. By the end of the Anglo-Saxon period the manor of Bruton was credited with some 9000 acres of woodland in Selwood *(Thorn and Thorn 1980)*. It has been suggested above that the forest once extended as far as Wells in the west, and the collection of woodland settlement names around Frome is probably the result of extending settlement on the Frome estate, which encroached into the forest round about. At an early date in the Anglo-Saxon period there also existed a forest on the Quantock Hills called *'Cantucuudu'* in 682 (S237). To what extent this forest still existed as a coherent unit in the tenth century it is impossible to say but it is noticeable that many of the surviving *hyrst* and *leah* names cluster around the slopes of the Quantocks.

2.7 *Man cutting cereals, from document c.1280*

FARMING PRACTICE

The question of how the Anglo-Saxon landscape was farmed in the eighth to tenth century is clearly of great importance in any attempt to reconstruct the landscape. The first question must be to what extent this was a landscape of open-field farming. Writing in 1972 Finberg expressed much hesitation about the existence of an open-field system in Wessex in the eighth century *(Finberg 1972)*. More recently, Della Hooke has shown that in the west midlands in the tenth century there are many references in charters to systems of farming involving not only common wood, pasture and meadow but also arable land, which look like an emerging form of open-field cultivation *(Hooke 1981)*. Some other references in charters point to the existence of infield–outfield systems in Gloucestershire *(Finberg 1972 and Hooke 1981a)*. Hall has demonstrated the antiquity of open-field systems in the East Midland counties, placing the origins in that area at a time before 1160 *(Hall 1981)*. However the evidence in Somerset, though inconclusive tends to suggest that open-field agriculture was not well established in the tenth century. Charter evidence at Weston (S508), Corston (S593), Batcombe (S462), Cheddar *(Liber Albus 2 fo. 246—no S number)*, Taunton (S311), Pitminster (S1006), Bishops Lydeard (S380), Ile Abbots (S740), and Rimpton (S571) shows that the word *feld*, 'a field' or 'an open space', occurs often enough for us to know that the word was in regular and common use in the tenth century. However the names in the Somerset sample are not good candidates for open field systems. At Weston, near Bath, the field was *clænan feld*, that is the 'bare' or 'clean field'. This suggests a contrast with open ground which was covered with scrub rather than ploughland. A similar usage occurs in the tenth century charter for Manworthy in Milverton (S709) where there is a reference to *clænan mor*, the 'bare moor', now Clean Moor in Milverton. At Batcombe the *feld* lay next to a wood and a part of the estate not later associated with the open fields. At Cheddar the *feld* was on top of the Mendips, close to the edge of Cheddar Gorge, and in an area which was then part of the hunting grounds of the Anglo-Saxon kings and which was later a part of the royal Forest of Mendip. At Pitminster the *feld* was called *Oxenafeld*, 'the field of the oxen' and lay on the broken slopes of the Blackdown Hills in the south of the estate. The *feld* in Fideok cannot now be identified, but the *fasingafeld* in Bishops Lydeard lay on the slope of the Quantocks while at Ile Abbots, *theodenesfeld*, 'the lord's field' was on low ground close to a river. Generally, these fields look as if they were open pasture areas and grazing grounds rather than land for arable cultivation. Only the field at Corston, near Bath, lies where a later open field lay and may have been arable in the tenth century.

References to 'acres' seem generally to refer to isolated plots of land rather than giving much information about their state of cultivation. The charter for Weston (S508) uses acres as boundary points, in one case *oden aecar*, 'the threshing acre', in another case a 'single acre in the wood', which looks like an assart. At High Ham where the 'king's thirty acres' can still be identified as an isolated piece of ground in Wearne, now part of Huish Episcopi parish, the land in question is detached from the rest of the estate by a river, and although it was probably arable at the time of the charter, it could not fit into a larger area of open field. It must always have been isolated as it is now.

Only one reference to furlongs survives in all the Somerset charters and this is in the charter for Marksbury (S431). There the 'east end of the east long furlong' and 'the east end of the furlong' both occur in areas associated with the later open field cultivation. However there are grounds for thinking that the bounds of this charter are not of the tenth century, but are probably an updated twelfth century description *(Costen 1983)*.

It is possible that some open field cultivation was being organised in Somerset in the later tenth century. Ann Ellison *(1983)* and Nicholas Corcos *(1983)* have demonstrated the existence of planned medieval villages in Somerset at Long Load, Ilton and Shapwick. Corcos, following Harold Fox *(Fox 1981)*, has argued that this reorganisation of the settlement pattern accompanied a reorganisation of the farming system and connects this change with the break-up of multiple estates. We should perhaps look to the reformed monasteries of the tenth century, with their acquisition of estates and resumption of the lands lost to their control in the eighth and ninth centuries, as the sources of this reorganisation of the landscape in Somerset. Perhaps this occurred in the search for more effective exploitation of demesne lands at a period when the status of the peasant farmer was declining while markets were growing in which large sums of cash might be made from the efficient production and sale of surpluses.

If the open-field landscape of Somerset was just developing, it is also possible to distinguish elements in the late tenth century landscape which had survived from an earlier age and only slowly disappeared. The *hiwisc* *(Costen 1988)* was a unit which has left its mark on the landscape in the place-names of Somerset at places such as Huish Episcopi and Huish Champflower. It is a name which ultimately derives from the Old English word for a family, so that a *'hiwisc'* is the landholding necessary to support a family. There is evidence that some of these units may have functioned independently as farmsteads in the late Anglo-Saxon period. A very few are mentioned as *hiwisces* in the tenth century charters of the county. This is the case for Burnham-on-Sea *(Liber Albus 2 fo. 246—no. S number)*, and Rimpton (S441). Others appear as independent manorial units in the Domesday survey, for instance Beggearn Huish and Huish Barton, now in Nettlecombe. Others can now only be distinguished by the survival of field names, as at Somerton and Yeovil. There is evidence that the hiwisces which once existed at West Hatch and at Somerton lay in what later became two separate estates. Thus the West Hatch example had lands both in the present West Hatch and in Thornfalcon, while the Somerton example extended into Kingsdon. This points to the existence of the *hiwisces* before the division of the estates which created the later units we see fossilized as parishes. Some *hiwisces* lay on low lying marshy ground, as at South Brent and Yatton. They may have

been pioneering units. Other estates are found spread across the county in the relatively rich lands of the south-east, at Rimpton and Lovington and on the higher ground of the Mendips, at Shepton Mallet and Radstock, on royal estates, at Crewkerne, and on the high ground of the far south-west, at Nettlecombe and at Rodhuish. Thus there is nothing to suggest that they were tied to a particular kind of landscape. On the contrary they were found everywhere, suggesting that they were part of a common social and agricultural organisation. There were probably many more that the 18 examples currently recognised. The size of these units varies considerably. Those at Lovington and Rimpton were of about 200 acres each, while the Nettlecombe examples were each of about 400 acres in extent. Rodhuish near Carhampton, although only rating one virgate for the geld in the Domesday Book, covered an area of 1450 acres as is shown in the Tithe Award 1842. These differences probably show that the *hiwisc* was a unit which really did vary in size according to the quality of the land, as indeed it would need to, in order to support the family unit in different terrains.

In west Somerset small settlements with 'worthy' or 'worth' names are quite numerous. Examples are at Woodworthy Farm in Chipstable, Clatworthy—a parish name, Elworthy—another parish name, Lexworthy in Enmore, and Almsworthy in Exford. Settlements with this type of name are much rarer in eastern and northern Somerset, but the field name 'worth', common everywhere in the county, together with a few parish names, Closworth and Badgworth, and a few minor settlement names— 'Baneworth', a lost settlement in Wellow, Ebbor, a deserted settlement in St Cuthbert Without parish, suggests that settlements and farmsteads with this type of name may have been common all over Somerset in the late Anglo-Saxon period. This points to an agricultural pattern which included many small farm units rather than a landscape uniformly farmed in open-fields. It seems possible that the Somerset landscape was much less differentiated as between upland and lowland than it later became. The farming pattern of the far west is perhaps a survivor of a pattern which existed everywhere once.

THE BOUNDARIES OF ESTATES

The charters of the tenth century show that the estates of that period, for which we have evidence, were clearly defined by well established boundaries, even in places like the wetlands. But that does not always mean that the boundaries were physical objects. Some were and still are impressive features. Thus the various charters for Pitminster (S440 and S475) mention a hedge which ran from the modern Woodbrook Farm (ST202184) to Dipford (ST205219) a distance of about two kilometres. The hedge still exists and is easily the longest and largest hedge mentioned in charters and still surviving. In many other places hedges described in charters do not survive. The *gemaere hagan* of the same Pitminster charters, which was probably close to Hayne in Corfe cannot be identified. The *maer hagan* at Bathampton (S627), the 'mere hawan' at Marksbury (S431), the *hagan* at Lottisham (S292) and the *maer hagen* at Rimpton (S571) can all be identified, but do not all survive as hedges. That at Bathampton is now a wall; at Marksbury the hedge has vanished. However at Lottisham it survives and at Rimpton the hedge which is described as a *scaga* in the charter S441 is still in use as a stout hedge for part of its length, Fig. 2.3. Here the whole hedge existed until recent years and has only lately been bulldozed. These *'hagan'* are usually very large dense hedges and they are associated with woodland or areas which were once wooded. They were probably formed by leaving a thick line of trees and bushes along the line of the boundary when the woodland was cleared. Such hedges were probably a common feature of wooded estates and it is likely that detailed fieldwork would reveal further examples which are not recorded in charters.

The less impressive *heges* of the charters occur almost everywhere and were probably planted as boundaries. More important were *dices,* sometimes *gemaer dices* (boundary ditches). In the surviving charters for Somerset there are thirty-two separate estates which have *dices* as boundaries, but nowhere was an entire estate surrounded by them. But what was a *dic?* Despite the obvious answer of 'a ditch', investigation shows that the same word was used to describe two different features. Usually a 'dic' was a bank of earth with a ditch formed when the bank was constructed. However in lowlying areas, out in the marshes, the word was used to denote a water filled furrow.

Some of the banks were described as being *micel,* that is 'big'. At Mells the *muchil dich* (S481 of 942) is the rampart of the Iron Age Tedbury Camp, while at East Pennard the *miclan dic* (S563 of 955) is the bank which separates Pennard from Ditcheat and gives Ditcheat its name. This bank is in fact a roadway of late Roman origin running from the Fosse Way to the temple on Lamyatt Beacon *(Leech 1986),* but was clearly not recognised as such, either in the tenth century or in the seventh or early

eighth centuries when Ditcheat was named. At Otterford the Taunton Charter (S311) has a *widan dic,* which is in fact the county boundary and is a large bank reinforced with stone facing.

More common than big dykes are old dykes. They occur at Weston, Charlcombe, Stanton Prior, Priston, East Pennard, Batcombe, Bleadon, High Ham, Taunton, Pitminster, Henstridge and Wellington. The concentration indicated in charters was heaviest in the Bath area, around Pilton and around Taunton. In many cases the banks and ditches are still discernible. The name 'old dyke' seems to suggest that the boundary followed a feature which was so old that it was thought to predate the estate boundaries themselves. Usually these banks are a formal feature rather than a major obstacle and their frequent occurrence in charters suggests that they were a feature of almost all estates and that consequently large numbers must survive unrecognised today. Furthermore, if such features were frequently thought to predate late Anglo-Saxon arrangements it could be that they actually marked internal divisions in older and perhaps much larger units. It has been noted *(Costen 1983)* that in the northern part of the county (around Marksbury) Wansdyke is not a local boundary. This suggests that the estates in that area pre-date the dyke. On the other hand the dyke does form the boundary in the Clifton—South Stoke district, pointing to these two estates being laid out after the construction of the dyke. Old dykes of other types may have been used also as bounds in making new divisions. Both estates created in the ninth or the tenth centuries and those which were ancient subunits of earlier multiple estates, existed side by side.

ROADS

Towns appeared in this landscape rather late in the Anglo-Saxon period. Hodges has pointed to their creation in the ninth century as part of the process by which the forces of the newly emerging state retained power over a developing economy and tapped part of the proceeds of that growth *(Hodges 1982).* Towns grew at points which were in most cases already centres of royal or official power, hence the Domesday Boroughs or earlier mints at Taunton, Bruton, Ilchester, Milborne Port, Crewkerne, Milverton and Axbridge *(Hill 1981).*

Important in shaping the relationships between the nascent towns were the long distance routes. Ilchester, with 107 burgesses in 1086, was the most important market centre in late Anglo-Saxon Somerset, apart from

Bath, and it held that position because of the existence of the Fosse Way.

There is some evidence from the charters of the district that roads ran from Ilchester into Wiltshire, heading towards the south-coast ports and towards Winchester. Rimpton, in south-east Somerset, was for long the staging post of the Bishops of Winchester on their journeys to Taunton, and an examination of its charters shows that it was on a major road *(Costen 1985)*. The same area has a large number of 'ford' names, implying that the routeways in the area were both early and very important. Thus Alford, Ansford, Blackford, Bayford, Lattiford, Mudford, Sandford Orcas and Sparkford are all in this south east area. Blackford, Bayford and Lattiford are on a route leading from Ilchester into Wiltshire, via Mere. Mudford and Sandford Orcas are on part of a route which runs further south, while it is also likely that there was a road which ran through Sherborne, northwards to Frome and so on into northern Wiltshire. References to roads and tracks are extremely common in the charters. No less than forty-nine of the estates for which charters survive use roads, tracks and paths as boundaries. So common are they that we must assume that everywhere roads were used as boundaries as a matter of course. There are of course numerous other routes, not referred to in the charters, such that nowhere in Somerset could anyone have been far from a highway, and often one which would take him on long journeys.

CONCLUSION

Late Anglo-Saxon Somerset was full of people. A well developed road system; estates whose boundaries were clearly marked or at the least well-known; woodland which was relatively small in area and well protected; moorland whose exploitation was regulated; all these are features which point to a landscape where land-use needed to be carefully regulated and apportioned. The contrast between large and small estates was the most conspicuous feature of land ownership and such large estates were to be found all over the county, where the administrative centre of a king or a monastery provided a focus. Agricultural methods were probably also markedly different as between large and small estates and contrasts were developing between the highland and lowland districts. Above all it was a rich landscape in which the population was increasing and where the country gentlemen of the late Anglo-Saxon era were reaping the rewards of the expansion of economic activity.

Note 1 This differs from Oliver Rackham's figure of 74 (p 19) but the total depends on whether several versions of the same charter are counted separately and whether estates within estates are individually distinguished.

Note 2 S in S236, S563 etc. refers to the serial numbers given to Anglo-Saxon Charters in Sawyer 1968. There is no S number for the charters for Banwell etc. (see below).

Note 3 The sources for the charters consulted here are very varied. The charters for Bath Abbey are in Corpus Christi College, Cambridge (ms 111) and are published by the Somerset Record Society (Hunt 1893). Glastonbury Abbey's cartulary (ms Longleat 39) kept at Longleat House, Wiltshire has also been published by the Somerset Record Society (Watkin 1947–56) as have those of Athelney Abbey and Muchelney Abbey (Bates 1899). The charters relating to the estates of the Old Minster at Winchester, later the property of the Bishop of Winchester, have not been printed, except in Birch and Kemble (Birch 1885–93, Kemble 1839–48); they are in the Codex Wintoniensis, British Library Additional ms 15350. The charters of Banwell and Compton Bishop, Wellington and West Buckland, and Wellow are in the Liber Albus in the Library of Wells Cathedral; and the British Library contains the charter (ms Harley 61) for Hentridge S570.

Note 4 See Smith 1970 for the Old English place-name elements and their meanings.

Note 5 OE is used for Old English throughout.

Note 6 It is likely that the element 'ing' which occurs quite commonly in names such as 'Lullington' is of the type described by A H Smith (1970) as -ing-4. This is a connective particle denoting the association of a place with a particular person whose name forms the first element in the name i.e. 'Lullington'—'the tun associated with Lulla'. The 'ing' has a genitival function but does not necessarily denote ownership.

DITCHEAT AND ITS CHARTER

The Longleat Chartulary of Glastonbury Abbey includes a charter (S292 of 842) for the Abbey's estate at Ditcheat. The grant is for an area which later appears as the ecclesiastical parish of Ditcheat. Two separate units, Ditcheat and Lottisham, were granted and Lottisham continued as part of the estate and part of the ecclesiastical parish, although completely detached on the western side of the Fosse Way, until modern times. Here only Ditcheat is considered. Both parts of the estate were surveyed and provided with a boundary clause in the charter, but the Lottisham part has not yet been solved. Although the Ditcheat clause is not certain at every point enough can be elucidated to make it a worthwhile example.

Ditcheat was an important estate in the Abbey's lands and it is clear that its origins are tied up with an estate of the late Roman period. Within its bounds there is a Roman villa site *(Haverfield 1906 p 320)*. The existence of an extensive area of the parish with the modern name *Old Floors*, probably denotes an otherwise unknown site of Roman origin (see 'A', Fig. 2.8), while at Sutton there is a site of an extensive Romano–British village (see 'B', Fig. 2.8).

In addition it is possible that a Dark Age *wicham* site also existed (see '8' below). However, the bounds of the estate, as we see them, are not entirely of Roman origin, since the northern boundary is a late Roman landscape feature, so that the boundary must be post fourth century in origin. It is also noteworthy that the late Romano–British temple on Lamyatt Beacon is less than two kilometres away in the next parish. Lamyatt itself was often appended to Ditcheat in the early middle-ages and in 1086 Lamyatt and Hornblotton were both included in the Ditcheat entry in Domesday Book, as was the estate inside Ditcheat at Alhampton *(Thorn and Thorn 1980)*.

The Bounds

1—First to the ford at the dyke . . .
At a point on the northern boundary there is a stream which cuts the boundary and runs through the parish to meet the river Alham. This stream separates the outlying parts of East Pennard from Evercreech. The ford is therefore a meeting point for several boundaries and the obvious place at which to start a perambulation. The ditch or dyke referred to probably gives Ditcheat its name (*dic+geat*), referring to the gap in the dyke through which the stream passes. This dyke is a large ditch and bank, which is probably a road linked to the nearby Lamyatt temple towards which it runs *(Leech 1986)*.

2—Along the course of the Alham to the thorntree at the boundary ford . . .
The boundary runs along the river Alham. At the point at which it leaves the river and turns in a generally southerly direction the field is called **millfords** (T661). There is no evidence for a mill here and it seems likely that this is actually a corruption of the Old-English *gemaereford*.

3—Thence south to a farm . . .
This point cannot be traced, but may be near the point at which the present parish boundary crosses the road.

4—To the road . . .
The boundary runs along Holwell lane.

5—Along the road to a post. . . .
Fields (T906 and 907) *(Note 7)* here are called Stable Acre. This is clearly the Old-English *stapel*, a post and enables this point to be fixed.

6—To the birdswood . . .
It is clear that, since the next point is close this one must lie near T912.

7—Thence to the clearing where garlic grows . . .
(Note 8)
Field T913 is **ramsley**.

8—South to the boundary ditch . . .
The boundary turns south and joins a stream deeply cut into the land which runs south to the river Brue. This is still the parish boundary. The names of the fields close to this boundary, T924–931 **castle** and T934 **wickham ash**, point to this as an area of early settlement. **Wickham Ash** is very close to the medieval *wykhamstyle (Note 9)*. This might be a *wicham* site.

9—Along the ditch to the River Brue . . .

10—Along the stream to the confluence with the river Alham . . .
The river passes the Roman villa site at **laverns** as well as a Romano–British village at Sutton.

11—Up the Alham to Bula's tree . . .
It is likely that the name Bula's tree is preserved in the name of Bolter's Bridge (bolamtre—bolter). The modern boundary goes on a little way beyond the bridge before turning, but this is probably what the original boundary did and it is the name which has migrated a few yards. Several fields around this area carry the name **bolters** (T1338 and T1339).

2.8 Ditcheat Charter

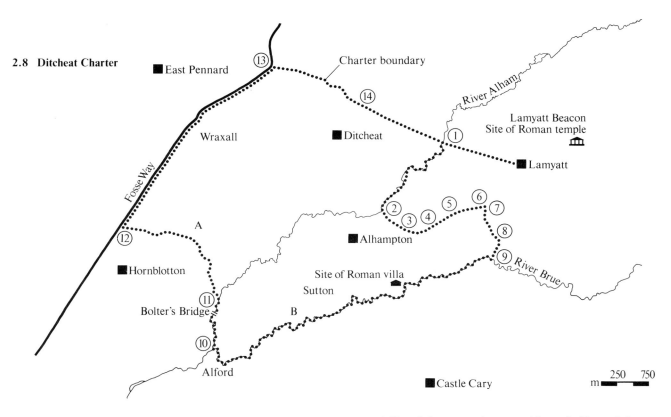

12—*Along the ditch to the Roman road...*
The modern boundary follows a small ditch which
divides Ditcheat from Hornblotton and runs to the
Fosse Way.

13—*Along the Roman road to the gap on the Roman
road...*
The boundary runs to the point where the Fosse
reaches an escarpment and plunges down to the plain.
The dip through which the road runs is probably the
"gate".

14—*Along the dyke once more to the ford at the ditch...*
This takes the boundary along the dyke until it
reaches the starting point of the charter. The charter
boundary and the modern parish boundary may
diverge slightly for part of this stretch, but the
divergence, if any, is very small.
The modern parish boundary and the charter
boundary seem to correspond for the whole of this
estate. Glastonbury had little reason to alter the
bound of its estates once they were fixed, and the

stability of the monastic ownership probably explains
why there were no changes in this boundary from the
ninth century until the establishment of parochial
boundaries in the early middle ages.

Note 7   *Tithe map and award for Ditcheat 1840 in the County
Record Office, Taunton.*

Note 8   *The transcription of this charter is late and many of the
spellings are actually Middle-English rather than Old-
English. It is therefore impossible to distinguish between
'hramsa', OE 'garlic', which is often spelt* hraemes *in
place-names and 'rammes' the genitive singular of OE
'ramm,' a 'ram'. In view of the very common association
between wild garlic and woodland, and the unlikelihood
of sheep in this context it seems best to treat this as
another example of* wild garlic.

Note 9   *British Library Manuscript Egerton 3321. A Survey of
the lands of Glastonbury Abbey of 1308–10.*

Chapter 3

THE CHURCH *in the* LANDSCAPE
Part 1 The Anglo-Saxon period

Michael Costen

*I*t is important to recognise that religious belief and practice was an integral part of Anglo-Saxon society and that the beginning of the Anglo-Saxon period in Somerset coincided with the growth of the alliance between the Anglo-Saxon kings and the newly trained native English hierarchy and clergy. This was a quite natural event, since the pagan Anglo-Saxon rulers seem to have been the leaders of religious cults for their subjects. This relationship inside the new church is clearly demonstrated in the work of Bede.

The West-Saxon King Cynegils was converted in about 635 *(Bede)* and although his successor, his second son, was not a Christian at first, he was converted while in exile in Essex. However, Cynegils had set up an episcopal centre at Dorchester on Thames and this institution survived, moving to Winchester in 662. Bede makes it clear that a bishop was normally established as the result of the request of the king and his people; he was not imposed by clerical authority from outside. The bishop exercised his authority inside the territory of a king and was clearly felt to be the bishop of a people, not of a territory. In those circumstances the conversion of the king and of his household was clearly the first priority for any missionary.

The arrival of the Anglo-Saxons in Somerset took place soon after their conversion, and it would be a mistake to imagine that paganism did not exist among them. There are some signs of paganism, which survive even into the late Anglo-Saxon period. At Taunton the bounds of the charter S311 *(Note 1)* preserve a remark about an ash tree, *"which the ignorant call 'holy'"*. In addition the parish of Staplegrove, near Taunton, probably preserves a remnant of a fertility cult in its name. It is significant that a field name in the middle of the parish preserves the name 'halgrove'. It seems possible that this was a site of phallic worship.

The building of churches was the responsibility of the king and in the face of continuing paganism his example was of the greatest importance. The existence of churches among the Anglo-Saxons from an early date is well attested *(Morris 1983)* and the foundation of both conventual monasteries and minsters in Somerset probably took place in the late seventh and early eighth centuries. However the actual dating of such institutions is very difficult and caution is necessary. The earliest church known in the county was the monastery at Bath founded about 676 (S51), but that was probably in the territory of the Hwicce and so should be regarded as Mercian rather than West Saxon. The only other churches which have foundation (or refoundation) dates in the seventh century seem to be Glastonbury, about 688 *(Garmonsway 1953)* and Muchelney about 693 (S240). The early foundation of minster churches must be inferred. At least on royal sites minsters were probably in existence by the early eighth century. Recent work has drawn attention to the difficulty of drawing a clear distinction between the monasteries, properly called, and the secular minster churches *(Blair 1985)*. However this does not mean that all the minsters founded to provide religious services to the secular community were founded as monastic communities in the strict sense, but that they all share the characteristic that both minsters and monasteries held land for their support.

3.1 *The central crossing under the tower at Milborne Port church. The Romanesque arches date from just before the Norman Conquest*

3.2 *Saxon crypt, Muchelney Abbey*

MONASTERIES

It would be unwise to assume that the early foundations at Glastonbury and at Muchelney had enormous lands at their disposal in their early years. The picture drawn in the Domesday Book is many centuries later and long after the refoundations of the tenth century. Consequently despite their political and social importance their predominance as landowners was probably far from established in the eighth century.

The situation of Glastonbury Abbey has often been remarked upon as suitable for a "Celtic" monastery, built in the marshes as it was. Whether of not it was a religious

site of significance prior to the late seventh century is still an open question, but it is indisputable that the site is also very convenient for the chief early royal 'tun' of Somerset, at Somerton, while Muchelney, also deep in the marsh lands, is also within easy reach of Somerton as well as another royal estate at South Petherton.

Nothing is known about the way in which monasteries exploited their early estates and we must assume that they merely fitted into the existing pattern of large centralised units which has been suggested for the secular world. However, the monastic revival of the mid-tenth century, affecting Glastonbury first among all English monastic institutions, produced a profound change in the relationship between the monasteries and their estates. It is clear that, as on the continent, the ninth century had seen a dispersal of the lands of monasteries among secular landowners. This alone would explain the moves to have Dunstan exiled from the court of King Edmund in 939, since a revival of English monasticism would have involved considerable financial loss for the local nobility *(Knowles 1963)*. As it was, the monastic resurgence from 940 onwards led to an enormous expansion of monastic property and turned Glastonbury into the largest landowner in the shire after the royal household.

The administration of monastic estates took place in the context of the new, individualistic landscape of the tenth century. In most cases the monastery was simply administering what it had been granted but there are some grounds for thinking that, where the monastery held large "multiple estates", it may have reorganised them to meet the new social conditions of the age. Work on Shapwick *(Corcos 1983)* suggests internal reorganisation of the estate in the tenth century, which provided for a nucleated village settlement and newly laid out fields. But Shapwick itself was only a part of a much larger unit and it may well be that the laying out of new estates along the top of the Poldens marks another part of the same enterprise.

MINSTERS

The siting of minster churches, often close to Roman villa sites as at Cheddar, Banwell and Keynsham *(Pearce 1982)*, or near Roman cemeteries as at Ilchester *(Dunning 1975)*, or late Roman mausolea as at Wells *(Rodwell 1982)*, suggests that kings were often constrained by relationships and religious forces which predate the period of foundation in the early eighth century. Other sites may also betray the need to take account of existing sacred sites. The minster on the royal estate of Williton, St

Decumans, is not close to the royal 'tun' which gives the estate its name, but out in the country, near to the sacred spring of St Decuman, itself probably a pagan site connected with celtic severed head and spring cults.

Despite its relatively late foundation (909) as the head minster the choice of the site at Wells is clearly constrained by the presence of a major cult there, which may have been powerful enough to have commanded the whole of the 60 hides which was credited to the cathedral in Domesday Book *(Thorn and Thorn 1980)*, even before it was the head minster.

Where such constraints did not operate the king was free to found churches at places convenient to the major royal secular sites, reflecting their use by the community of high ranking people and the need for those of a lower social status to turn towards the social centre of their community to meet their religious needs.

In Somerset we have regrettably little information about the extent or pattern of church building during later Anglo-Saxon times. The well known ordinances of King Edgar concerning tithes, issued between 959 and 963, give valuable information about the relationships between churches and show that by the mid-tenth century a hierarchy of status, probabaly related ultimately to date of foundation and the prestige of the founder, was clearly defined:

> *"And all payment of tithe is to be made to the old minster to which the parish belongs and it is to be rendered both from the thegns, demesne lands and from the land of his tenants according as it is brought under the plough.*
>
> *If however there is any thegn who has on his own bookland a church with which there is a graveyard, he is to pay the third part of his own tithe into his church.*
>
> *If anyone has a church with which there is no graveyard he is then to pay to his priest from the nine parts what he chooses. And all church scot is to go to the old minster from every free hearth."*
> *(Whitlock 1955 p 395).*

3.3 *East Pennard Church, listed as Pennarminster in The Domesday Book, although none of the Saxon fabric remains*

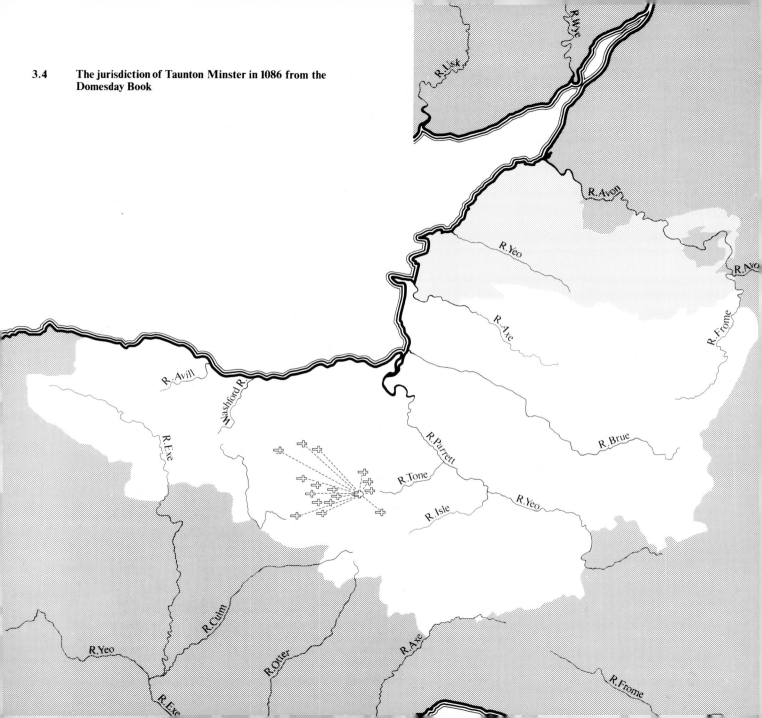

3.4 The jurisdiction of Taunton Minster in 1086 from the Domesday Book

The hierarchy of churches was: the chief minster (the cathedral), the old minster, the church with a graveyard and the field church or chapel without a graveyard.

The old minster had around it a parish in which might stand other less important churches. Even in 1086 some of these 'parochiae' can be recognised. The case of Taunton is a good example. The Domesday entry for Taunton shows vestigial ecclesiastical rights still attached to the minster in Taunton for many of the places inside the Bishop of Winchester's manor of Taunton, although these places are often some miles distant from the centre of the borough. The communities mentioned as being tributary to Taunton had clearly been a part of its parochia at an earlier date (Fig. 3.4). The fact that only the lords of these subsiduary settlements needed to be buried in Taunton shows that this was a symbolic link with a mother church and that even at this date the rest of the population were being buried in graveyards in their own communities. This suggests that they mostly had churches of their own by the end of the Anglo-Saxon period, although it does not imply that they **all** had graveyards or churches of their own.

Church building has left very little evidence from before the Norman Conquest and no Anglo-Saxon church at the 'estate' level can be recognised anywhere in the county. However it is possible that in many communities there were chapels in existence before 1086 and that they were later absorbed into the growing parochial system, either vanishing completely, or surviving only as 'free chapels'. At Alston Sutton in the parish of Upper (formerly Nether) Weare a free chapel existed throughout the Middle Ages *(Woodward 1982)*. Although it existed inside the parish of Upper Weare, this chapel had its own tithes *(Tithe Map for Alston Sutton, ref. D/D/Rt92 in the Somerset County Record Office, Taunton)*. The chapel stood on a site next to the manor house of the estate *(Tithe Map number 110, Chapel Hay and 111 Court Hay)*. Alston Sutton is one of a small group of estates on the Isle of Wedmore which includes Stone Allerton, Chapel Allerton and Badgworth which were probably laid out as newly planned communities in the tenth or the early eleventh centuries. The chapel at Alston Sutton would have been part of the village amenities provided when the site was founded, which was certainly pre-Domesday. Chapel Allerton lay in the ecclesiastical jurisdiction of Wedmore of which it was a dependency. However it eventually broke free to become a parish church in its own right, unlike the chapel at Alston Sutton. Probably many other small chapels which have now vanished appeared in the tenth century and it seems likely that many of the village churches with graveyards were also in existence by the eleventh century, judging by Edgar's Laws.

It seems that the hierarchical development of local churches was the consequence of the break-up of the multiple estate system. As smaller economically independent units emerged with a more numerous body of rural landholders the local church also multiplied, built and owned by this class for the usual mixture of social, religious and economic reasons. The local church, standing next to the lord's hall, proclaimed his independence and his social status. It drew his peasantry into a closer relationship of dependence, since the priest was also his creature, and it also increased his income, by diverting a proportion of the tithes into the lord's church and so into his pocket *(Whitelock 1955)*. The parish church can be seen as a monument to the rising affluence of the tenth century countryside and to the growing influence at the local level of the secular landholders.

3.5 *Wilton Church near Taunton. Probable long and short Anglo-Saxon masonry. (Vertical joint to the right of the window)*

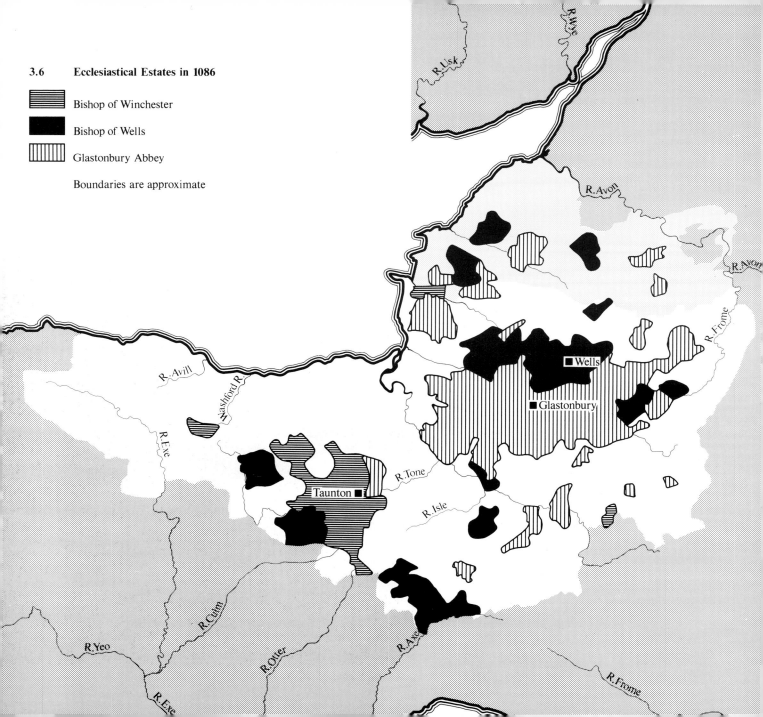

3.6   Ecclesiastical Estates in 1086

Bishop of Winchester

Bishop of Wells

Glastonbury Abbey

Boundaries are approximate

Wells

Glastonbury

Taunton

R.Wye

R.Usk

R.Avon

R.Avon

R.Frome

R.Avill

Washford R.

R.Exe

R.Tone

R.Isle

R.Yeo

R.Culm

R.Otter

R.Exe

R.Axe

R.Frome

Part 2 From the Norman Conquest to the Reformation
Joseph Bettey

The Church had a greater impact upon the medieval landscape of Somerset than any other human agency. Throughout the Middle Ages few secular buildings could compare in size and grandeur with those of the Church; the towers of the parish churches were everywhere to be seen rising above fields and dwellings, the monastic houses dominated the landscape, the ecclesiastical estates in Somerset included more than a third of the county (Fig. 3.6), while not even the wildest stretch of moorland, the most secluded valley or the deepest marsh were out of earshot of the church bells. The Church dominated the economic life of many Somerset parishes no less completely than it controlled the spiritual life of all the medieval inhabitants of the county. As a major landowner, employer of labour, purchaser of services and goods, as the patron and founder of markets and fairs, the Church exercised a powerful economic influence throughout Somerset as in all other parts of England.

In Wells the Church held total power, and the great cathedral, the palace of the bishops, the Vicars' Close and the parish church of St Cuthbert, all served to emphasise the power of the Church in the city. Monastic houses dominated several other towns; Glastonbury, Bath, Keynsham and Bruton all existed beneath the shadow of wealthy monasteries, and monastic houses such as Cleeve, Montacute, Barlinch, Muchelney, Athelney, Woodspring, Witham and Hinton Charterhouse each controlled the surrounding countryside with their lavish buildings, numerous servants and widespread lands.

Apart from its religious buildings, the Church also had a major effect upon the landscape as the initiator of land reclamation and drainage projects, the promoter and financer of mining schemes, the founder of towns and

3.7 *The Bishop's Palace, Wells*

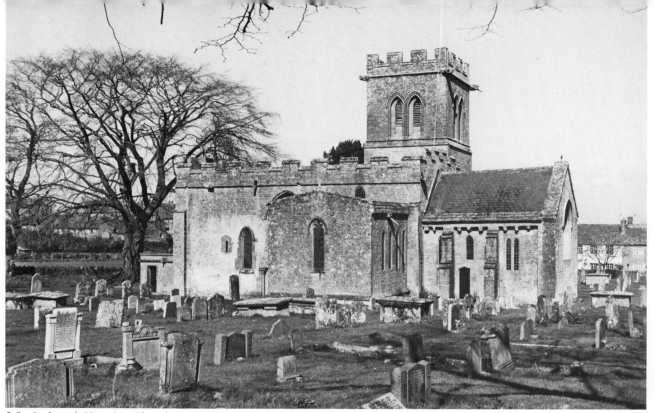

3.8 *Stoke sub Hamdon Church, south elevation*

ports, and as the builder of farms, granges and barns.

The period from the Norman Conquest to the Reformation saw a constant process of church building, alteration and enlargement. Examples of small Norman churches survive in a few places, notably at Culbone, Sutton Bingham and Swell, or can be clearly recognised beneath later work as at Stoke-sub-Hamdon, Compton Martin, Englishcombe or Lullington; but most Somerset churches were so much enlarged or so completely rebuilt during the prosperous years of the later Middle Ages that often only fragments survive of the earlier parts of their structure. Only seventeen Somerset churches are listed in the Domesday Survey of 1086, but more than 150 surviving Norman fonts and numerous doorways or fragments of carving are evidence of the number of early churches in the county. During the next four-and-a-half centuries many new churches were built and existing churches enlarged; aisles were added, chancels extended,

roofs were raised and clerestories built, while the later Middle Ages saw ever larger and finer churches with wide naves and aisles, soaring pillars to support the fine wooden roofs, large chancels for the increasingly elaborate ritual, and most impressive of all, the elegant western towers which continue to provide such notable landmarks throughout the county.

The Norman fonts and the surviving Romanesque carvings in Somerset churches bear witness to the beliefs and attitudes of parishioners during the eleventh and twelfth centuries, and show the impetus which led to the great increase in the number of churches. A major motive was the certainty of the ever-present power of evil in the world and the urgent need for the Christian soul to seek the protection of the Sacraments of the Church. The incessant battle between good and evil and the constant danger from the powers of darkness can be appreciated in the sophisticated carving of the battle between St Michael and the dragon on the north wall of Stoke-sub-Hamdon and in the galaxy of monsters which decorate the corbel table of the chancel, in the conflict between the four sphinxes and four devils on the font at East Pennard, in the carving of St Michael and the dragon above the Norman doorway at Flax Bourton, in the monsters, grotesques and demons at Stogursey, in the four figures which clasp the font and repel the snakes at Locking. Best of all is the font at Lullington where the ornate Norman carving shows the flower-strewn heavenly mansions which may be attained through adherence to the Church and its Sacraments, while all around are depicted the grotesque powers of evil, including the pagan horned god, which lie in wait for the unwary soul, and around the bowl of the font is the deeply-cut inscription **'HOC FONTIS SACRO PEREUNT DELICTA LAVACRO'** *(In the sacred washing of this font are sins cleansed)*. Lullington also possesses the remarkably fine Romanesque figure of Christ above the north door, as well as a collection of monsters and mythical figures in the corbel table and on either side of the chancel arch.

The continuing process whereby new parishes were founded, new churches built, or existing chapels and daughter churches acquired parochial status with rights of baptism and burial, is very clear from the surviving documentary evidence. So also is the way in which large sums of money were raised for the new buildings and the methods by which the building work was organised. Bishops' registers include many licences granted for the founding of chapels and oratories, as well as licences by which subsidiary chapels were given rights of burial and baptism and gradually acquired parochial status. For example, between 1332 and 1338 Ralph of Shrewsbury, Bishop of Bath and Wells 1329–1363, granted licences for the establishment of chapels and oratories in no less than seventy-six places all over Somerset *(Scott Holmes 1896 p-lxix–lxx)*. Some chapels-of-ease soon became parish churches in their own right; others continued for several centuries to be subsidiary to their mother churches, even though some chapels were enlarged and rebuilt on the grandest scale. St Mary Redcliffe remained as a daughter church of Bedminster throughout the Middle Ages; Leigh-on-Mendip continued to be a daughter church of Mells notwithstanding the fact that the worshippers there raised enormous sums of money to rebuild their church and to erect one of the finest of all the Somerset towers; as late as 1455 the inhabitants of Leigh-on-Mendip were admonished by the bishop for failing to recognise their

3.9 *Locking font*

3.10 *Detail of Lullington font*

allegiance to Mells and for not providing bread to be blessed on Sundays in the parish church *(Hobhouse 1887 p 257)*. The large parish of Crewkerne continued throughout the Middle Ages to be surrounded by a ring of subsidiary churches or chapels—Wayford, Misterton, Seaborough and others *(Dunning 1978 p 28–9; Dunning 1976a)*. When the antiquary John Leland visited Chew Magna in c. 1540 he noted that

> *'There be dyvers paroche chirches there aboute that once a year do homage unto Chute (Chew Magna) their mother chyrche'* *(Toulmin Smith 1906 p 103).*

3.11 *High Ham Church*

As late as the eighteenth century the responsibility for repairing specific sections of the churchyard wall of the ancient minster at Chew Magna was still laid upon the daughter churches at Chew Stoke, Norton, Stowey and Dundry who continued to bury their dead at the mother church *(Aston 1985 p 48–9)*. The gradual progress from the status of chapel-of-ease to that of parish church can be seen at Witham where a chapel had been established during the twelfth century for the lay brothers who were attached to the Carthusian monastery. By the fifteenth century there were no longer any lay brothers and paid servants were employed to cultivate the monastic lands; these men were of course married and brought with them their wives and children, so that in 1459–60 the bishop gave permission for a baptismal font, a churchyard and a place of burial to be established at the chapel of 'La Frary' and for a chaplain to be appointed to minister to the spiritual needs of the monastic servants *(Maxwell-Lyte and Dawes 1934 p 312–3 and 318–9)*. Likewise at Chewton Keynsham in 1460 the inhabitants of the hamlet which was within the parish of Keynsham were given licence to appoint a chaplain and have services in their chapel of the Holy Cross because they were more than a mile from the parish church and the road was made dangerous by the strong stream and floods of the river Chew *(Maxwell-Lyte and Dawes 1934 p 350)*.

Ashwick church was originally founded as a chapelry of the minster at Kilmersdon, and evidence of the way in which it gradually acquired rights of its own including rights of burial in 1413 comes from the cartulary of Buckland priory which was a major landowner at Ashwick. In 1413 the Bishop of Bath and Wells caused a churchyard to be dedicated at Ashwick and rights of burial were given to the church because of its distance from Kilmersdon

> *'it being distant three English miles and more, and the difficulties of the ways, deep with water at many times of the year and covered with snow . . .'*

Ashwick was also permitted to have its own chaplain to celebrate mass there; but as a sign of their continuing dependence upon the mother church at Kilmersdon all the inhabitants of Ashwick were to attend mass at Kilmersdon on the patronal festival and offer three pence at the high altar *'in sign of their subjection and obedience'* *(Weaver 1909 p 95–6)*. Bishops' registers also provide evidence for the decline of some settlements, the desertion, decay or demolition of churches and the union of some parishes. For example the parishes of Berkley and Fairoak were united in 1460 on account of their poverty, their nearness to each other and the small number of their parishioners; and in 1454 the church at Standerwick was described as having been long deserted and in utter ruin *(Maxwell-Lyte and Dawes 1934 p 242 and p 403–4)*. An example of the way even a well-established parish church could fall into disuse and disappear so completely that even its site is uncertain, is Wittenham alias Rowley on the borders of Wiltshire and Somerset. The village was situated along the Wiltshire side of the river Frome and was in the diocese of Salisbury. The first reference to the parish church occurs in 1299, but no doubt a church existed long before that for a settlement is referred to in a charter of 987. By the fourteenth century it was an independent parish with its own rector and churchwardens; the church was dedicated to St Nicholas, and consisted of a nave and chancel together with a churchyard. By the late fourteenth century the village was in decline, possibly because of the Black Death or perhaps because part of it had been destroyed to make a park for the Hungerfords at Farleigh Hungerford castle which is on the Somerset side of the river Frome. In 1428 Lord Hungerford was granted a licence to unite the parishes of Farleigh Hungerford and Wittenham on the grounds that the latter was depopulated and impoverished. Thereafter Wittenham church seems rapidly to have fallen into decay; there is a brief entry in the **Valor Ecclesiasticus** of 1535, but no subsequent references. By the nineteenth century all memory of its situation had been lost, although the most likely situation, a piece of open common, was still known as Holy Green *(Crittall 1953 p 69--75 and Jackson 1872 p 227–51)*.

The situation and surroundings of other churches provide evidence of desertions, movements of population or other changes in the settlement pattern of the parish, for since parish churches have tended to cling to their original sites in spite of later changes of settlement, they provide an invaluable fixed point for all aspects of landscape study. A good example is Holcombe where the isolated Norman church is surrounded by earthworks of the original settlement; other churches which are now isolated because of medieval or later population movements, economic changes, or the creation of mansions, parks and formal gardens include Babington, Cameley, Hardington, Broadway, Stocklinch Ottersey, Alford and Nettlecombe.

One of the principal questions which must trouble any thoughtful visitor to the splendid parish churches of Somerset is how the small medieval communities could have raised the enormous sums of money which were required to build, furnish, decorate and maintain these large buildings. Considerable evidence survives from the later Middle Ages concerning the ways in which money was raised for church building and on how the work was organised. In a few places new churches or aisles, chapels and chantries were paid for by one or more wealthy benefactors. The Hungerford family who acquired widespread estates in Wiltshire and north-east Somerset during the later fourteenth century were notable founders of chantries and almshouses, and in Somerset contributed lavishly to church buildings at Farleigh Hungerford and Wellow *(Hicks 1985 p 123–33)*. North Cadbury church was rebuilt on a grand scale during the early fifteenth century by Lady Elizabeth Botreaux who intended to found there a college of priests *(Wickham 1965 p 32)*. Two of the last abbots of Glastonbury, John Selwood (1456–93) and Richard Bere (1493–1524), were generous in their contributions to building work on parish churches, and their initials are to be found in several places, including East Brent, Chedzoy, Bruton, Othery and Westonzoyland. An account of the rebuilding of High Ham church was inserted in the parish register by an Elizabethan rector, Adrian Schaell. He records that much of the cost of the work in 1476 was paid for by several persons including John Selwood, the abbot of Glastonbury, John Dyer the rector, Sir Amias Poulett and various local gentry.

> '. . .lest the remembrance of that Churche newly erected from the foundation, together with diverse other thinges perteininge thereunto, throughe the continuance of time and death of the auncient inhabitantes thereabout, should utterly perishe, . . . I have thought good, as well for the love of antiquity as for the commodity of the parishe, to comitt those thinges unto writinges . . . The Church of Higham . . . was builded anew from the foundacon and troughly finished in the space of one yeare, which was from the nativity of Criste 1476, and this was performed by John Selwood, then Abbot of Glaston, . . and certain other personages. . . which at that time in the thicke mist of error and superstition (with a certaine devoute intent as they thought) did both bountifully and readily contribute charges to the same.' (Crossman 1894 p 117–22).

But the great majority of parishes had no wealthy benefactor, and in such places the rebuilding, enlargement or furnishing of the parish church rested entirely upon the

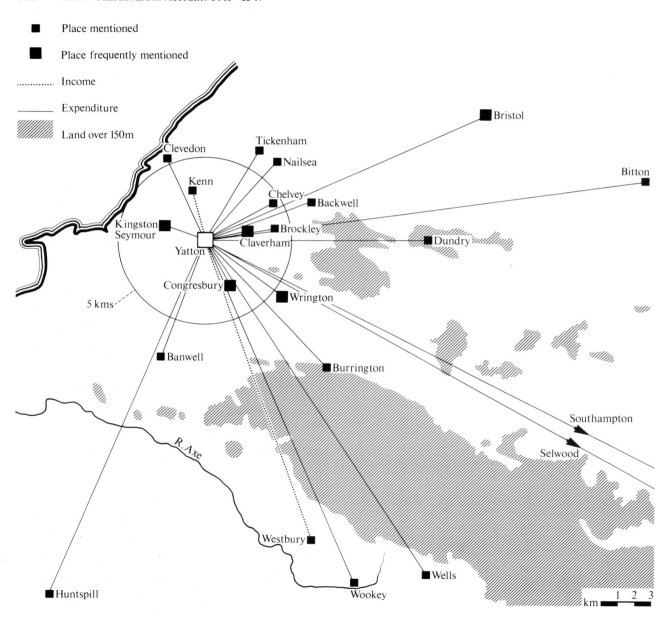

3.12 Yatton Churchwarden Accounts 1445–1547

■ Place mentioned

■ Place frequently mentioned

.... Income

——— Expenditure

▨ Land over 150m

Bristol

Bitton

Tickenham

Clevedon

Nailsea

Kenn

Chelvey

Backwell

Kingston
Seymour

Brockley

Yatton

Claverham

Dundry

5 kms

Congresbury

Wrington

Banwell

Burrington

Southampton

R. Axe

Selwood

Westbury

Wells

Huntspill

Wookey

km 1 2 3

Yatton Churchwardens Accounts 1445–1547

Recorded expenditure on goods or services at a particular place.

Backwell
—*oak, carpenter*
Banwell
—*ringers for church ale*
Bitton
—*riding to*
Bristol
—*buy vestements, cope, bells, boards, paint*
Brockley
—*oak*
Chelvey
—*stone to grind colours*
Claverham
—*lightmen, chapel*
Clevedon
—*fetch a horse*
Congresbury
—*church ale, smithy, timber*
Dundry
—*stone for spire*
Huntspill
—*speak to clerks*
Kingston Seymour
—*writing of a book, a wheel, church ale*
Nailsea
—*stone, tile*
Selwood
—*timber*
Southampton
—*boards*
Tickenham
—*wood*
Wells
—*carriage of altar table to be blessed*
Wookey
—*to bless chalice at Bishop's manor house*
Wrington
—*fetch a horse, church.*

parishioners. The evidence of late-medieval wills and the churchwardens' accounts of St Michael's, Bath, Yatton, Croscombe, Pilton, Tintinhull, Banwell, Yeovil and elsewhere, shows that the necessary money was raised by the parishioners themselves through 'church ales', collections, gifts and fund-raising activities, and that the building work was arranged and supervised by the churchwardens *(Hobhouse 1890; Dunning 1976 p 11–18)*. At Yatton the fine set of detailed churchwardens' accounts starting in 1445 show how very large sums of money were raised in the parish for successive projects on the church (Fig. 3.12). Almost all of the money came from the parishioners, with few contributions from wealthy families like the Newtons of Court de Wyck at Claverham in Yatton. Money was raised by collections and above all by church ales, organised by the churchwardens and held in the church house which they built on the edge of the churchyard. Many gifts were received in kind—rings, livestock, wheat, timber and household utensils. The Yatton accounts, like those of other parishes, leave no doubt of the enthusiasm which existed for enlarging, furnishing and decorating the church in the grandest possible style; whether this enthusiasm was engendered by an understandable desire to escape the fires of hell, by rivalry with neighbouring parishes, or by genuine devotion to set forth the greater glory of God, makes no difference to the result of all the activity which was to produce superb churches full of the most elaborate and colourful furnishings. The work was organised and supervised by the churchwardens, and their accounts show lavish expenditure on stone from Dundry, timber, lime, scaffolding and roofing materials including a ton of lead which they bought from Mendip in 1489, as well as on masons, carpenters, carvers and painters. The whole nave was remodelled, although the central tower from the earlier church was retained, a notably fine west front was created surmounted by a carving of the Trinity, and an ornately carved porch was built, all in Dundry stone. At Yatton, as in other west-country churches, a result of all this late-medieval building work is to leave a marked contrast between the lofty nave on which money has been lavished by the parishioners, and the small low chancel of the earlier church. The chancel was the responsibility of one of the prebends of Wells cathedral and was not rebuilt or enlarged like the nave *(Edwards 1986 p 536–46) (Note 2)*. At Dunster, the central tower was built during the 1440s, and the contract for the work survives, made between the churchwardens and John Marys, a mason from Stogursey.

The contract stipulated that the height of the tower was to be 100 feet, and that it was to be paid for at the rate of 13s 4d per foot, the parishioners supplying all the materials. The upper windows in the tower were to be made according to the pattern or design of Richard Pope, a free mason who was at that time engaged in work on Sherborne Abbey, but apart from this, very few conditions were laid down about the manner in which the tower was to be constructed, and it was left to John Marys to build it 'sufficiently' and 'after reason and good proportion.' An interesting point which emerges from the Dunster contract is that few men were employed on the work, and consequently the contract provided that if any of the stones was so large that John Marys and two of his workmen could not lift it then the parishioners were to provide the necessary muscle power.

> 'Allso if there be any stone y-wroughte of such quantity that ii men or iii at moste may not kary hym, the sayde parishe shall helpe hym.' (Salzman 1952 p 514–5).

The construction of the elegant spire at Bridgwater in 1366–7 was paid for by parish collections and by the gift of money and goods by the parishioners; nearly £137 was raised for the project by the enthusiasm of local people *(Dilks 1933 p 63–7; Dunning 1980 p 46).* At Mells the church was rebuilt on a lavish scale during the early sixteenth century and the money was raised by the parishioners; John Leland in c. 1540 commented that it was built *'yn tyme of mynde . . . by the hole paroche' (Toulmin Smith 1906).* The fine late-medieval churches in the Somerset towns bear witness to the wealth and prosperity of the period as well as to the piety of those who contributed so generously to rebuild churches such as those at Ilminster, Crewkerne, Axbridge or Yeovil. The great outburst of building activity on Somerset parish churches during the later Middle Ages is most evident in the landscape in the ornate and expensive towers. There can be no doubt that parishes vied with each other in the size and magnificence of these towers, some of which were still being constructed during the 1530s when the early Reformation legislation was being passed by Parliament. The evidence of wills from Chewton Mendip shows how money was being left during the early sixteenth century to complete the magnificent tower there with its finely carved figure of the Risen Christ, and the evidence of wills can also be used to date the late-medieval towers of Batcombe, St Mary's, Taunton, Mells and Leigh-on-Mendip *(Weaver 1901; Dunning 1976; Wickham 1965; Harvey 1982).* Bequests from Taunton merchants for the tower of St Mary's included money, cloth, iron, wine and woad while the humbler townsfolk left money, valuables and household goods *(Dunning 1983 p 45).* The tower at Dundry which provides such a notable landmark on the hill above Bristol was erected in 1484 and paid for by the Merchant Venturers of Bristol.

It was not only through its religious buildings, the cathedral, abbeys, priories, parish churches and chapelries, that the medieval Church dominated the landscape of Somerset, for the Church was also one of the greatest of

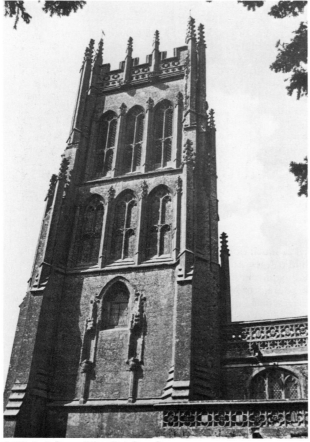

3.13 *Leigh-on-Mendip church tower*

3.14 *Meare Fish House*

medieval landowners. By the time of the Domesday
Survey in 1086 Glastonbury abbey already possessed one-
eighth of the land of Somerset while several other
monastic houses were also extremely wealthy, and these
rich institutions had a profound effect upon the landscape
and the evidence of their impact is still very apparent.
Great monastic barns survive at Pilton, Doulting,
Glastonbury, Ditcheat, Kelston, Woodspring and
elsewhere; the early fourteenth-century fish-house at
Meare which belonged to Glastonbury abbey, the
dovecotes at Stogursey, Witham, Stoke-sub-Hamdon,
Dunster, Kelston and Blackford (Selworthy) or the
remains in the Levels are all reminders of the way in which
the ecclesiastical landowners exploited the resources of
their estates. Glastonbury, Wells, Athelney and Muchelney
between them owned two-thirds of the Somerset Levels as

well as much of the surrounding uplands through the
Middle Ages, and these wealthy institutions played the
leading part in medieval drainage work *(Williams 1970)*.
Large areas of Mendip were owned by various
ecclesiastical bodies, the Bishop, the Dean and Chapter,
Glastonbury abbey and several other abbeys and
institutions including Bath, Witham, Hinton Charterhouse,
Keynsham, Stanley abbey in Wiltshire, the Knights
Templars, St John's Hospital in Bristol and the hospital of
the Holy Cross in Winchester. A few place-names preserve
the memory of these former owners; the Carthusians gave
the name to Charterhouse-on-Mendip, the Knights
Templars to Templedown farm, there is a St Cross farm in
Litton and a Chancellor's farm in West Harptree *(Neale
1976)*. The memory of the estate on Mendip owned by the
Carthusian monks of Hinton Charterhouse was still alive

forty years after the monastery was dissolved, for in an action before the Court of Exchequer during the reign of Elizabeth elderly witnesses could recall the monks' farm at Green Ore and the monastic sheep flock which was kept there. One witness declared that

> *'the priors kept upon Greeneworth als Grenewore a thousand sheep by the great hundred, viz upon Furzhill 800, upon Stockhill 400. And as touching Whitnell als Whitnalls this deponent remembereth not whether the priors dyd farme it out or held the same in their owne hands.'*

He also remembered in great detail the cattle, colts and pigs which the prior of Hinton Charterhouse kept upon Mendip, and the furze and turf which was cut there for the monastery *(Note 3)*. The ecclesiastical estates were carefully managed by literate overseers, and it is upon the surviving account rolls of Glastonbury abbey and the bishopric of Winchester that much of our knowledge of the medieval economy, farming and trade of Somerset is based. The surviving records of Glastonbury abbey show the large-scale farming activity, with enormous sheep flocks and carefully planned use of the arable lands, while this monastery with others was also involved in lead mining on Mendip and was active in land reclamation and in providing sea-defences along the coast *(Watkin 1947–56; Keil 1965)*. During the thirteenth century under the energetic leadership of the notable abbot Michael of Amesbury (abbot 1235–52) the arable lands of Glastonbury were extended, land was drained, enclosed and reclaimed from the sea and from the marshes, new barns, sheep houses, dairies and dovecotes were constructed and stock was increased until there were some 1,300 cattle and over 7,000 sheep *(Williams 1970 p 25–70)*.

The Church also possessed deer-parks like the park at Evercreech which belonged to the bishop, or that at Pilton belonging to Glastonbury. Many of the quarries at Doulting were owned by the Church, and a new town at Chard was founded by Bishop Jocelin of Wells during the early thirteenth century, although an earlier attempt to found a port at Rackley on the Axe proved abortive. Fulling mills were owned by Cleeve, Glastonbury, Hinton Charterhouse and St John's Hospital at Bath among others, while the canons of Wells owned mines on Mendip and leased a quarry at Doulting *(HMC 1907; Shorrocks 1974)*. The Cistercian monks of Cleeve abbey were actively engaged in large-scale farming enterprises, while the hospitality which they provided for travellers in that part of west Somerset was remembered in their favour at the time of the Dissolution *(Dunning 1985a p 58–67)*. The Church also actively encouraged contributions to roads, bridges and other public works. For example, in 1445 Bishop Thomas Bekynton granted forty days indulgence to all who contributed to the repair of the road from Bristol to Dundry which was dangerous to travellers; and when in 1458 the harbour at Watchet was destroyed by a storm all parishes in the diocese were exhorted by the Bishop to send alms for its reconstruction *(Hobhouse 1887; Maxwell-Lyte & Dawes 1934)*. Earlier, Bishop Bubwith (1407–24) had encouraged the laity to contribute to the repair of roads, causeways and bridges, as well as giving money for religious projects *(Scott Holmes 1913–14)*. Some religious guilds also had a practical purpose, like the guild associated with the chapel of Our Lady on Bristol bridge, which was charged with the task of maintaining the bridge

> *'to keep and repair the Bridge of Bristol, piers, arches and walls, for the defence thereof against the ravages of the sea, ebbing and flowing daily under the same' (Bettey 1983 p 5)*.

The houses and estates of church officials were also a prominent feature of the landscape. In addition to the palace at Wells, the bishops possessed manor houses at Banwell, Evercreech, Wookey, Wiveliscombe and Chew Magna; the Treasurer's House at Martock, the Chantry House at Trent (now in Dorset), the Priest's House at Muchelney and the medieval vicarage at Congresbury are a few of the many ecclesiastical domestic properties. Evidence of the wealth and widespread possessions of Glastonbury abbey and of the style in which the last abbots lived can be found in the description of the abbey and its estates sent to Thomas Cromwell by the royal commissioners in September 1539,

> *'The house is great, goodly and so princely as we have not see the like; with 4 parks adjoining, the furthermost of them but 4 miles distant from the house; a great mere, which is 5 miles compass, well replenished with great pike, bream, perch and roach; 4 fair manor places, belonging to the late abbot, the furthermost but 3 miles distant, being goodly mansions; and also one in Dorsetshire, 30 miles distant from the late monastery' (Bettey 1986 p 158–9)*.

Late-medieval monastic buildings like the abbot's lodging at Muchelney, the gatehouses at Cleeve and Montacute or the abbot's Kitchen at Glastonbury add further weight to the idea of a sumptuous life-style enjoyed by the high-ranking clerics on the eve of the Reformation.

During the Middle Ages the church dominated the social life of most towns and villages, and many Somerset parishes had 'church houses' or parish meeting places in which social gatherings, ales, feasts and plays were held, and where money-raising activities for the church took place. Many of these survive and remain attractive and interesting features of the village scene. Good examples may be seen at Crowcombe and Chew Magna where they continue to be used for their original purpose. At Yatton and East Harptree the former church houses are now dwellings, at Stoke-sub-Hamdon and Long Ashton they have become public houses *(Cowley 1970; Bettey 1985 p 24)*.

Finally, two of the finest inns in Somerset were both originally monastic lodging houses, and continue to serve as a reminder of the range of activities undertaken by the medieval church. These are the George and Pilgrim at Glastonbury with its remarkably fine late-medieval building, and the George at Norton St Philip, which was the centre of a great medieval fair and a collecting point for wool from all over that part of Somerset. The George, like the whole of Norton St Philip and its great fair, belonged to the Carthusian monks of Hinton Charterhouse.

Note 1—The charters are numbered from Sawyer 1968
Note 2—Somerset Record Office, Yatton Churchwardens
*   Accounts 1445–1560*
Note 3—Public Record Office E134/19 Elizabeth Hil 3

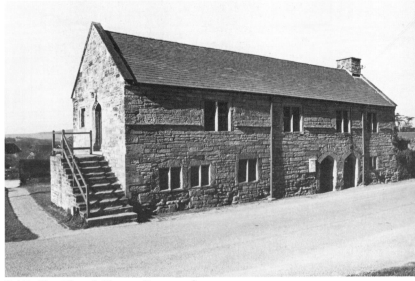

3.15 *The Church House, Crowcombe*

3.16 *The George Inn, Norton St. Philip*

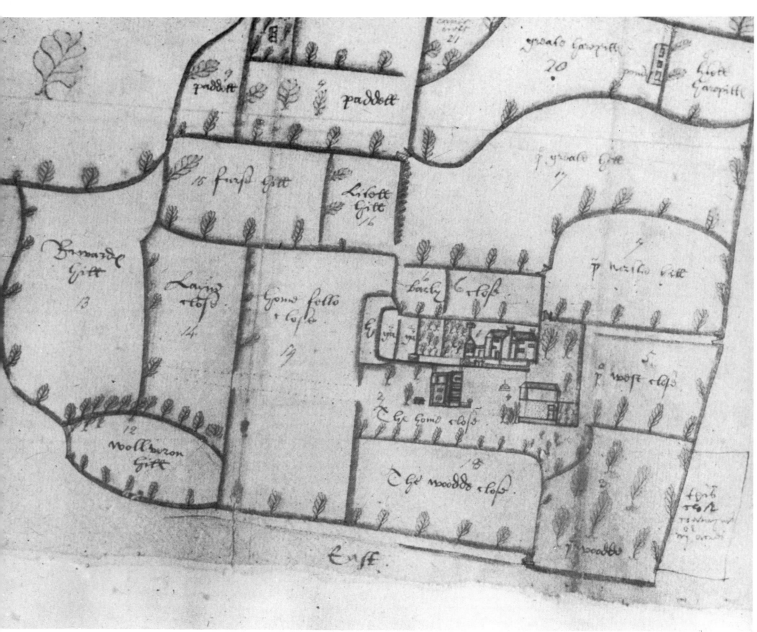

4.1 *Hazelgrove village in Queen Camel parish from a map of 1573*

Chapter 4
SETTLEMENT PATTERNS *and* FORMS

Michael Aston

Today, most people live in towns, even in a largely rural county like Somerset; yet we are all aware that the countryside around the towns is full of farms and villages. Usually, it does not occur to us to ask when these farms and villages began, why they look like they do, or whether they have changed at all. Nor do we ask why in some areas there are a lot of villages, while in others they are few and widely separated. Yet, when looking at any landscape, these are some of the first questions we should ask.

When, and how, did the pattern of settlements originate, and why do the villages and hamlets look like they do today? These are questions which are not easy to answer, and indeed, even the mechanisms for beginning an investigation of them are not readily available, although in most parts of the country they have been under examination for a long time. Yet nowhere are these problems more acute than in Somerset, which has a large area, a very varied topography, geology and relief, and a great variety of present-day settlement patterns and forms. It is, therefore, the purpose of this chapter to point out some of the differences in settlement pattern and form within the county of Somerset, to discuss something of the origins of the settlement pattern, and to consider the origins of the plans and forms of a few of the villages in the county. This will be set against the background of research carried out elsewhere in the country, particularly on the origins of nucleated settlements *(Roberts 1977; Taylor 1983).*

Examination of vertical air photographs (such as the RAF series taken around 1947) or the larger scale maps (1:50000, 1:25000, or 1:10000 series by the Ordnance Survey) quickly reveals great diversity in the pattern of farmsteads, hamlets and villages, and in their individual forms, in different parts of Somerset. Recent considerations of 'village England' as opposed to 'hamlet and farmstead Britain' show that Somerset lies on the border of the main division between the two *(Thorpe 1964; Roberts 1977).* Studies of what have been called the 'planned' and the 'ancient' countryside of England likewise locate Somerset on the border area *(Rackham 1986 p 3–5).* The general impression, then, is that Somerset is not really a county of villages (depending on the definition of villages which is adopted), although villages certainly do occur, and can most readily be identified in the centre, south, and south-east of the county. Nevertheless, the abiding impression is of a county of hamlets and farmsteads—particularly noticeable in the west of the county on and around Exmoor and in the Vale of Taunton Deane.

SOURCES OF INFORMATION

As already mentioned, in seeking to investigate settlements in this way we are confronted by great difficulties. Most villages and farms do not have any really old **buildings** in them which might tell us something about the earliest types of housing and arrangements of farmsteads. The church, if the settlement has one, is usually the oldest building, and there may be a manor house, parsonage, or vicarage, perhaps of late medieval date; but the earliest cottages and farms will probably be of 16th or 17th century date, if not later. Generally speaking, then, an examination of surviving buildings and the way they are arranged does not necessarily tell us anything about the medieval settlement, although it is immensely useful in showing us something of the disposition of dwellings and farms in the centuries immediately following the Middle Ages *(Austin et al 1982).*

We may think that **documents** might help, and certainly the abundant medieval records for the county contain much topographical information which can be used to suggest general arrangements in some settlements—perhaps even the disposition of elements like churches, manor houses, wells, roads, lanes, and so on. But nowhere is there a clear description of a village or farm in, say, the 12th or 13th century. Nor do we have anywhere a clear reference to the establishment of a village in the medieval period (or earlier), or any one example of rebuilding, development, extension, or depopulation in Somerset.

Another type of document, **maps,** ought to be extremely useful: but medieval maps are extremely rare, only some 50 or so being known for the whole of Britain, and none for Somerset. The earliest map of a village is that of Boarstall in Buckinghamshire (1444): for Somerset the earliest known so far is that of 1573 for part of Queen Camel parish (Fig. 4.1). This is Tudor rather than medieval, but it does show the plan of Hazelgrove, a village which has now gone, with its houses, village green, and even its village cross. Even for the 16th century, though, such maps are rare, and so we cannot rely on them as a source to show us what medieval villages looked like by the end of the Middle Ages.

Of course, the best way forward would be to **excavate** a village and record all the earlier buildings, their contemporary closes, roads, and lanes, together with the pottery, bones, metalwork, and so on that would indicate to us how earlier people had lived there. But there are difficulties in this approach, not the least of which being that modern excavation is both very expensive and time consuming. The greatest difficulty, however, is that most medieval villages are still occupied, and short of evicting all the modern inhabitants (a method of research not yet considered respectable!), little can be achieved in a village which is still lived in and flourishing. The archaeological information will remain buried beneath houses and gardens for the future. Some progress could be made, however, just from collecting pottery samples from the garden soil of each house in the village. The different types of pottery sherds represented would at least indicate to us likely areas of occupation for different periods.

How, then, can we say anything about the form of Somerset's villages—why they look like they do, and how (and when) they came into existence? At the moment, two main approaches and methods are used. Firstly, we use archaeological **fieldwork,** particularly in the location and recording of surface features like earthworks and scatters of stone and pottery in ploughed fields. More important, however, is the examination of the **plan elements** in villages—the layout of properties, the arrangement of such features as village greens, patterns of lanes, and the disposition of churches, manor houses, and farmsteads. In particular, we look for degrees of regularity or otherwise, which might suggest deliberate planning, and clear cases of a succession of features, where a road or property alignment definitely overlies or cuts through earlier features. Secondly, we have to be aware of research elsewhere in the country, where either better documentation or greater archaeological opportunities have produced new information, enabling new ideas to be developed about how and when villages developed, and why they have their present appearance. Such research will be referred to below as we consider the settlements in Somerset.

OLD AND NEW IDEAS

It is often assumed by some local historians, or was until recently, that villages were introduced by Anglo-Saxon invaders in the centuries following the Roman period, the so-called 'Dark Ages' between AD 400 and 700. New work, however, has cast great doubt on this interpretation of events. It is clear, for example, that far from being forested and marshy wildernesses, counties like Somerset were actually well settled in the preceding prehistoric and Roman centuries. There is abundant evidence for numerous Roman villas in Somerset, and other types of settlement have recently begun to be recorded. Roger Leech has excavated a Roman village at Catsgore, near Somerton, and air photographs are revealing large numbers of contemporary farms showing up as cropmarks in ripening crops *(Leech 1978, 1982)*. Similarly, in addition to hillforts and such sites as the Glastonbury and Meare 'lakes villages', there is increasing evidence that there were large numbers of farms in the landscape before the Roman conquest *(Burrow 1982)*. At the other end of the Roman period, it is now clear that there was much greater continuity of occupation and land use in the post-Roman period, especially in Somerset, than was hitherto thought, and we can no longer assume that a lack of Roman pottery and coins on a Roman settlement in the 5th and 6th centuries means that it was abandoned by that time *(Rahtz 1982)*.

According to the documentary sources (and there is nothing from the archaelogical record to contradict this), the Saxons arrived in the county in the 7th century, by which time they were already Christian and it is by no means clear what is meant by either 'Saxons' or 'arrived'.

The 'post-Romans' of Somerset had been around for some 200–300 years by this time. The idea of an Anglo-Saxon invasion, then, is not really credible: it is most likely that there was some sort of aristocratic takeover, with little large-scale folk movement, and hence little need for large numbers of new settlements.

Moreover, even in eastern England the 'Dark Ages' cannot now be seen as the time when villages were first developed. The Anglo-Saxon settlements that have been identified for the early period (for example, West Stow in Suffolk *(West 1985)*, Mucking in Essex, and Eynsham in Oxfordshire *(Gray 1974)*), and even those for the 7th and 8th centuries (for example, Chalton *(Addyman & Leigh 1973)* and Cowdery's Down in Hampshire *(Millet & James 1983)*, and Catholme in Staffordshire), largely consist of scatters of farmsteads and buildings with no obvious focus, such as a village green; they often seem to be set between existing Roman settlements, which occupied the better land. There is nothing so far from archaeological investigation to indicate the regular village with its green and farmsteads which is still seen as the archetypal Saxon settlement in many text books. Rather, the picture is of a dispersed pattern of Romano-British farmsteads and villages with a few Anglo-Saxon settlements founded between. There appears to be no regular plan to any of the Saxon sites investigated so far, although some of the Romano-British settlements do look like large, regularly planned, villages.

In Somerset, then, we should be looking for evidence of prehistoric and Romano-British settlements continuing into the 6th and 7th centuries and perhaps beyond. We should expect these to be mainly farmsteads and hamlets, rather than large villages, and we should not expect them to possess particularly regular plans, but to appear as irregular groups of buildings. Can we see any of these settlements in the county?

SAXON SETTLEMENTS IN SOMERSET

It must be said from the outset that nowhere in the county can we see a clear example of a farm, hamlet, or village of the period from the 5th to the 12th century. None has been excavated, and although we have place-names and references in documents, none of these can be applied with any certainty to a particular place, nor in any way that helps us to appreciate what it looked like at that time. There are, however, lots of clues to where such settlements might lie, and by using evidence from elsewhere in the country we can get some idea of what they might have looked like.

Firstly, it is possible that a great many medieval settlements are on the sites of Roman settlements. This is clear from the finds of Roman pottery and other material from within and around them. The large number of both Romano-British and medieval settlements means that there is bound to be overlap in many cases. Continuity of occupation, however, cannot automatically be assumed in every case; it is not clear from any example whether there has been **continuous** occupation of the same site from Roman times to the present day, but in many cases this may be true. Finds of Roman and medieval pottery on a site may well indicate that it was occupied in the period from 400 to 1100, as well, but we would not expect to find much evidence in the form of Saxon pottery or other objects without a lot more excavation; pottery does not, in any case, seem to have been produced or used in Somerset throughout most of the Saxon period.

It is also unclear whether any of the **plans** of present settlements which have produced Roman material are of Roman date (or earlier). In many cases there must have been great changes, since there seems to be little apparent relationship between the disposition of known Roman features and the plans of the later settlements. Elsewhere in the country, however, at Wharram Percy in Yorkshire and Hound Tor on Dartmoor for example, it has been shown that some of the boundaries within the medieval settlement plans are considerably older—of late Bronze Age and Romano-British date at Wharram *(Hurst 1983)*, and Bronze Age date at Hound Tor *(Beresford 1979)*. How many more early boundaries are lurking undetected and unrecognised in our village plans?

Non-alignment of boundaries could be considered as an argument for **discontinuity** of occupation, or at least some later changes of settlement plan. Nevertheless, such apparent discontinuity does not exclude the possibility that people continued to live and farm in the immediate vicinity over a very long period. Continuity of community, of agrarian regime, or of estate structure could all have occurred without the element of continuous unbroken habitation on one site.

Roger Leech felt that the abundant evidence for some sort of Romano-British occupation beneath many documented medieval settlements meant that many of the villages had Roman origins *(Leech 1977)*. In many cases they may be on prehistoric sites. This idea is supported particularly by the research of Professor John Coles and members of the Somerset Levels Project, who have argued that settlements around the Somerset Levels in the early prehistoric period are most likely to have been sited a third of the way up the slopes of the higher land around the Levels—very much where the medieval and modern villages are, particularly those around the Poldens and along the south side of the Mendips *(Coles 1982)*. It is thus probable that the Roman, and indeed prehistoric, settlements that have been found by archaeological fieldwork may well represent only those sites which were **abandoned** in the post-Roman period. The settlement patterns of Roman and medieval sites in several parts of the county certainly suggest this, as Roger Leech has shown.

The western part of Somerset was never as Romanised as the eastern part, and the 'native' types of late prehistoric settlements and farmsteads, such as 'hill-slope enclosures' and 'rounds', seem to have continued in use right through the Roman period. The inhabitants may have used Roman pottery and coins, but perhaps never built rectangular Roman-style buildings, used Roman roads, or took part in the commercial Roman economy other than in a peripheral way. This western area seems to have had the same kinds of settlements as Devon and Cornwall.

It is likely that many of the farmsteads and hamlets which can be documented in the 12th and 13th centuries around Exmoor, the Brendon Hills, and the western side of the Quantocks lie near to and on the same land units as such earlier farmsteads *(Aston 1983)*. Only one has been excavated, at Hurscombe in Brompton Regis, where a farmstead documented to the 14th century produced pottery of probable 12th century date *(Leach 1982)*. The excavations were not extensive, and we should not expect any pottery of obviously earlier date to be immediately recognisable. Although there was no Roman pottery, the occupation of such a site may well have begun long before the 12th century.

Elsewhere, the proximity of probable prehistoric enclosures to medieval farm sites suggests continuity of land units, if not actual settlement sites, from later prehistoric to medieval times. Examples include Spangate in Wooton Courtenay, where a ruined farmstead occupies a circular enclosure, and Road (or Rode) in Winsford, where the ruins and earthworks of a farm in existence by the 14th century (as implied by a surname in the 1327 Lay Subsidy) lie below a knoll crowned by a small circular earthwork. The best example, however, is probably in the Bagley–Sweetworthy area in Luccombe parish. Here, two ringworks of unproven but probable prehistoric date have

been superceded by two farmsteads: one, Sweetworthy, probably abandoned in the Middle Ages; the other, Bagley, in use until the late 19th century. The latter is a Domesday estate of 1086, and so is probably at least late Saxon in origin, while Sweetworthy has the 'worth' element in its name which Michael Costen has suggested is associated with Saxon farmsteads. It is thus at least likely that here we have two late prehistoric farms which have continued in use right through the Saxon period into the Middle Ages, although the actual **sites** of the farm buildings at each date were slightly different.

If this analysis is correct, the fact that these settlements are high up, above 1000 feet, on the north side of Dunkery Beacon suggests that settlement was dense and ubiquitous on Exmoor even before the Norman period, and if it was so in those conditions, how much more intensively occupied were the lower and more fertile parts of Somerset likely to have been *(Aston 1985 p 85)*? Such ubiquitous upland settlement has been demonstrated elsewhere: for example in Cornwall, on Dartmoor, and in the Pennines at Ribblehead in Yorkshire *(King 1978)* and at Simy Folds in County Durham *(Coggins et al 1983)*.

It is thus likely that much of the settlement pattern in Somerset has Romano-British or prehistoric origins, even if individual settlements are not on exactly the same sites, or in the same form and arrangements, as later on. Can we say anything, then, of when the present plans and alignments of Somerset's villages developed, and why there are such differences in settlement pattern in the county—from predominantly hamlets and farmsteads in the west, to villages and hamlets in the east?

VILLAGE ORIGINS

It is a little easier to consider such problems now than it was a decade or so ago, largely because research elsewhere has indicated a number of general lines of development which are as likely to apply to Somerset as they seem to apply to everywhere else. It now seems clear, for example, that there were few large, nucleated, agglomerations of farmsteads in central and eastern England before the late Saxon period. In the north, particularly in Yorkshire and Durham, many seem to begin in the 12th century *(Allerston 1970; Roberts 1977; Sheppard 1976)*. Before then, the general pattern seems to have been one of dispersed settlement, apparently in the form of farmsteads or groups of farms in small irregular hamlets. Few of these have been excavated but many have been located from scatters of potsherds found in ploughsoil during fieldwalking, particularly in

4.2 *Lyncombe in Winsford. An isolated medieval farmstead still occupied*

Northamptonshire by Glenn Foard *(Foard 1978)*, Christopher Taylor, David Hall and others, in Essex by Tom Williamson *(Williamson 1985)*, and in Norfolk by Peter Wade-Martins *(Wade-Martins 1980)*.

The pattern of Saxon settlement suggested by these pot scatters for eastern England is very different from the large villages several miles apart which we tend to think of as the normal arrangement for the English countryside. But it is very similar to what can be seen all over Somerset, and indeed elsewhere in western Britain. Is it likely, then, that the pattern of farms and hamlets in much of Somerset is Saxon and early medieval in date? In the past, farmsteads and hamlets which are poorly documented, or even not recorded at all before the 13th or 14th centuries, have generally been considered to represent a phase of population and settlement expansion in the early Middle Ages. It has already been shown for west Somerset from the Lay Subsidy lists of 1327 *(Aston 1983)* that the present pattern of farmsteads, including those now deserted, is of 14th century date or earlier. Where further research on the

documents has been undertaken, many sites can be shown to be in existence by at least the 12th or 13th century, and some from the time of Domesday Book in the 11th century *(Everett 1968 p 54-60)*. It is likely, therefore, that this dispersed pattern of settlement is the more normal pattern in many areas of England, with villages being a later development—an 'aberration' as John Hurst has called the development of the nucleated village at Wharram Percy in Yorkshire *(Hurst 1984)*.

Despite earlier suggestions that the sites around Exmoor were farmsteads, it is probable that a large part of the earlier pattern consisted of dispersed, irregular **hamlets**. This can be demonstrated for Brompton Regis, for which we have an unusual document of 1629, listing the seats in the parish church and the particular farms and tenements in the parish to which they were attached. But is was certainly also the case for other places in the 14th century; many that are now farms, even deserted—like Mousehanger in Winsford—were probably hamlets in 1327, and perhaps earlier *(Aston 1983)*.

71

The picture is clear, then, for west Somerset: it was an area of hamlets and farmsteads in the Middle Ages, with early origins, and little alteration of sites. There was little, if any, village development, except at a few important centres like Brompton Regis and Dulverton (the latter more of a small market town), and on the north coastal plain between Porlock and Quantoxhead. Any substantial villages, such as Wheddon Cross, Simonsbath, and Exford, can be shown to be largely post-medieval developments.

Why are eastern and southern Somerset so different? These are the areas of Somerset with most villages, many of them large, like South Petherton, Martock, West Coker, Queen Camel, and so on. Yet these are not like the large, ancient parishes with single, large, regular, nucleated villages in them, each with a church and a manor house, such as exist in Midland England—we will not find such clearly defined settlements in Somerset. The ancient parishes in Somerset contain a mixture of settlements, with one or more villages (ie those places with churches), several hamlets, and a number of isolated farmsteads—the latter can often be shown to be in use by at least the Middle Ages.

Not only is the settlement pattern made up of a mixture of types, but the forms of settlement are very variable, ranging from small irregular clusters of buildings to large agglomerations with numerous elements in them, and some places with very regular layouts. When the deserted part of the settlement pattern is also considered, it can be shown very clearly that the medieval countryside of this part of Somerset contained a large number of relatively small hamlets, and that in each area there was great variety. In **Mudford** parish, for example, there were seven separate settlements in the early parish, of which only one was a village with a church (Mudford itself), and two were hamlets with chapels (Nether Adber and Hinton); of the seven, six are now partially or totally deserted (Aston 1977). Similar examples could be demonstrated for many places in the eastern and southern parts of the county.

If we consider the field names and local place names which contain some habitative element—such as wick, cote, ton, worth, or huish—which might indicate former settlements, the picture which emerges is one of a dense but dispersed pattern of settlement. This is comparable to that in the west of the county and eastern England, but with a few larger and more complicated villages. Nicholas Corcos in his examination of Shapwick, for example, has drawn attention to the names of a number of medieval land parcels which, by their endings, suggest former habitation: 'manycrofte', 'langenworthy', 'shortenworthy', 'purycrofte', langworth', 'enworthie', 'shortgoldworth' and 'worthie'. He is, however, cautious—"they are not strictly habitative names, but many contain 'enclosure' elements, suggesting a field system based on farming in severalty, perhaps with isolated farmsteads" (Corcos 1983). A similar example is probably demonstrated by the names 'byneworth' and 'kylworth' which occur later as openfield names in Kingsbury Episcopi parish (Aston 1985a). As elsewhere in the country, part of this pattern in Somerset was abandoned both during and after the Middle Ages. More relevant to village development, however, is the likelihood that part seems to have been abandoned in much earlier times—in the late Saxon and early medieval periods.

Michael Costen's research suggests large numbers of small, late Saxon estates centred on farmsteads or small hamlets which can only be traced, via Saxon land charters and tithe maps, from place name elements such as 'huish' and 'worth'. At Rimpton, for example, he has shown that beyond the stream to the north of the village there were two holdings in the 10th century. One, later called Woodhouse, was a one-hide unit added by Brihtric Grim to the east of the original area of land at Rimpton (of similar size), while to the south was another unit later called Weathergrove. He suggests that "this area was made up of several one-hide units" and that "we would expect to see some settlement on those areas rather than the concentration in Rimpton village" (Costen 1985). This looks like a comparable situation to that discussed by Christopher Taylor in **Village and Farmstead** (1983), whereby large numbers of scattered Saxon farmsteads are replaced by fewer, but larger, villages and hamlets later on; part of the earlier pattern is abandoned and the rest of the settlements are developed and enlarged.

Again, it must be emphasised that at the moment there is little archaeological evidence and even less documentary corroboration for these developments in Somerset. But the fragmentary picture which does emerge is at least consistent with current ideas in placename studies, and on the development of estates and ecclesiastical organisation, and indeed the picture from elsewhere in the country (Aston 1985). What we have to imagine in the late Saxon period, perhaps the 9th and 10th centuries, is a pattern of dispersed farmsteads and villages all across the county, more densely packed in the more fertile parts, but nevertheless extending up to the highest parts of Exmoor and probably down to the more easily drained parts of the

Levels. Later on, parts of this pattern were abandoned, especially in the centre, east, and south of the county, where some settlements were developed into villages; in the west, the older pattern persisted. But when, and why, did certain settlements become large agglomerations?

VILLAGE DEVELOPMENT
Current research elsewhere in Britain suggests two main lines of development of villages, in two main periods, but these are not directly related *(Taylor 1983)*.

New Villages
Firstly, there are clearly **new** villages, probably originating in the late Saxon period, and certainly in the early Middle Ages. It has been known for some time that the 12th and 13th centuries were a time of **town** development, with the plantation and planning or large numbers of new market centres *(Beresford 1967)*, and more recently research has shown the development of many Anglo-Saxon towns and market centres, especially in the Wessex region, of which Somerset was an important part *(Haslam 1984)*. But it now seems likely that such urban developments were merely one part of a more widely developing economy in the period 800–1200, involving the greater definition of land units associated with the buying and selling of estates, the reorganisation of field systems *(Fox 1981)*, the defining of woodland and pasture rights and, as now seems probable, the development of newly-planned settlements. Nationally there is little in the documentary record to indicate any of these changes, and so far little archaeological evidence has been found.

In Somerset, placenames like Newton in Martock, and West and North Newton in North Petherton, suggest **new** settlements at some time and in relation to other places, but generally it is very difficult to show when any particular settlement was new—when it originated. Most of the examples for Somerset are late, and they are all special cases. At Mells there is an unusually documented example of the creation of part of a new village plan, when Abbot Selwood intended to lay out a number of new streets in the shape of a cross—only one, New Street, was finished *(Aston 1985a)*. However, being of the 15th century this example is rather late in date.

Witham Friary is another village whose date of development can be suggested with reasonable certainty, but its unusual origin as the lay brothers' hamlet for the adjacent Carthusian monastery of Witham means that it will not assist us much in understanding village development generally in the county. A population other than of celibate men is indicated in 1459, when Bishop Beckington caused his suffragan to consecrate a churchyard, confirm a licence for a font, and appoint a chaplain following a request from the prior of Witham *(Maxwell-Lyte & Dawes 1934 p 313 & 319)*. Also connected with the Carthusian priory of Witham is the probable foundation (or extension?) of Knapp, in North Curry, to where it is suggested the dispossessed tenantry of the pre-existing village of Witham were sent in the late 12th century *(Farmer 1985 p 17)*.

The best clue to the construction of new villages lies in their **plans**, and most research has concentrated on identifying those places with regular rectilinear layouts of properties and rectangular patterns of streets, lanes, and greens *(Roberts 1982)*. In many ways, the places possessing such plans are comparable to the contemporary new towns—the only difference being that the towns are more completely documented. Many of Somerset's villages fall into this rectangular-plan category, and are likely to have originated as planned settlements in the early Middle Ages. Two have been discussed by the editors of the Victoria County History. Of Hinton St George it is said "The village east of the cross, with its regular plots and a surviving southern rear access known as the Lane by 1717 and Back Lane by 1745 is characteristic of a medieval planned settlement" *(Dunning 1978 p 39)*. At Bicknoller "in the 11th century the recorded settlements were Newton and Woolston, the former perhaps an alternative name for Bicknoller, whose regular street pattern shows characteristics of a planted village" *(Siraut 1985 p 13)*.

Detailed appraisal of each settlement in the county has hardly begun (although Brian Roberts has completed a preliminary general survey of the county's plans), but obvious examples include most of the Polden villages, including Shapwick, Edington, Cossington, Woolavington, and Greinton in particular. As Nicholas Corcos has written of Shapwick, it must have originated in its present form, "as the morphology of both its fields and of the settlement itself suggest, as a result of a deliberate and planned wholesale reorganisation" *(Corcos 1983)*. Many such settlements lie in south-east Somerset and have been identified by Ann Ellison *(1983)*; examples include Long Load, Wearne, Limington, Mudford, Winsham, and Compton in Compton Dundon.

Before research can progress much further, careful comparative analysis needs to be made of the settlements' plans—degrees of regularity will need to be assessed and

4.3 Shapwick
 a. from 1764 map

b. from Tithe Map 1839

Manor House

Barn Dovecote

Barn
Dovecote

Church

Moat

Pond

Lake

Park

Church

Mill

74

m 50 100 150

Spring

Spring

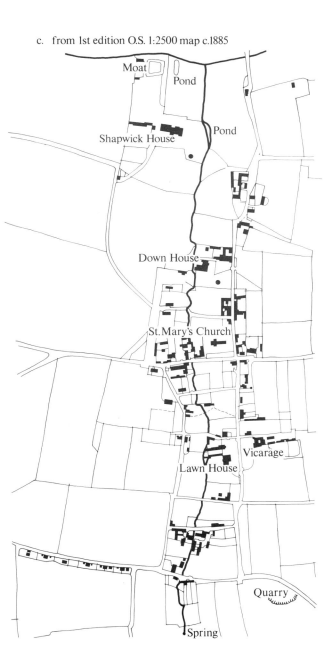

Moat

Pond

Shapwick House

Pond

Down House

St. Mary's Church

Vicarage

Lawn House

Quarry

Spring

quantified, based on how rectilinear a plan is, and particularly how close to a right-angle the junctions of property and road alignments are. Consistency in plot widths and lengths will also need to be demonstrated, together with some common order of measurement and laying out, before a clear case for planning can be made. For Yorkshire, June Sheppard was able to do this, and discovered a regular series of measurements in use in the north in the 12th century *(Sheppard 1974)*.

It is, as yet, not clear in Somerset when such regular plans were developed, but I have argued elsewhere that it was a long process taking place between approximately 800 and 1200 *(Aston 1985a)*. On the Glastonbury Abbey estates, the plantation of new villages was probably completed before the Norman Conquest, with many of the village plans there probably dating to the 9th and 10th centuries; but it may still have been going on in the period 1066–86 in south central Somerset. No doubt other places were laid out in the 12th and 13th centuries, as has been observed in the north of England.

Before more certainty can be given to these statements, a great deal of analysis needs to be undertaken, particularly of the correlation between **ownership** at certain dates and places having regular plans. In the north, there seems to be a close correlation between very regular village plans, places damaged in the 11th century, and high-status landowners *(Sheppard 1976)*. It is almost as if the more important barons and monastic houses were applying a consistent 'estate policy' to the settlements on their lands. The villages on the estates of Glastonbury Abbey look as if they have been treated in the same way, but much more research is needed before we can be sure.

We would expect the process of village planning and development to be over by around 1300 at the latest, when documents begin to enable us to see something of the disposition of properties, lanes, and buildings in villages, even if only vaguely. There is no indication in these documents of post-1300 changes in village plans in Somerset, so, by a process of elimination, developments must have been completed by that date. However, although it is likely that the development of planned villages in Somerset spans a long period, reflecting general trends observed elsewhere in the period either side of the Norman Conquest, a lot more research on individual settlements is necessary before even tentative conclusions can be drawn: research such as that carried out by Nicholas Corcos for Shapwick *(Corcos 1982; 1983)*, Harold Fox for Milton Podimore *(Fox 1986)*, and Christopher

Thornton for Rimpton (the latter two rather more concerned with the origins of field systems).

The most spectacular examples of new settlements in the Somerset landscape are the medieval planned villages, but at the moment we can only imagine the processes involved in laying out the plots (probably with rope and pegs), and the gradual building of the new farmsteads. We have little idea yet of the reasons for such new developments, the ways in which people were brought together, and the fiscal and tenurial background to such changes, although these have been hinted at elsewhere.

Composite Villages

Rather more common than newly-planned regular villages are those places which are made up of numerous units, some regular and some irregular. Christopher Taylor calls these 'polyfocal villages' *(Taylor 1977)*, although Brian Roberts' term 'composite' is perhaps more useful *(Roberts 1982)*. These seem to have originated as dispersed but closely juxtaposed hamlets, or as small settlements clustered around small centres (such as a church, manor, green, or road junction). Later, the spaces between were infilled, often with regularly laid out units, presumably to accommodate new people as the population increased, or perhaps as a reflection of changing social structure or economic activities.

In those areas of Somerset where there are many villages and hamlets, 'composite' village plans are well represented, and some of the larger settlements are of this type. Sometimes, separately named elements within a large village enable us to see that it is truly 'composite' and that what appears as a single place is really an amalgam of several separate hamlets. More often, separate names (if they ever existed) have not survived but we can still detect the separate units from different manorial ownership in the Middle Ages. Thus, Lopen has two main parts, each with a separate owner in the Middle Ages *(Aston 1985a)*, and Barrington, Long Sutton, and Merriott are similar *(Dunning 1974; 1978)*. The villages which best demonstrate their composite nature—with numerous units, separately named elements, and in some cases different manorial holdings—are Charlton Horethorne, South Petherton, Martock, Combe St Nicholas, and Bishop's Lydeard, but many others will be identified with further research.

Even a settlement which seems on first examination to be insignificant can often be shown to have separate units within it; frequently, both a regularly planned part and several, possibly earlier, irregular centres can be

4.4 Limington village earthworks

⋯⋯ Remains of medieval fields

⌁⌁ Earthworks

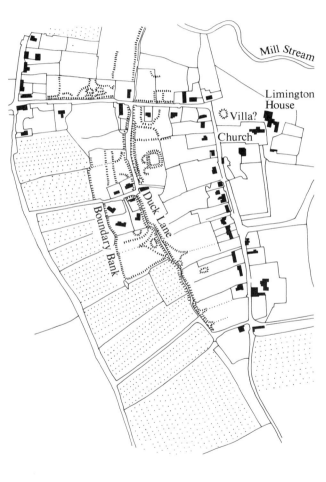

Mill Stream

Limington House

Villa?

Church

Duck Lane

Boundary Bank

m 50 100 150

4.5 Lamyatt village earthworks

⋯⋯ Remains of medieval fields

⌁⌁ Earthworks

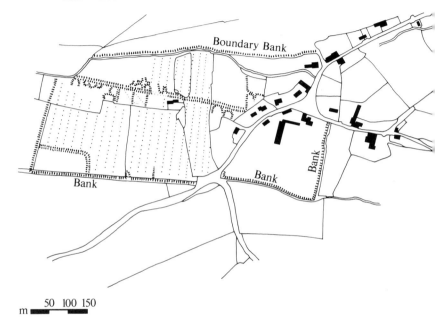

Boundary Bank

Bank

Bank

Bank

m 50 100 150

recognised. Limington probably developed as a planned village, but it also has two other centres—around the church, where there was also a Roman site, and at the manor farm. The whole plan is now obscured since the present village occupies only the back lane of the medieval village. At Marston Magna three separate elements can be seen in the plan—one at Lambrook to the north, and two others which demonstrate a sequence of construction in the village *(Aston 1985 p 76)*. At Lamyatt a regularly laid-out block of properties and a separate element around the church have been replaced by a linear row of houses and farms cutting across the earlier plan and linking the two units. South Cadbury is a very small village today, but nevertheless its eastern end seems to have been a separate settlement called Littleton, judging by the topography of the village and the openfield name nearby *(Hardwick 1978)*.

77

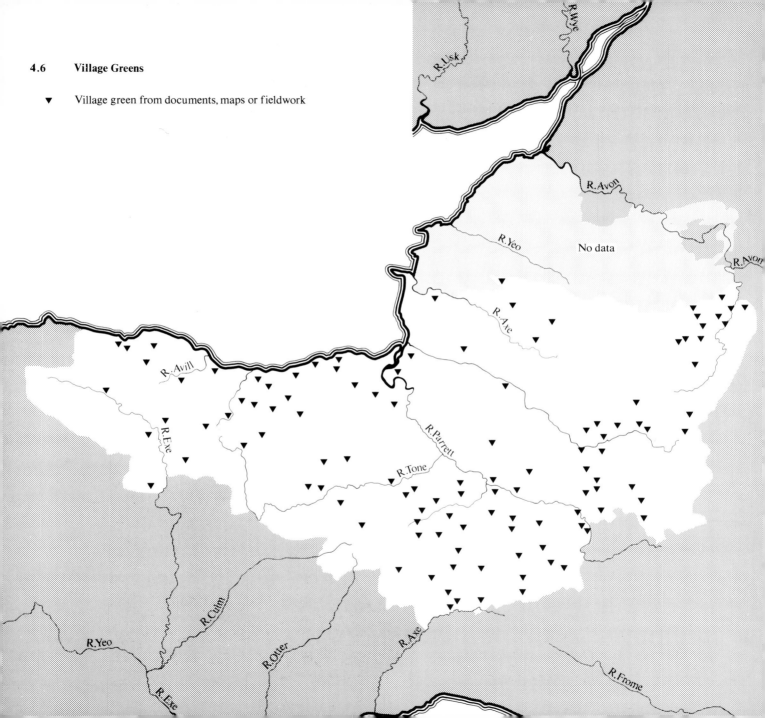

4.6 Village Greens

▼ Village green from documents, maps or fieldwork

CHURCHES AND VILLAGE GREENS

Where do those most obvious features of the English village—the church and the village green—fit into this scheme of village development? Up until very recently it would have been argued that the medieval village **church** site represented the most ancient area of settlement within a village. No doubt in some cases this is true, especially if the church reflects some development from Roman times, as at St Andrew's, Northover *(Dunning 1975)*, or represents some earlier 'celtic' centre based on a cemetery, holy well, cross, or other focus, as at Brean (St Bridget), or Carhampton (St Crantoc) *(Rahtz 1982)*. But in most cases the origins of the church will not be known, although generally the churches of Somerset were developed either from minsters (or 'mother churches') for their surrounding area in late Saxon times, and occasionally from an early monastic centre, or perhaps most commonly as proprietorial or private churches attached to the house and land of a local lay owner. Only from the 12th century were the latter brought under the full control of the church authorities as parishes and the related parochial organisation became fully developed.

Many churches, therefore, represent not so much the focus of an early settlement so much as an appendage to a pre-Conquest manor, which may have consisted of no more than a large house and farm buildings *(Cadman 1983; Cadman & Foard 1984)*. Many former hamlets, and indeed separate manors within later villages, could have had their own churches in the period before 1200. It is difficult to point to an unequivocal case in Somerset where one village with several manors had more than one church; but several later chapels which either have special status, such as Edstock in Cannington or Alston Sutton in Weare, or have produced burials such as Horsey chapel in Bridgwater parish, probably represent earlier more important ecclesiastical buildings whose status was eroded as parish organisation progressed.

In Somerset's larger villages and separately documented hamlets, therefore, we should in future expect to find more churches, either from re-assessment of documents or from archaeological work *(Morris 1983)*. Places with documented 'chapels of ease', or 'free' or 'royal' chapels from the 13th and 14th centuries should be looked at particularly closely, since if, like Horsey, they have produced burials (a prerogative of the most important church in any area) it may be that they were formerly of a higher status—the proprietary church of some unknown landowner, which was later demoted to be the chapel to a more important

parish church elsewhere.

Ideas on the origins and significance of **greens** have also altered dramatically as a result of recent research. Thirty were listed in Somerset (including south Avon) by W G Hoskins and L D Stamp in 1963. No particular concentration was noted, but they were shown to be distributed in south Somerset, from Exmoor to Yeovil, and in what is now south Avon. The average extent of each was just over an acre. It is not difficult to show that there are, and have been, more village greens than this—a more recent attempt is shown in Fig. 4.6.

Village greens have traditionally been associated with the founding of villages in the early Saxon period, and are regarded by many as an essential part of the English scene. However, we have already seen that villages, and therefore their greens, were not founded in the early Saxon period. Similarly, village greens, rather than being an entity in their own right, can best be seen as a part of the communal open space, like the roads and commons between the properties and precincts which make up the village plan. Such open spaces range from the small triangular areas where three roads join, to large commons with scatters of cottages and farms alongside. With the recognition of planned villages, and planned elements within composite settlements, greens and commons can best be seen as the open spaces left between rows of properties. They presumably imply some sort of pastoral element in the economy at the time they were defined, but where they have survived they reflect either the continuity

4.7 *Priddy village green*

of this pastoral element, or inertia, or conversion to some other use such as recreation. As such, we have probably been over-enthusiastic about their significance in the past.

Greens can be created and lost within village plans—both developments have been observed elsewhere in the country: they are not permanent or unchanging features in the village. In Somerset there is still an incomplete record of past and present greens, and only with detailed research in each settlement, such as that carried out by the editors of the Victoria County History, will all examples be recognised. Some of them are clearly related to planned settlements: Faulkland in Hemington, Curry Rivel near the church, and High Ham seem to be such cases. Others are in effect large commons in upland or formerly forested areas, such as those at Priddy, North Brewham (which has now been enclosed), Shipham, and Lottisham. On closer analysis, few settlements do not have some open space within the confines of their overall plans.

DESERTED VILLAGES
Many of the current ideas on village development have been derived from the study of deserted villages, and reference has already been made earlier in this chapter to the importance of fieldwork on the deserted parts of settlements.

Although settlements of all periods can be found abandoned in the landscape, in the last 40 years or so most attention has been paid to deserted medieval villages. Sites have been located from fieldwork, documentary research, and the examination of early maps and air photographs. The reasons for desertion have been examined, and these range from spectacular events like the Black Death, or the eviction of farmers by landowners to create sheep and cattle ranches, to the more mundane but less well documented slow social and economic changes in late medieval society *(Beresford 1954; Beresford & Hurst 1971; Dyer 1982)*. The latter reasons are the most common in Somerset. Two examples demonstrate this well— Speckington in Yeovilton and Little Marston in West Camel.

At **Speckington** the rents were reduced from the 14th century onwards, and agricultural works had been commuted to cash payments. In 1451 at least three 60-acre holdings, complete with farmsteads, were let at reduced rents *'until better tenants should come' (Dunning 1974 p 171)*. **Little Marston** was a separate manor with its own field system, manor house, chapel, and mill. The population must have fallen in the 15th century, since by

1503, judging from the evidence of field names, the arable fields had given place to pasture for sheep *(Dunning 1974 p 76)*: fewer people were needed for sheep than for arable cultivation. Similar reasons have been advanced for the demise of settlements in **Mudford** parish *(Aston 1977)*.

The attraction of deserted settlements, whether farmsteads, hamlets, or villages, for the study of settlement plans and patterns is that without later buildings and inevitable disturbances, a clearer view can be gained of earlier outlines. Generally speaking, most surviving settlements have some earthworks in them, so the researcher often has existing boundary features with the buildings and roads in use, as well as earthworks of abandoned areas. Many of the Somerset settlements are like this.

The location, distribution, and something of the desertion of sites has been discussed elsewhere *(Aston 1982; 1985a)*; the deserted farmsteads and hamlets of the west have also been examined *(Aston 1983)*. What, then, can deserted settlements tell us about earlier village and hamlet plans? There is great similarity between the plans of those places which survive and those which are deserted. If anything, there is rather more regularity in some deserted settlement plans, and such features as moats and fishponds are often more obvious in the surviving earthworks; the pattern of roads is often clear, too, although these are narrower than would be expected for vehicular traffic. However, other sites are very irregular in plan, often with confused or dispersed areas of earthworks

4.8 *A deserted village, probably Pignes, in Chilton Trinity*

which defy clear explanation. Some have later features associated with the village earthworks, such as industrial workings or the earthworks associated with formal gardens and landscaping schemes.

Only by allowing for the existence of abandoned settlements can any accurate assessment of earlier settlement patterns be made. We can usually be more certain of the contemporaneity of medieval settlements than we can for earlier periods, while from documents or earthworks we can gain some idea of their former size—both in terms of population and area of occupation. The picture which emerges is of a well-populated medieval landscape full of settlements of one description or another.

THE FUTURE

Why should we bother studying the plans and patterns of medieval settlements at all? Are they of any relevance to the present day? Academic considerations apart, there are several practical reasons in a highly developed, over-populated society like Britain in the late 20th century why such research should proceed. In the past, most people in most periods lived and worked in the countryside. Today, even though over 80 per cent of us are now urban dwellers, villages, indeed rural settlements generally, are still thought of as the places where most people would ideally like to live, and a house in the country is an aspiration of many. The English village is, then, an intrinsic part of our heritage and a focus for our nationalistic emotions.

But as I have tried to show, we know very little about our villages. For most we are not even sure when they originated, and usually we have no idea how and why they reached their present layout and appearance. If the general public living in and visiting such villages in the countryside does not know the answers to these basic questions, it has to be said that those studying villages have themselves only just begun to try to answer them—even our definition of the problems is still under discussion. There is no doubt though that if we knew more in detail of the origins and development of rural settlements, then our appreciation of them would be all the richer. The interest there is in other aspects of the past, such as churches and country houses, could be extended to the more mundane groups of farmsteads, houses, and cottages.

A second reason for study relates directly to the desire people have to live in the countryside. With greater mobility and wealth, more and more people are able to realise their ambition to live in a village, and in order to accommodate their desires, many villages have been expanded and developed. In a few cases this has been done sympathetically, and the age-old processes of adaptation and extension have proceeded apace. But it has to be said, particularly in Somerset, that expansion in villages has not usually been achieved with much sympathy either to the fabric of the villages, in terms of scale of architecture and building material, or to their historic plans. Very often, the amount of land taken up and the number of buildings erected since 1950 exceeds the total surviving development from the last 400 years! The layout of the roads, estates, and plots usually owes more to ideas from new towns elsewhere in this country and beyond than it does to the village alignments in Somerset in general, or those of the settlement undergoing expansion in particular.

This **is** a criticism, but those who could be blamed, councillors, planners, surveyors, developers, and builders, can rightly claim that either inappropriate advice or no advice at all was available to suggest alternative ways of developing rural settlements: the only exception so far is the splendid survey by Ann Ellison for part of the south of the county *(1983)*. If we are to avoid past mistakes, yet still allow villages to grow and develop in the future, we must ensure that any development is in keeping with the existing heritage. This can be achieved best if it is directly related not only to the present appearance of the particular place undergoing change, but also to what has happened in the past. Much can and is being done about the 'built' part of that appearance, but more remains to be done about the layouts adopted. The study and appreciation of the plans of settlements should help in pointing out the essential 'grain' of a particular place, which, if emulated, could lead to satisfactory rural settlement planning. It is to be hoped that **our** contribution to continuing village development, a process already at least a thousand years old, will be as satisfactory to future generations as the past usually is to us.

ACKNOWLEDGEMENTS
Joe Bettey, Bob Dunning and James Bond read and commented on an earlier version of this chapter; it has benefited considerably from the critical and editorial skills of Carinne Allinson.

Michael Costen and Nicholas Corcos provided stimulating discussion on some of the ideas here while Christopher Gerrard surveyed and drew up the plans of some of the sites. The staff of the County Record Office, particularly Robin Bush and Steve Hobbs, were very helpful.

Chapter 5

LAND USE *and* FIELD SYSTEMS

Michael Aston

An economy such as that operating in medieval Somerset required that people should have access to a variety of types of land in order to be able to grow the food, keep the animals, and gather the resources necessary to sustain life. Primarily, this involved access to arable land and pasture, but meadowland, upland and lowland waste, and woodland were also essential: ideally, every settlement should have within its borders, or within easy access, all these different types of land. In practice, some settlements would have had access to all of these resources; others would be well endowed with some but not others; a few settlements, however, would have found it difficult to sustain themselves.

There were two solutions to this problem. Firstly, they could travel (sometimes long distances) to the particular resources not available within their own borders, and there are many examples of this in Somerset. The Levels, for example, were extensively used both by surrounding settlements and by those at some distance *(Williams 1970)*. Upland pasture on Exmoor was used by many widely scattered settlements in the west of the county *(MacDermott 1911)*—Withiel Florey on the Brendon Hills was actually granted to distant Taunton manor as a piece of pasture of *'four mansae . . . for the pasturing of cattle'* in the eighth or tenth century *(Finberg 1964 p 115)*.

Secondly, settlements with few resources could go to market to purchase what they could not produce

themselves. The development of markets from late Saxon times onwards (if not before) facilitated the exchange of agricultural produce, and enabled settlements to trade their specialities or surpluses for products from elsewhere. Many markets were probably developed at the junctions between regions of different land use, but it is difficult to be sure of this for Somerset. Obviously, markets such as those at Frome and Bruton could have prospered on the exchange of goods between the wooded areas to the east and the Levels to the west, but this was probably only one of a number of contributory factors in determining their success as market towns in the Middle Ages *(Aston 1986; Gerrard 1987)*.

Many resources were often shared between settlements. Woodland was one of these and, as it may have been some distance away, it was usually very carefully managed to produce the timber and wood needed (this is referred to in the chapter by Oliver Rackham and will not be further discussed here). Upland and lowland pasture, in the form of commons and wastes, was another 'shared resource' and was possessed by many settlements, especially those near to Exmoor, the Brendon Hills, the Blackdown Hills, the Quantocks, and the Mendips, and those surrounding the Levels. The term 'waste' is a misnomer for such land, since it was important for the grazing of cattle, sheep, horses, and geese, and for supplying fuel and building materials in the form of wood, clay, rushes, and turf (from turbaries). It also acted as a source of wild food, which might include hunting in the upland and seasonal fishing and fowling in the lowlands, and as a reserve of land for future more intensive exploitation, particularly after investment in liming, clearance and draining.

As with woodland, settlements often had access to pasture some distance away, and some of the inhabitants must have been prepared to travel and stay away from

5.1 *Photograph of the area between Cheddar and Draycott (Nov 1971). In the centre, a medieval strip field system has been enclosed piecemeal forming long thin fields. Top right of these, there are medieval strip lynchets. The top of the Mendips (top right) and the Levels (bottom left) were enclosed in characteristically rectilinear shaped fields*

home looking after herds and flocks for some part of the year. Such **transhumance** to pasture and woodland must have been an important part of rural life in earlier times (although it does not seem to be particularly well documented for the Middle Ages in England *(Aston 1985)*), yet today it is usually only associated with Third World countries.

Meadowland was used to grow hay for winter fodder. Although any suitable grassland could be used, it was most common to find streamside and river valley land being used—not necessarily poorly drained, but probably annually flooded and wet enough for most of the year to promote rich growth. Such areas were often managed communally, with different areas of the grass being allocated to different farmers in complicated rotation arrangements. The strips, or 'doles', were often marked on the ground: the stones at Milton Mead (Ash) and at Ruishton, while of post-medieval date in their present form, preserve such early arrangements. Later on, certainly from the 16th century but possibly from the 14th century (see below), elaborate irrigation schemes were developed in these areas. Water meadow schemes are common in some parts of southern England, such as Dorset and Wiltshire *(Bettey 1977)*, but they seem to have been little developed in Somerset. The upland version, called 'gutters', 'waterleats', or 'catchwork water meadows' is mainly a post-medieval development, common in west Somerset.

Hay would have been cut from these meadowland areas several times a year and stored as winter fodder. As such it was immensely important, and this is reflected in the high value given to meadowland in medieval records—usually higher than any other land, including arable land. It is perhaps worth emphasising that the animals were fed over the winter and not slaughtered, since the latter is a myth that is still often quoted.

In earlier times, many settlements would have had adequate pasture within their boundaries, while others would have shared pasture with neighbouring settlements; however, as the entries in Domesday Book imply, specific **areas** of land were allocated to each settlement although there would probably have been no physical boundaries between them *(Thorn & Thorn 1980)*. In such circumstances there is no real need to rotate arable and pasture on the same area of land.

Arable land ideally needs to be located as near to the settlement as possible, as it needs intensive and persistent labour—ploughing and preparing the seed bed, planting, weeding, harvesting, and manuring. Areas worked close to the farmstead minimise the time taken in travel to and from the fields and the difficulties of carriage of manure and crops. Traditionally, however, the medieval agricultural system is thought of as having strict **rotation** of arable and pasture in large, open, common fields, usually three in number. As we shall see, this was certainly not the norm in Somerset; indeed, there is a great variety of types of field system in the Middle Ages in the county.

MEDIEVAL FIELD SYSTEMS

In a seminal article, Joan Thirsk has listed four characteristics which she considers a settlement should have if it is thought to have had a 'classic' common field system *(Thirsk 1976)*. These are:

1—Arable and meadow divided into strips among the cultivators, each of whom may occupy a number of strips scattered about the fields.
2—Arable and meadow thrown open for common pasture by the stock of the cultivators after harvest and in fallow times.
3—Common pasturage of waste with rights to gather timber, turf, and other materials.
4—The ordering of all these activities regulated by an assembly of the cultivators—generally the manorial court.

It is not difficult to show from medieval records that some of these aspects existed in many places in Somerset: but to qualify as a classic open field village a settlement must have all of them.

Of those places in Somerset that ever had open fields, some places had three large fields as we might expect, but very many more had only two. At Milton Podimore, Harold Fox has traced the change from a two to a three field system in the 14th century, while in many places the evidence for the change taking place is more clear for the 16th century. This suggests earlier arrangements in many settlements—originally half the land ploughed and half as pasture in any one year. Villages with two and three fields in the Middle Ages can be seen on Fig. 5.5—they are predominantly in the south, south-east, and centre of the county.

It is important to be clear about terminology when discussing medieval field systems: many of them seem the same because of the similar terms used, but there has been much confusion in the past which has tended to simplify the great variety of field systems in use *(Baker & Butlin 1973)*. Often, the complex origins of the systems are thus

5.2 *Ridge and furrow at Alford*

obscured; and those systems which evolved further are only seen clearly in later documents and maps. Here, the types of evidence for different field systems will be discussed and examples given; this will then be related to current ideas on how such systems developed.

FIELD EVIDENCE

There are four types of field evidence available to us:
1—earthworks, including features visible from the air
2—crop and soil marks visible on air photographs
3—evidence from hedges
4—the patterns of boundaries in the landscape.

Evidence from earthworks largely consists of areas of ridge and furrow and strip lynchets, although other features, such as water meadows, are also found. **Ridge and furrow** varies enormously in its form: the 'classic' large, wide, high-backed ridges with reversed 'S' shape, so typical of the Midlands, are not common in Somerset but they do occur, particularly in south-east Somerset. Many areas, clearly shown on air photographs taken in the late 1940s by the RAF, have now been ploughed out and destroyed, but there are still well preserved areas near Alford (Fig. 5.2) and in the Brue valley west of Castle Cary. The evidence of air photographs showing crop and soil marks is that this wide, curved ridge and furrow was once more extensive, but was still largely confined to the south, south-east, and centre of the county (Fig. 5.3).

Much lower, narrower ridge and furrow can be seen elsewhere in the county. Where it is straight and regular it probably dates to the 18th and 19th centuries; the irregular forms, however, are probably earlier and may in part have been dug and worked by hand using spades. Such early ridge and furrow occurs on the uplands of Exmoor (particularly on Winsford Hill and North Hill, Minehead), and on the Quantocks, and probably also existed on the Blackdown Hills before enclosure. It is recorded by James Savage in 1830 on the Brendon Hills before the area was improved. He says of Withycombe, for example,

> 'the remainder is a common called Withycombe Hill, and a sheep walk attached to Gupworthy Farm, called Black Hill. The former measures about one hundred and eighty-four acres, and a considerable part of it has been cultivated, the ridges still being very perceptible',

and also

> 'Most of the estates in this parish have rights of common on this hill, and as formerly the occupiers of estates having rights of common used in many instances to cultivate certain parts of the same, there can be little doubt but such was the case here, which accounts for the ridges and the decayed mounds that might have been boundaries, which are still to be seen' (Savage 1830 p 273–4).

These upland areas probably represent 'outfields' periodically worked from the settlements much lower

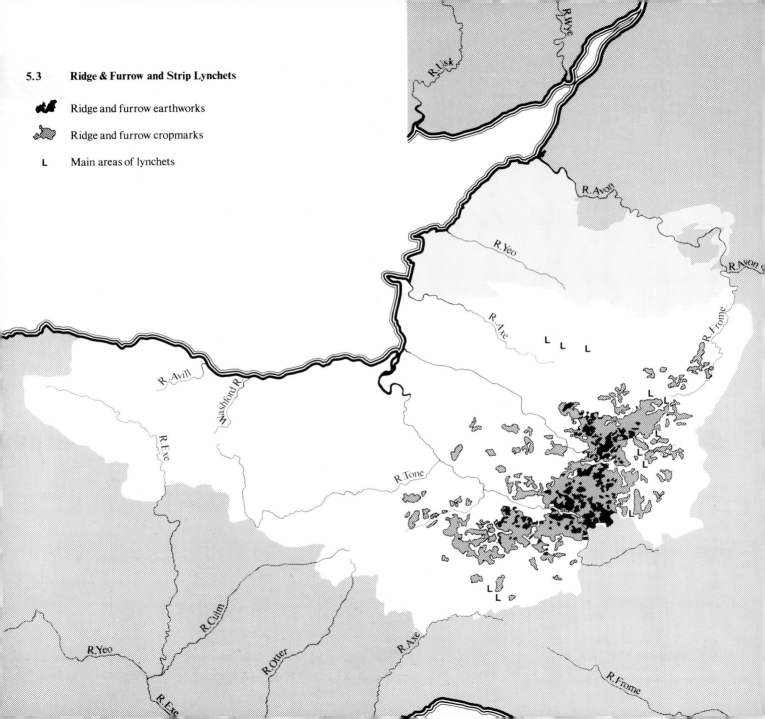

5.3   Ridge & Furrow and Strip Lynchets

  Ridge and furrow earthworks

  Ridge and furrow cropmarks

L   Main areas of lynchets

down, and therefore they would not have been the main areas of arable available to the settlements. The system of taking in part of the upland for arable crops for a few years is well known in the West Country. It is well documented in the 16th century at Wootton Courtenay on the north side of Dunkery Hill

> 'licence to sow corn upon the lord's common at North Hill and Duncrey this year' (1550)

and

> 'licence had to sowing wheat upon the common of the lord at North Hill for this year and Dounecrey' (1551) (Note 1).

Other earthworks resemble ridge and furrow but were probably not used for arable farming in the same way. Large areas of such earthworks exist all over the clay belt in the Somerset Levels, from the mouth of the Parrett to Weston Super Mare. Much of this must be the result of drainage operations, but the picture is more complex than that. Part of the function of 'normal' ridge and furrow is drainage, so this might be land which has just been more intensively drained. Once draining is achieved for a long enough period within the year, then arable crops could be planted on the ridges. Examination of the Glastonbury manor of Brent in the early Middle Ages, where arable farming is well documented, suggests that these low-lying ridged areas could possibly have been used for arable. While a lot of cultivation could clearly have taken place on Brent Knoll itself, this would not account for all the area under cultivation: but all around the base of the Knoll are extensive early drainage patterns—perhaps such areas were used for arable.

Another type of earthwork, strip lynchets, is common in the county. There are widespread isolated examples, but the main concentrations are in the south-east of the county: Yarlington parish and South Cadbury contain particularly dense clusters and good examples. Further north, Westbury sub Mendip has exceptionally well-preserved flights of lynchets. It used to be thought that such lynchets were either prehistoric or Anglo-Saxon in date. Recent research, however, particularly by John Hardwick in Somerset (1978) and Christopher Taylor elsewhere (1966), has shown that they were very closely related to commonfield farming patterns divided into strips and usually, where the evidence survives, are integrated into patterns of ridge and furrow. They seem to date to a period of land hunger in the 12th and 13th centuries when, in order to feed a growing population, hillside land was terraced to produce arable crops.

Often, areas of strip lynchets respect parish boundaries, suggesting that it is the individual fortunes of particular communities that we are seeing; and there are clear differences in the amount of land covered by strip lynchets even in adjacent parishes. Yarlington has more than neighbouring parishes, but then it has more hilly land—hence the need to build terraces if enough crops were to be grown. Westbury sub Mendip seems to have been terraced more than its neighbours because much of the better, flatter land lower down was unavailable for arable use because of the large park of the Bishops of Bath and Wells to the south of the village. Perhaps the villagers had no choice but to adapt the steeper slopes to grow their arable crops. Later, when the park went out of use, possibly in the 16th century, the higher strip lynchets were abandoned to rough pasture as the former park area was used for arable.

Hedges

It has been suggested that certain shrub species can be used to **date** hedges, thereby offering a useful field method for detecting early patterns in the landscape (Pollard et al 1974). However, the 'one species for every hundred years of age of the hedge' method which has been suggested elsewhere is too simplistic for Somerset. In the former forest of Neroche, for example, even the 19th century hedges had up to six species in them—while medieval hedges often had more (but different) species in them. A real relationship, therefore, cannot be established, and reliable dating of a particular hedge cannot be made without a lot of documentary and cartographic information being gathered beforehand. As Oliver Rackham says of the Neroche area, the "post-1833 hedges have averages of 6, 7 and 6.3 species; in this respect they are statistically indistinguishable from the medieval hedges. But the species are not the same. Elm and hazel are specially characteristic of the old hedges; furze of those of intermediate age; sallow, privet, and oak of the post-1833 hedges" (Rackham 1986 p 202). In addition to those listed by Rackham, it seems likely that spindle, guelder rose, and wayfaring tree are also indicators of ancient hedges in Somerset.

The contents of later hedges (ie from the 16th century onwards) probably relate closely to the activities of 'nurserymen' and their ability to produce and supply large numbers of plants for hedging (Harvey 1974). In earlier times, and indeed up to the 19th century in Somerset, hedges tended to reflect more their piecemeal formation

5.4   Medieval fields and enclosures in Alford

a. Extent of ridge and furrow from 1947 aerial photographs

b. 1805 enclosure map

Headlands and roads

Medieval settlement earthworks

?   Areas of uncertain extent of ridge and furrow

Ridge and furrow visible on aerial photographs

⇨   Church

Intended new hedges and roads

Strips in the open fields

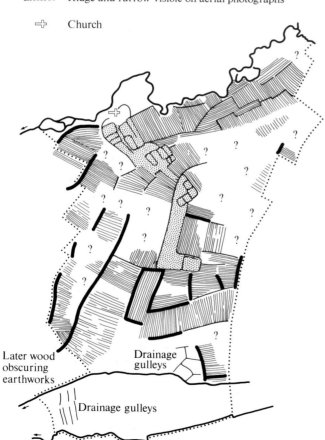

Later wood
obscuring
earthworks

Drainage
gulleys

Drainage gulleys

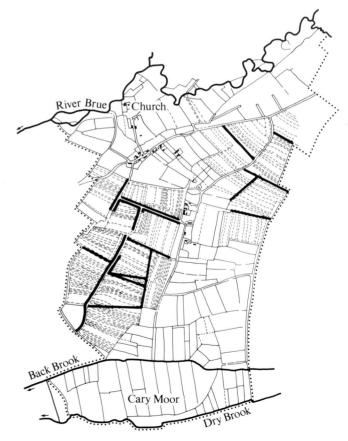

River Brue   Church

Back Brook

Cary Moor

Dry Brook

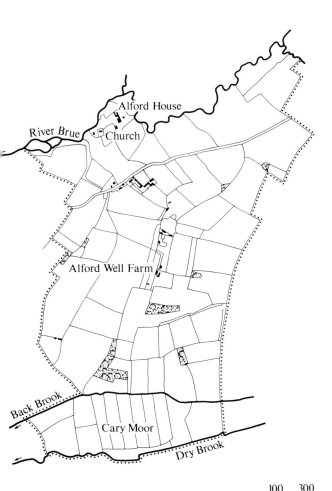

c. The late 19th century landscape

Alford House

River Brue

Church

Alford Well Farm

Back Brook

Cary Moor

Dry Brook

m 100 300

by the selection of cuttings and young plants from existing hedges and woodland. Whatever the mechanism, many of the hedges in Somerset have a large number and a rich variety of species in them, and very many were the result of medieval or immediately post-medieval enclosure.

Patterns

The patterns created on the landscape by hedges, walls, and banks are also useful clues to past land use. If we exclude areas of late enclosure (such as the Levels, various uplands, and a few parishes in the south and east of the county), much of the landscape of the rest of Somerset is made up of either irregular-shaped fields or patterns of hedges in a roughly strip-like arrangement, which reflect the two main aspects of the enclosure history of the county.

The irregularly-shaped fields represent areas of land taken directly into cultivation from woodland, waste, or unenclosed pasture by a particular farming group; in these areas there probably never was an open communal system of arable farming. Much of the west of Somerset, the north, the area now in south Avon, and the areas in and around the royal forests of Neroche and Selwood developed like this. In the Middle Ages, this process of woodland clearance was referred to as *'assarting'* the clearance and grubbing out of trees—and the place names—*'sarts'* and *'searts'* reflect this activity. A grant by the king to the prior and convent of Bruton in 1252 demonstrates the process. They are to have

> *'25 acres of purpresture in their manor of Brewham without the covert of the forest of Selwood with licence to bring them under tillage and till them as they will, quit of regard provided that the doe with her fawn and others of the kings deer have free entry and exit' (Calendar of Close Rolls).*

The exact course and chronology of the opening up and cultivation of the land in the early Middle Ages has yet to be studied in Somerset. The process is well documented in the 12th and 13th centuries and is very largely complete by 1300. But there is no reason why it cannot be going on in the 9th and 10th centuries (or earlier) under the influence of the powerful Wessex kings and the major ecclesiastical land owners in the county, such as the abbots of Glastonbury, Muchelney, and Athelney, and the Bishops of Wells.

The patterns of small linear fields found so frequently over the centre, south, and south-east of the county reflect

89

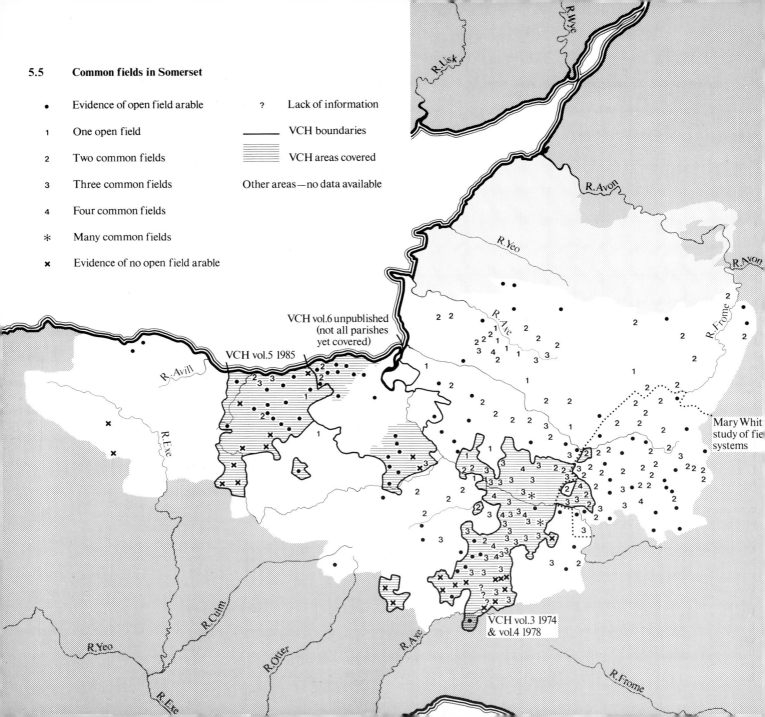

5.5 **Common fields in Somerset**

- Evidence of open field arable
1 One open field
2 Two common fields
3 Three common fields
4 Four common fields
* Many common fields
× Evidence of no open field arable

? Lack of information
— VCH boundaries
≡ VCH areas covered
Other areas—no data available

VCH vol.6 unpublished
(not all parishes
yet covered)

VCH vol.5 1985

Mary Whit
study of fie
systems

VCH vol.3 1974
& vol.4 1978

the piecemeal enclosure of former strips in common fields, by private agreement between freeholders, before the bureaucracy of 18th and 19th century parliamentary enclosure came along with its commissioners, surveyors, and map-makers *(Tate 1948)*. Such earlier enclosure is often poorly documented, and rarely mapped; the best evidence is in the field patterns and the dates of the accompanying farms. It is usually assumed to have taken place in the 16th and 17th centuries *(eg Whitfeld 1981 p 27)*, but there is no reason why the process cannot have begun somewhat earlier.

CARTOGRAPHIC EVIDENCE

Somerset is not well endowed with early **maps**, so it is not easy to find evidence in cartographic form of what the medieval field systems were like. There are few enclosure maps which might show us what a system was like before the present field pattern was created. By the time the tithe maps were drawn up in the 1830s and 1840s, most of the Somerset landscape looked like it does now.

The only way to see something of the former pattern is to look at estate maps, particularly those showing land use, and try to ascertain whether they reflect earlier agricultural arrangements. However, it is clear from many examples elsewhere in the country that the complexities shown on 16th and 17th century maps, and the way common field systems were operated as described in the documents, are quite different to what went on earlier. However, these maps do at least help in showing where the common field system has operated in the county, and something of the later arrangements. Such maps exist for Alford, Shepton Beauchamp, South Cadbury, Stoke sub Hamdon, and a few other places *(Tate 1948)*.

Enclosure maps cover two types of land use. We are not concerned here with enclosure of what had been upland and lowland waste into patterns of new fields *(Williams 1970a; 1971; 1972; 1976)*: rather, we are interested in maps showing areas which had been formerly common fields and which were to be enclosed into lands separately owned by individual farmers. However, there are very few enclosure maps of Somerset parishes *(Tate 1948)*.

DOCUMENTARY EVIDENCE

It is from documents, then, that most of our information can be derived at the present time about the field systems in use in Somerset in the Middle Ages. Many documents exist to show us how the estates of the major ecclesiastical landowners were run, such as those of Glastonbury Abbey *(Keil 1964)* and the Bishops of Bath and Wells *(HMC 1907; 1914)*; and the editors of the Victoria County History have done a splendid job in unravelling the agricultural arrangements in the parishes they have studied *(Dunning 1974; 1978; 1985)*. Elsewhere, without considerable very detailed work, such as that done by Mary Whitfeld on Bratton Seymour *(Whitfeld 1974)* and other parishes in the south-east of the county *(Whitfeld 1981)*, it is usually difficult to give a full picture of how agriculture was conducted in the Middle Ages (Fig. 5.5)

Field systems in west Somerset have been studied by Robert Dunning, Robin Bush, and Mary Siraut as part of their research for the topographical volumes of the Victoria County History *(Dunning 1985)*. Their studies of 23 parishes between Old Cleeve and Lilstock in the north and Raddington and Chipstable in the south cover the north and south sides of the Brendon Hills, and the northern area of the Quantocks. The landscape of these uplands and the vale between, and the north coastal strip, contrasts greatly with that of the parishes in the south and east of the county, and their field systems reflect this, as will be discussed below.

Many of the parishes in this western area have never had any open field arable; this is particularly true of the parishes around the eastern end of the Brendon Hills. Thus we find "no common fields" at Chipstable *(Dunning 1985 p 26)*, "no trace of open-field arable cultivation" at Huish Champflower *(Dunning 1985 p 83)*, "no evidence of common arable fields" at Nettlecombe *(Siraut 1985 p 111)*, and "no evidence of open-field arable cultivation" at Raddington *(Dunning 1985 p 136)*. These parishes probably did grow some arable crops for their own use, however, but clearly the fields were not like the large, open, common fields held communally in strips elsewhere.

The system in use in the west may have been more akin to an infield/outfield system, with perhaps only one infield close to the settlement used for arable. This may be indicated by the *'Great field of Leigh'* in Crowcombe in 1352 *(Bush 1985 p 58)*, by the arable recorded at Rowdon in Nettlecombe in the 14th century *(Siraut 1985 p 116)*, the open field at Sedgeborough in 1300 in Clatworthy *(Bush 1985 p 31)*, and the possible open field at Currill in Holford at about the same date *(Dunning 1985 p 2)*.

In the infield/outfield system, there was usually abundant pasture, common, and waste available for periodic arable use: on both the Brendons and the Quantocks this is referred to frequently in the Middle Ages. Thus, at Bicknoller in the 16th century rye was being grown on Bicknoller Hill on the Quantocks *(Siraut 1985 p 15)*. In Crowcombe, the next parish southwards, small plots of common on the Quantocks were being ploughed in 1405, and in the 1430s parts of the common at Heddon and Heathfield were ploughed for growing rye—this was called *'betelond' (Bush 1985 p 58)*. At East Quantoxhead in the 15th and 17th centuries parts of the common were cultivated for rye *(Dunning 1985 p 125)*.

These examples of single open fields look like common field farming, but the arable crops were not worked by all the farmers of the parish. Other aspects of these agricultural regimes also look like common field farming, but fail to meet the criteria of the classic Midland system. In most of these parishes there was abundant pasture, and it was usually held in common: this was the case at Holford, Bicknoller, Clatworthy, Old Cleeve, Crowcombe (where a third of the land was common—both upland and lowland), Nettlecombe, Raddington, Dodington, Huish Champflower, Elworthy, and elsewhere. There were disputes about common at Bicknoller resulting in the laying out of bounds *(Siraut 1985 p 16)*, and we hear of the erection of baulks and stones in 1502 to define the boundaries on the common in Clatworthy *(Dunning 1985 p 36)*. In St Decumans the open common on the Brendons was enclosed in the 16th century *(Dunning 1985 p 158)*; and there were large areas of common pasture in Stogumber *(Siraut 1985 p 178)*. Better quality areas were used as meadow, but again this was held in common: at Sampford Brett there was common meadow in Molland Mead and Sampford Moor *(Siraut 1985 p 171)*. In St Decumans in the 14th century water meadows were created with waterleats west of Williton at Outmoor; and there were also waterleats at Doniford by 1418 *(Dunning 1985 p 158)*.

The overriding impression across west Somerset, therefore, is of a pastoral landscape, with a lot of enclosed land around scattered settlements which had been founded very early on. The main activity was sheep and cattle raising. Brompton Ralph was almost entirely enclosed by 1383, and pasture for sheep was of prime importance; the same was true of Chipstable and Clatworthy. In Raddington the "grazing of cattle and sheep seems to have been the important part of the parish economy" *(Dunning 1985 p 139)*. Robert Dunning also suggests that "the ten freeholders of Huish manor recorded in 1333 may represent scattered farms, characteristic of the Brendons", as a farmer at Stolford in the parish in 1573 had the right to take timber from the 'out hedges' of his enclosed farm *(1985 p 85)*.

At the other end of the scale there were clearly some open-field villages in west Somerset in the Middle Ages. Open fields are recorded for many of the manors on the coastal strip, which seem to have been operating a more or less 'normal' system of common field agriculture. Old Cleeve had open fields north-east and south of the village *(Dunning 1985 p 42)*. At Crowcombe "open field arable survived into the early 15th century in parts of the parish", and there may have been separate sets of fields for some of the outlying farmstead hamlets *(Bush 1985 p 58)*. The same is true in the large parishes of Stogumber and St Decumans: in the latter, traces survived until the 19th century, with open fields at Williton, Watchet, and probably Doniford (where there may have been three fields). Watchet in the 13th century had two fields 'Almyr' and 'Wrisland', after which terraces of houses were named in the 19th century. Williton almost certainly had three open fields—open field is recorded in 1288, Gothangre field mentioned in the late 14th century, while a Tregose field east of Williton existed in the 16th century, and a North field in the 17th century *(Dunning 1985 p 158)*—but, as we shall see, there may be other explanations for these references.

Nether Stowey had two open fields (north and south) *(Siraut 1985 p 191)*, Lilstock two (east and west) *(Dunning 1985 p 103)*, as did Kilton, where 'Kilton' and 'Sessons' fields (or east and west) are referred to—"strips were not usually located by their furlongs (but) rather by the fields in which they lay" *(Dunning 1985 p 89)*. Elsewhere, we usually just know of the existence of open field arable (Bicknoller, Halse, Monksilver, and West Quantoxhead). Only at Kilton do we get much idea of what was going on in the landscape. There, between 1377–81, the arable crop consisted almost entirely of wheat grown on a three-year cycle with very small areas of beans and peas and, in one year only, barley. Stock comprised pigs and cattle for draught, and 120 sheep. The manorial tenants owed 891 services, of which more than a third had been commuted to cash rather than labour *(Dunning 1985 p 93)*.

There were clearly a range of agricultural economies in west Somerset in the Middle Ages. There were open field villages, and there were scattered communities of farmers with enclosed land. The majority of places lay somewhere between the two, with some involvement in common open fields, but with pasture held in severalty and arable held in common. The large number of hamlets and farmsteads in existence by 1200 means that there can never have been a proper fully developed common field system. There was always a lot of enclosed land, and there was plenty of rough pasture and waste for future expansion. Such mixed areas with complex settlement patterns and varied field systems have not been much studied in the past, either in Somerset or elsewhere. Stogumber and Crowcombe parishes furnish the best examples in west Somerset in the areas studied so far *(Siraut 1985; Bush 1985).*

In great contrast are the parishes which have been studied in central and southern Somerset by Robert Dunning and Robin Bush for earlier Victoria County History volumes *(Dunning 1974; 1978).* Between Aller and Lydford in the north and the county boundary in the south some forty parishes have been examined. Something of the same contrasts can be seen here as in the west of the county, but they are not so marked.

In the hilly land between Crewkerne and the Devon border there was formerly a lot of woodland. There, the settlement pattern is scattered and there are a number of parishes with no recorded open field land, or where any open fields that had formerly existed had been enclosed early. In Chaffcombe, for example "no reference has been found to open-field cultivation" *(Bush 1978 p 125),* while at Cudworth "field names from the late 14th century onwards suggest well-established enclosures" *(Dunning 1978 p 144),* and at Cricket St Thomas "any former open field arable system seems to have been disrupted by inclosure before the 15th century". There may have been one field at Cricket called the Great or Corn field— perhaps, again, the infield of an infield–outfield system *(Bush 1978 p 136).*

Such parishes contrast with estate after estate in the lower land to the east, where there were more or less 'normal' common field systems. Exact numbers of fields cannot always be ascertained for particular dates, but the picture is generally clear and consistent. By and large, in this part of Somerset the 'Midland' system is the norm and conforms to our textbook idea of what common fields should be like. Examples are legion: **Barrington** had three fields—east, middle, and west—with common pasture land at Westmoor and Nidons *(Dunning 1978 p 113).* **Lopen** had the same field names in the 19th century as in the 12th; there were three fields, two sown with crops and one fallow each year. In the 14th century, wheat, rye, and barley were grown with smaller quantities of oats, hemp, beans, and peas. Although there was limited pasture and meadow on the small manor, there was a new flock of sheep in 1370 *(Dunning 1978 p 166).*

Within the large parish of **South Petherton** there were common fields at Compton Durville (two in 1558), Stratton (four in the 14th century), Drayton, Wigborough (three), and Petherton itself (four); there was common pasture and meadow at Yellands and South Mead in the south, and Drayton Mead in the east. In the 17th century there were still merestones dividing the meadows into doles on the Petherton manor *(Dunning 1978 p 172).* At **Shepton Beauchamp** the open fields, which survived until 1807, were said to be arranged on a three-year rotation in 1343, although there were more than three fields—a reminder that the actual working of the system could be more complicated than is implied in the recorded number of open fields. There was meadow and pasture in the north of the parish *(Bush 1978 p 215).*

The large parish of **Martock** shows clearly the association of nucleated groups of farmsteads with commonfield systems. The nine or ten separate villages and hamlets in the medieval parish each worked sets of open fields. At Ash there were three fields by 1273, with pasture in the north and west and meadows at Langmead and Yellowmead. Bower Hinton and Hurst shared three open fields—west, east, and south—in the 15th century, with common meadow at Hinton Mead and Ham and pasture at Wetmoor. At Coat there were two open fields in 1243, with meadow held in common. Long Load and Milton had three fields each, growing wheat, beans, and fallow. At the former there were three common moors or pastures at Outmoor, Foremoor, and Rottenham, and meadowland at Barland, Gosham, and Mare Mead; while at Milton there were still dole strips at Milton Leaze and Milton Mead in 1841. There were similar arrangements at Martock and Witcombe as well *(Bush 1978).*

Hinton St George provides a typical example of a village and its fields. It had three fields, west, south, and north, which were finally enclosed in the 16th century. There was meadow in the north of the parish and pasture and woodland in the south. In 1347 we hear that on the Carent manor the West Field had wheat and rye, while the North Field was planted to oats and beans, and the South Field was part fallow and part newly broken. In 1362 on the Denebaud estate two-thirds of the land was sown to arable each year, and twenty acres of grassland were held in severalty for hay production *(Dunning 1978 p 45).*

It is clear in these commonfield parishes, however, that the situation was not at all stable. Land which had been moor or permanent pasture was brought into arable cultivation on some manors, while there is widespread evidence for settlements increasing the number of their open fields by subdividing earlier groups of two or three main fields. Such division was recorded at Dowlish Wake, where "by the 16th century the medieval open fields had been divided into several smaller units" *(Bush 1978 p 153)*; Compton Durville (two in 1558, four in the 18th century) *(Dunning 1978 p 185)*; Stratton (four in the 14th century, later six) *(Dunning 1978 p 172)*; Witcombe in Martock (three? to four by the 18th century); Coat (two fields in 1243, three by 1555, and four later in the 16th century) *(Bush 1978)*; Crewkerne (two fields in the 13th century, three in the 16th century), where it is said that there had been some reorganisation *(Dunning & Bush 1978 pp 19–20)*; and Wayford (two medieval fields, three by 1610) *(Dunning 1978 p 69)*. At both Charlton Adam and Charlton Mackrell medieval two-field systems were replaced by four-field systems in the 16th century *(Bush 1974 p 82 & 96)*, while at Somerton the four medieval fields were rearranged in the 16th century *(Dunning 1974 p 129)*.

It will be noted that much of this change came about in the 16th century, at which time elsewhere there was replacement of common fields as more and more land was enclosed into individual holdings. The division of common fields probably enabled greater food production when the population was rising, while at the same time keeping less land fallow. The pressure on land that is implied is well shown for Mudford in 1554. A survey of the manor of Mudford and Hinton states that there were no commons or wastes in the manor, *'but only the common fields that are in tillage';* in other words, there was no room for any settlement expansion or increased arable production. The former demesne of the lord of Mudford, who lived at Hinton, had been subdivided between the tenants because the *'tenantries were so small and so little land belonging to them that no tenant was able to keep hospitality, to provide for his wife and children, and to pay the lords rent until about the year . . . 1400'*, when the reallotment took place *(Tawney & Power 1924 p 60–63)*.

That such division of common fields occurred earlier has been discussed by Harold Fox from the excellent documentation for Milton Podimore. The change was anticipated in 1330–1, when 200 yards (31 'ropes', each of approximately 20 feet) of ditch six feet wide and four feet deep were dug between *'the furlong of Port path and la Fosse'*—what was going to be the new middle field and the southerly field. A charter of around 1265 and an extent of 1332 refer to strips in West field and East field. Between the harvest and the autumn sowing of 1333, however, a three-field system was introduced, so that

when a terrier was made a few months later the furlongs were grouped into three fields, at first called the first, second, and third fields—these lasted until enclosure in the 18th century *(Fox 1986 p 533–4)*.

That such changes in field arrangements occurred elsewhere is extremely likely. Where two, three, or four fields are recorded in the Middle Ages, it is now at least possible that there were originally one or two open fields and that later subdivision has taken place. Such developments need to be discussed in the light of the origins of the Somerset field systems.

THE ORIGINS OF THE SOMERSET FIELD SYSTEMS
All sorts of explanations have been put forward in the past for the present appearance of Somerset's landscape *(Morland 1938)*. Most of these have been based on the idea of little pre-Saxon activity, colonisation by Saxon settlers, and nucleated settlements of farmers exploiting the land communally—none of which is now seen to be normal, general, or likely. How, then, did the variety and complexity of field systems which we have examined come about?

In earlier societies, such as those operating in late prehistoric, Roman, and post-Roman Somerset, land would have been used in the most productive way. It is very unlikely that low-lying land would have been used for arable; steep slopes and land at some distance from the settlements would perhaps be used as woodland. Arable might be expected to have been adjacent to each settlement for ease of access, and on this basis we might suggest that many settlements had their arable field nearby; with the application of farmyard manure and domestic refuse it would be possible to keep this field under cultivation almost indefinitely *(Aston 1985)*. The field may have been divided into strips among the families living in the hamlet; it would thus have the appearance of a common field, and it would be open between the strips, but this is a different sort of arrangement to that seen in the classic Midland commonfield systems. Extra areas could be ploughed from time to time, taken out of the pasture beyond. This is in effect an infield–outfield system *(Baker & Butlin 1973 p 655–6)*.

Something of this sort may have been operating at Codsend in Cutcombe in earlier times. A series of late 18th century maps show five small farmsteads, some with their holdings scattered in several areas of arable separated off from the commons beyond by massive field banks (Fig. 5.6).

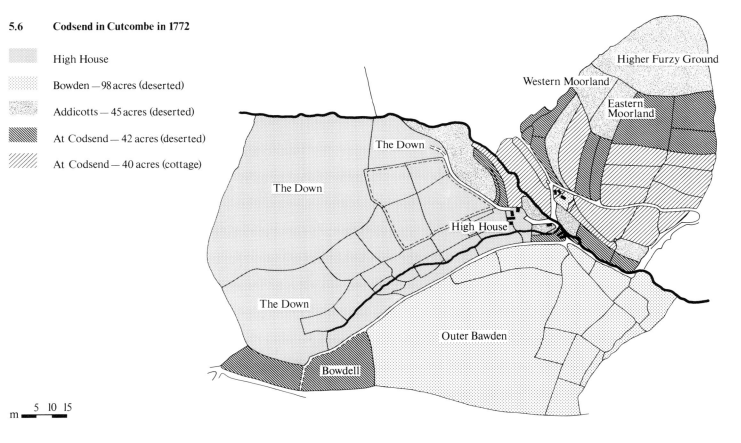

5.6   Codsend in Cutcombe in 1772

High House

Bowden — 98 acres (deserted)

Addicotts — 45 acres (deserted)

At Codsend — 42 acres (deserted)

At Codsend — 40 acres (cottage)

Higher Furzy Ground

Western Moorland

Eastern Moorland

The Down

The Down

The Down

High House

Outer Bawden

Bowdell

m 5 10 15

It would not have been necessary to expand or intensify arable production until the population increased markedly, as new people could have been accommodated either in an enlarged settlement and fed from an increased area of arable, or in new settlements with their own fields.

Such a situation may have been the norm in Somerset in the 6th, 7th, and 8th centuries following the Roman interlude, with many Romano-British settlements continuing the exploitation of the land on a less intensive, more subsistent basis. At this time the land was organised into large 'multiple estates', with numerous settlements dependent on and serving the needs of a 'caput', 'villa regalis', or lord's hall. Any excess production of a commodity, or speciality of a particular settlement, was probably exchanged with other neighbouring settlements on the same estate *(Jones 1979)*.

Harold Fox has argued that it is the break-up of these large estates in the late Saxon and early medieval periods that begins the development of the common field systems we see in the 13th and 14th centuries *(Fox 1981)*. Rising population and the need to feed more people would have led to an increase in the amount of land being used. Arable would need to be expanded at the expense of pasture in some areas. Markets and other exchange activities were developed to facilitate the movement of foodstuffs and other commodities between settlements in any area.

Only when population levels reached a certain level, and all the land that could be used for arable farming had been taken into cultivation, would some change in the field

5.7 ``Old´´ names which may indicate earlier field arrangements

◻ Oldfield

◯ Oldland

■ Other ``old´´ names

system be necessary. In order to accommodate the animals it would have become imperative to rotate the use of land so that pasture could be provided alternately with arable on the same ground. This may well have been associated with greater intensity of farming and with increased concern for the use of manures to maintain or increase fertility. In such circumstances, an estate with what had been a single arable field with pasture beyond would have become an estate where all land usable for arable is under cultivation at some stage.

The earlier stage seems to be recognisable in some parts of the country from field names. It has been suggested that 'innox' and 'breach' names, for example, perhaps represent new land associated with 'outfield' exploitation; while in Yorkshire 'old' field names have in places been shown to refer to earlier field arrangements before common fields were introduced *(Allerston 1970)*. Names such as 'oldfield' and 'oldland' occur widely in Somerset and may well refer to ancient infield arrangements (Fig. 5.7).

Later, simple division would enable one half of the original single arable field to be used for pasturing animals while the other half produced crops. Further division would result in two-thirds being used for arable and a third, the fallow, for pasture. Later rearrangements would produce more arable open fields and greater complexity and regulation of farming activities. This may well be the explanation of what we see in Somerset.

Only where there are large nucleated settlements do we get well-developed commonfield systems. In such areas there is a shortage of pasture, meadow, and woodland, as we are told at Lopen and the Seavingtons, for example, and there is careful management of the arable land with provision for pasture by rotation. There is no spare waste for expansion, as we have seen in the Mudford example. At the other extreme, in the hilly areas and in the woodland areas, there is little evidence of commonfield farming. Settlements are small and dispersed, the land is enclosed, and there was great emphasis on pastoral farming; probably equally important, however, were wood pasture and woodland management.

In between come the settlements and field systems that cover the majority of Somerset. These are the most common in the Somerset landscape, and indeed, it could be argued, generally represent the 'normal' English countryside. In these areas there is great variety and diversity of settlement, with a mixture of villages, hamlets, and farmsteads of different origins and ages. There is

abundant pasture and waste, both on uplands and on moorland, plenty of scattered woodland, and varying amounts of meadowland. A variety of land uses reflects the levels of population, the great areas of land available, and the variety of terrain.

In such areas there **is** arable, often on a large scale, but there are rarely fully developed commonfield systems. This is reflected in the difficulty of determining exactly how many open fields were in existence at any one time, how extensive they were, and when they were finally extinguished. Because of the large areas of pasture, there was never the pressure for rotation of arable with pasture, although the manure produced by grazing animals would have been important: single open fields and permanent cropping could have been the norm, and we have seen references to this above. The arable may have been open and worked communally, but such areas had most land enclosed and held in severalty; by the time documents become available in the 12th and 13th centuries they are often already fully enclosed. Elsewhere, enclosure of what open arable there had been is complete by the 15th and 16th centuries. The current pattern of scattered farms and hamlets with enclosed pasture fields with thick hedges is the result. Much of what we see today is, therefore, a landscape fully created for the most part by the 16th century, though it is certainly based on older and very persistent foundations.

Note 1   The quotations are from the Court Rolls of Wootton Courtenay 3 and 4 Edward 6 1550–1 for which an English translation exists in the County Record Office DD/CCH 7/6.

ACKNOWLEDGEMENTS
Joe Bettey, Bob Dunning, and particularly James Bond read and commented on the text; Carinne Allinson applied her considerable editorial skills and made useful critical comments.

I would like to thank Bob Dunning and Mary Siraut for access to unpublished VCH material and for useful discussion; my debt to them will be apparent from the references. The staff of the County Record Office, particularly Robin Bush and Steve Hobbs, were very helpful.

Frances Neale, Hazel Hudson, Vince Russet, and Michael Costen provided details of field systems in individual parishes; permission to use illustrations was provided by Derek Shorrocks of the County Record Office and John Hardwick.

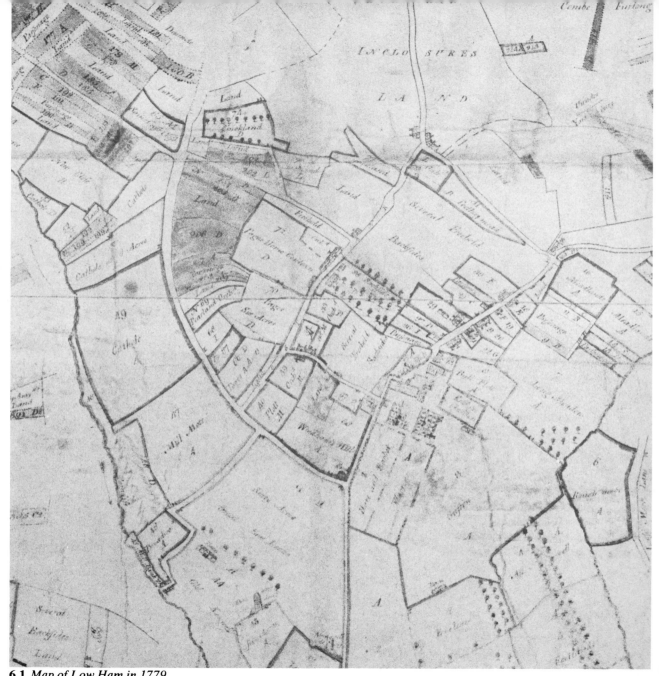

6.1 *Map of Low Ham in 1779*

Chapter 6
PARKS, GARDENS *and* LANDSCAPING
John Harvey

Until quite recently it was usual to consider our landscape as either open or wooded, and to divide the latter into 'natural woodland' for the most part, and 'the English landscape garden' as to a small proportion. This remained the basic approach of the late Miles Hadfield in his masterly **Landscape with Trees** *(Hadfield 1967 p 9)*. Within the last few years it has become clear that the historic facts are far more complex. On the one hand, major human interference with nature can by archaeological method be carried back to a remote period; while on the other, documentary research has shown that the age of the landscape garden—in its wider sense—began not later than the generation of the Norman Conquest *(Harvey 1972 p 59–68)*.

Here we are concerned with these last nine centuries of development in a single ancient county: the deliberate interference with Somerset's pre-existing landscape (whether 'Natural' or not) to form parks, gardens and scenic effects, from the time of William the Conqueror to the present day. Though not proceeding at a constant rate, this interference and the creation of new aspects of the landscape has been continuous and substantial. Somerset is but a single unit in a much greater whole, yet it has played a distinctive part in the history of English landscaping and horticulture.

Starting from the Conquest, we must first note the extensive holdings recorded in Domesday Book, 1086 *(Thorn and Thorn 1980)*, of the bishop of Coutances, Geoffrey (I) de Montbray (Bishop 1049–1093). Out of an immense estate, comprising 75 manors in Somerset alone, the bishop kept 14 in his own hands *(Note 1)*. Four of these manors: Long Ashton (with 100 acres of wood in 1086), Newton St Loe, Orchardleigh (with woods 6 furlongs by 2 furlongs or about 120 acres), and Wraxall (with 150 acres of woodland) were later to have extensive parks. This may

have considerable significance for the history of English landscaping. For it was this bishop who, after a journey to southern Italy to visit his Norman kinsmen who had conquered the country, returned to lay out the first recorded pleasance in North-Western Europe *(Note 2)*. This certainly reflects his contact with the Arab influences on the South. Before 1066 he had acquired a large area of land by Coutances, surrounded it with a double ditch and palisade, planted a garden and vineyard and made two pools, and in the park sowed acorns and took pains to grow oaks, beeches and other forest trees *(quercus et fagos caeterumque nemus studiose coluit)*. Then, at a date after the Conquest, he filled the park with deer from England *(Note 3)*.

Here is an implication that deer-parks were already better established in England than on the Continent, but it is the fact of direct interrelation between the bishop's estates on both sides of the Channel that is of supreme importance. We cannot doubt that Bishop Geoffrey's interest in sowing and planting trees extended also to his English demesne manors and provided an exemplar for future arboriculture in this country. Thus there was, well before 1100, a direct personal contact between Somerset and the source of three linked concepts: the enclosed pleasure-ground; its deliberate planting with trees; and its association with pools or lakes *(Note 4)*.

Contrary to the received tradition (still accepted by Hadfield) that it was only in 1580 (well after the end of the Middle Ages), that the first regular plantation of trees was made in England, it is now known that substantial tree planting and the sowing of acorns and nuts went on from the thirteenth century or earlier until the time of Henry VIII *(Note 5)*. This was not only a matter of monastic policy in respect of timber, but was also carried out on the private estates of bishops, abbots and lay landowners.

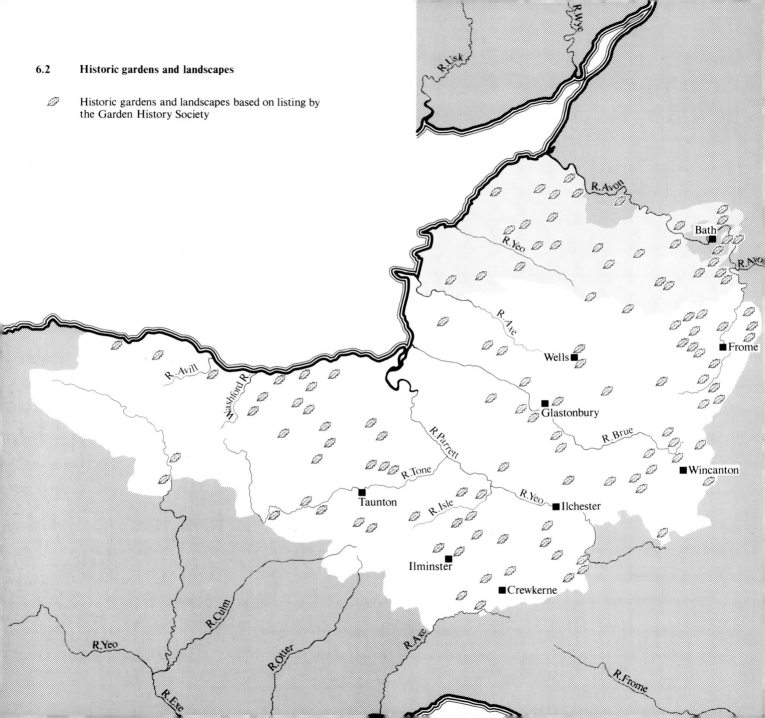

Historic gardens and landscapes based on listing by
the Garden History Society

Among the earliest recorded instances of deliberate landscaping is the mention of small elms planted *(hulmellos plantatos)* near the new west front of Wells Cathedral by 1243 *(Note 6)*. In this we have one of the first examples of the association of trees, and the accompanying turf of the Green, with a great work of architecture. The beauty of trees was again recognized at Wells in 1326, when the orchard of the bishop's palace was divided, and a medlar tree specially reserved on the bishop's side of the new boundary *(HMC, 1907 p 214–15)*.

The major estates of Somerset in the Middle Ages were largely those of churchmen: the abbot of Glastonbury, the bishops of Bath and Wells and of Winchester, and the prior of Bath. The palaces of the abbot, with very large deer-parks, included East Brent, Meare, Mells, Pilton, and several close to Glastonbury itself: Norwood, Shapwick, Sharpham and Weston. At Glastonbury the last Abbot, Whiting, had an important garden with an arbour formed of bay trees. In addition to Wells the bishops had country seats at Banwell, Chew Magna, Claverton, Evercreech and Wiveliscombe; the priors of Bath had Prior Park to the south of the city and St. Catherine's on the north. Besides all these there were Butcombe Court belonging to the abbot of Thame in Oxfordshire, and Halsway Manor, a favourite retreat of Cardinal Beaufort early in the fifteenth century. Two of the great parks near Taunton— Nailsbourne and Poundisford—originated in the immense estate of the bishops of Winchester.

In a few cases something is known of planting and management during the Middle Ages. This is hinted at in the charter which Bishop Reginald obtained from Richard Coeur-de-Lion about 1190, allowing him and his successors the right to keep sporting dogs throughout Somerset; and further indicated by the charters of 1207 and 1221 which permitted the inclosure of the park to the south of the palace at Wells and the diversion of several public roads which had run across the area *(Note 7)*. Bishop Beckington (1443–65) made *'a most beautiful orchard with divers wonderful fruits'* at Banwell; at East Brent Abbot Selwood of Glastonbury about 1475 planted an orchard of over three acres with apples and pears of the finest sorts, and also with elms and oaks *(Harvey 1969 p 296–7, Note 8)*. His successor Abbot Beere enlarged the earlier pleasance at Meare by walling in more than three acres, forming moats, pools and orchards; and it was probably he who built the great buttressed wall of the garden to the north of Mells Manor *(Harvey 1981 p 136)*. At the same period Prior Cantlow of Bath was forming or

enlarging the terraced gardens at St. Catherine's Court *(Country Life, XX, p 738, p 774)*. Less is known of the secular estates, but at Merriott Manor in 1369 there was a garden with a nursery *(la noresirie)*, the earliest known use of the word in the horticultural sense, as well as a park and a wood *(Dunning 1978 p 57, Note 9)*. Ashton Park near Bristol was enclosed and planted by Thomas de Lyons in 1391, but is likely to have taken the place of a much earlier planting of the bishop of Coutances *(Murray 1882 p 368)*.

After the Dissolution of the monasteries, complete in 1540, the lay purchasers of the church estates began a new campaign of emparking and gardening. The pleasure garden as a major feature took on increased importance as the trickle of new plants introduced from abroad grew to a flood. Bruton Abbey and Witham Friary were converted to secular dwellings and their precincts became—if they were not already—important gardens; on a smaller scale the abbatial manor-house at Mells was converted to a layman's mansion with a walled garden complex. The immensely influential works of Sir John Thynne at Longleat lay on the borders of Somerset and from 1550 onwards exercised a strong pressure upon regional

6.3 *Deer and goats, from a medieval manuscript*

development. Before 1640 Edmond Figgins had a large tree nursery covering six acres of ground at Westbury, Wiltshire, specialising in many named varieties of fruit. This was, it is true, three miles outside Somerset, but at the same time there was another large nursery, of which less is known, at Mudgley near Wedmore. These are among the very earliest trade nurseries recorded in the English provinces and imply extensive interest in planting in the region. Many sorts of fruit trees were ordered for the Earl of Cork's new orchard at Stalbridge, Dorset, some 30 miles from Westbury and as far from Mudgley *(Note 10)*.

Later Elizabethan gardens of importance were at Fairfield near Stogursey, Hardington Park *(Aston 1978)* and, above all, at Montacute. Thomas Gerard, writing in 1633, described Montacute as

> *'a very beautifull peece. . . whether you consider the fairness or neate building of the house, or ye conveniences about it, such as are large and spacious Courtes, gardens, orchards, a parke, &c.' (Bates 1900 p 99).*

Historically the most interesting Somerset garden of the time is that of the (Old) Deanery at Wells, cultivated in 1551–54 and 1561–68 by Dean William Turner, the Father of English Botany *(Note 11)*. Under James I there were large-scale garden designs at Low Ham (c.1605–20) *(Aston 1978)* and at (East) Coker Court about 1620; and the greater Renaissance garden was exemplified under Charles I at Hinton St. George in 1630–40 and again at Ashton Court. What was done at Hinton must have been unusual in its effect, for it elicited commendation from Cosmo III, Grand Duke of Tuscany, at his visit in 1669, because the gardens and terraces were *'very different from the common style' (Murray 1882 p 436; and see Appendix)*. Another estate which had evidently been greatly developed was Brympton D'Evercy, described in 1633 as *'daintily sceated and furnished with all manner of conveniences as gardens, orchards, groves, &c.'* The gardens of Brympton have been re-made several times since *(Note 12)*.

Before Somerset could become typical of the monster landscapes of the day, the Civil War struck, and was followed by a wave of puritanical and equalitarian vandalism *(Strong 1979)*. Even after the Restoration very little was done in the county and Redlynch Park, which still preserves the Orangery from the layout of c.1670, seems to have been the only first-class development during the reign of Charles II. About 1685–90 this was followed by the second great mansion and gardens at Low Ham

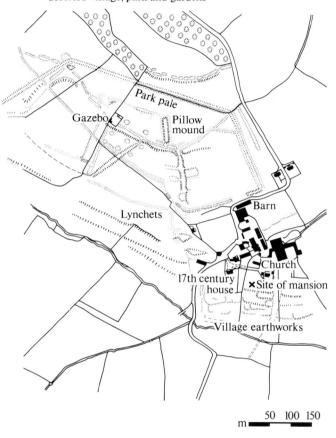

6.4 Hardington earthworks
deserted village, park and gardens

(Aston 1978). After the Revolution there was activity near Taunton, notably at Orchard Portman (which by 1633 had had 'a parke and all other delights') *(Bates 1900 p 61)* and Poundisford, but the next wave of garden making did not come until the reign of Queen Anne. Soon after 1700 works began at Clevedon Court, Combe Hay, Hutton Court, and Standerwick Court, and in some cases lasted well into the reign of George I. In 1708 the ancient abbatial manor-house at East Brent was demolished, but stone figures were saved from its gardens to adorn that of one Dr Westover in Wedmore *(Note 13)*. There was a fresh

6.5 Low Ham earthworks
lynchets, gardens and warren

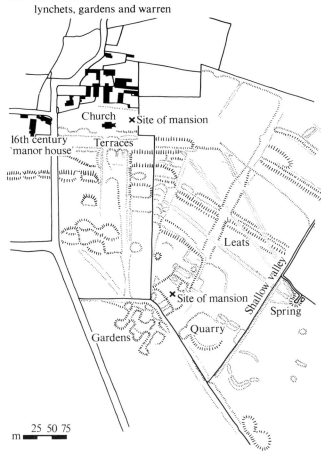

Church
× Site of mansion
16th century
'manor house'
Terraces

Leats

× Site of mansion

Spring

Shallow valley

Quarry

Gardens

m ▬▬▬ 25 50 75

phase of garden activity at Brympton D'Evercy in about 1710–23, along with the building of the Stables and Clock Tower. Crowcombe Court, Dunster Castle, Midelney Manor and Sandhill Park all had works in progress in the 1720s, but it was at Marston House near Frome that the most notable things of the time were done. It was there that Stephen Switzer designed a semi-formal garden for the Earl of Cork, with water-spouts to the south of the mansion. There had already been *'orchards, gardens and pleasant walks'* around the old house of c.1610–30, but it is uncertain how much of this survived Switzer's

replanning of 1724 and the activity of the next twenty years. This new garden was destroyed about 1820 by Sir Jeffery Wyatville, but is recorded in Badeslade's print of 1739 *(McGarvie 1974 and 1987)*.

There is known to have been an important period of gardening at Orchard Wyndham in 1730–40 under Sir William Wyndham and his head gardener William Brown. Brown was a subscriber to Philip Miller's first folio **Dictionary** in 1731 and to Switzer's **Practical Husbandman and Planter** of 1733. About the same time were the plantings around Hazlegrove House in Queen Camel, remodelled in 1732 by the Blandford architects John and William Bastard. Of this much survives, but a total loss are the splendid gardens on the monastic site of Witham Charterhouse, designed for William Talman's 'Old' House of 1710–17 with its important garden front. The site of the Great Garden, known from a plan of 1812, largely disappeared beneath the Weymouth main line of the Great Western Railway *(McGarvie 1981)*.

Except for Switzer's documented work at Marston, most of the early landscaping is anonymous or was directed by the landowners and their chief gardeners. Of the Somerset gardeners we know little, though Sir John Smyth at Ashton employed one Thomas Baylis in 1733 and the Hon. S. Copplestone-Bampfield at Hardington was served in that capacity by Robert Brown who died in 1739. His memorial is in the north chapel of Buckland Dinham Church*(Kellor 1924 p 21)..* He may have been related to William Brown and to the later Robert Brown *'of Hill Farm, Somersetshire'* (perhaps at Otterhampton) who published **The compleat Farmer; or the whole art of husbandry** in two small volumes for six shillings in 1759 *(Green 1902 II p 200)*. The most famous gardener of the time was John Searle, who had been gardener to Alexander Pope at Twickenham for twenty years until Pope's death in 1744, and then moved to Bath to take charge at Prior Park for Ralph Allen *(Hadfield 1969 p 187–8)*.

Roughly from the accession of George III in 1760 a new pattern emerges with the setting of fashionable trends, first by Lancelot Brown and later by Humphrey Repton *(Stroud 1975; Carter, Goode & Laurie 1982)*. Known works by Brown include his masterpiece of Prior Park Bath (1762–65), Burton Pynsent (1765–75), and Kelston Park (1767–68) overlooking the Avon. Repton worked at Ston Easton Park from 1794 and at Newton Park, Newton St. Loe, about two years later; he was at Ashton Court around 1801, though the terrace walls there are thought to go back to the later years of Elizabeth I. Repton was also in charge of landscaping at (East) Coker Court about 1803, and his latest work in Somerset was at Leigh Court where he laid out the extensive gardens and park around the new house of 1814 by Thomas Hopper. Later in the century these were described as *'beautiful grounds . . . in finest order' (Murray 1882 p 364)*. The grand scale of work can be judged from the case of Ammerdown, where the landscaped estate was made from a large area of open sheep down from 1788 onwards, and over 20,000 trees were planted from 1795 to 1799 *(Allan 1970, p 75; Country Life, LXV, p 216, p 292, p 330)*. At the end of the Georgian period came the grotto and follies of c1830 at Barwick House *(Jones 1974 p 227)*.

Although no famous names are on record as designers of Somerset gardens or landscape in the Victorian period, several estates carried out extensive planting or re-planting. Notable among these were Newton Surmaville near Yeovil, and Orchardleigh close to Frome. Newton goes back to the important house of 1602–12 and preserves some remains of a mid-eighteenth-century landscaping, notably the summerhouse on a hill to the west; but its splendid trees belong mostly to the 1860s *(Note 14)*. Orchardleigh was laid out by a Mr Page in 1855–56. This was very likely William Bridgewater Page (1790–1871), the Southampton nurseryman, son-in-law of John Kennedy of Hammersmith, and founder of the firm later Toogoods *(McGarvie 1983 p 130–7; Willson 1961, p 52, Harvey 1974, p 99–100)*. There was also some activity in the grounds of the Bishop's Palace at Wells where important specimen trees were planted, and where the tradition is being continued by the Jubilee Arboretum of 1976–77 *(Sales 1980 p 137; Wells 1983)*.

Coming down to the present century, gardens designed by Sir Edwin Lutyens include Ammerdown (1901–03), Hestercombe (1904–10) and Redlynch Park (c.1910). At Hestercombe the planting was controlled in detail by Gertrude Jekyll, who also suggested the planting of the new garden at Barrington Court in 1920–25. Another personal style is exemplified by the garden at Wayford Manor (1900–10) by Harold Peto. Since the passing of the historic era with the deaths of Miss Jekyll in 1932 and of William Robinson in 1935, the gardens of Somerset have again taken on fresh importance, this time as a centre of plantsmanship. The lead was taken by Walter and Margery Fish at East Lambrook Manor near South Petherton where the 'cottage garden' of little over an acre became, between 1938 and Mrs Fish's death in 1969, a model and an inspiration for many gardeners throughout the country. Another private enterprise of great importance was that of Captain and Mrs Reiss at Tintinhull House, given to The National Trust by Mrs Reiss in 1953 and since maintained by a brilliant succession of tenants of the house.

Now a modern garden but with a long family tradition behind it, is Clevedon Court, a medieval house and the home of the Eltons since 1709, when the terraces were made and the Octagon summerhouse added in 1720. There was tree planting throughout the eighteenth century and this was romanticised about 1840. Later on, commonplace bedding earned the scorn of Gertrude Jekyll in 1901, but the estate has since been revolutionised. Other splendid new gardens formed on an ancient basis are those at Hadspen, Montacute and Lytes Cary, where the atmosphere of the Elizabethan garden of Sir Henry

6.6 *Hestercombe House gardens*

Lyte, translator and enlarger of **A Niewe Herball** (1578) has been skilfully evoked *(Note 15)*.

It is not possible here to consider the many garden buildings which survive on the older estates, such as the gazebos at Montacute. A few highly unusual structures, however, must be mentioned: the Keeper's Lodge at Hardington (Fig. 6.7), built for defence but apparently incorporating a first-floor banqueting chamber, dated to 1582; *(McGarvie & Harvey 1980)* the famous Palladian Bridge of 1750 in Prior Park; and the Conservatory by Decimus Burton at Ven House, Milborne Port, built in 1836. Of undoubted age is the small stone building at Lodge Farm, Farleigh Hungerford, scheduled as an Ancient Monument on the suggestion of Abbot Horne that it was a Falconry. Far more impressive in their effect on the landscape are the hilltop towers, columns and follies, a selection of which may be named in chronological order. Earliest are the towers of churches or chapels built on high places. The most conspicuous is the Perpendicular tower on Glastonbury Tor visible for many miles around. On the southern boundary of the county (and in recent years actually transferred to Dorset) is the 14th-century spired tower of Trent Church, another landmark. St. Michael's Chapel on Burrow Mump, both genuine and artificial (a rebuilding of c.1793), and the conspicuous church towers of Dundry and Leigh-upon-Mendip (both of c.1480), had also set their mark on the scene before the end of the Middle Ages.

The later monuments begin with the one to the Civil War Battle of Lansdown (1643) erected above Bath in 1720; the Dunster summerhouse on the Tor of 1727; and then a crop of the 1760s: the Sham Castle on Bathwick Hill (1762), an eye-catcher; the Conygar Tower at Dunster; Lancelot Brown's column at Burton Pynsent (designed in 1765 and built over the next two years); followed later by Alfred's Tower (1776) above Stourhead but just in Somerset. Then came a pause, but after the Napoleonic Wars the hills burgeoned with the Wellington Monument on the Blackdown Hills (1817 and later); the Monument to Sir Samuel Hood on Windmill Hill (after 1814); Willett's Tower, Elworthy (by 1782) and Cothelstone Beacon, not far away; then the eccentric Beckford's Tower on Lansdown (1825). Finally there was a Victorian group including notably the Banwell Tower built for Bishop Law and Brown's Folly on the Wiltshire border east of Bath (both 1840), the Ammerdown Column of 1853–55, and (East) Cranmore Tower of 1862. There are others, and were many more.

6.7 Keeper's Lodge, Hardington Park

East elevation

Cross section

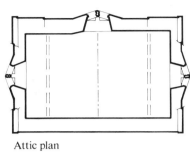

Attic plan

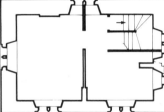

First floor plan

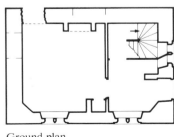

Ground plan

m ▬ 1 2 3

North

The Hood Monument is of unusual interest in that it was linked to Butleigh Court, the home of the Hood family, by an avenue a mile long planted with Cedars of Lebanon, of which many remain. A short distance off is another Cedar Walk at Kingweston House; but both these plantings are modern compared with that of the Cedar Piece at Hinton St George, where the trees are believed to date from 1684. Other trees of note are the oaks and beeches at Hazelgrove in Queen Camel, the oak plantations of the Trevelyans at Nettlecombe, and the great chestnuts at Halswell Park, also noted for its temples and obelisks. Cothelstone had a giant walnut with a girth in 1875 of 19 feet 3 inches at three feet above the ground *(Kelly 1875 p 198)*.

In retrospective survey, Somerset presents a paradox: as Michael Havinden has brilliantly put it, the county "was characterised by a surprising absence of resident peers" *(Havinden 1981 p 239)* and this in turn implied that it was apparently almost devoid of those famous great estates which in the past three centuries have played such a prominent part in the English landscape as a whole. Yet we find on closer examination that our shire has played an exceptionally distinguished part in the development of what makes up the man-made landscape of garden and park. On the Somerset estates of the Bishop of Coutances it is probable that England received the first impact of a new art-form: the oriental 'paradise', within the first quarter-century from the Conquest. It was at Wells Cathedral that, at the very moment of consecration on 23 October 1239, young elms were being planted in relation to what was to remain henceforth the greatest of our church fronts. Within another three or four generations it was in Somerset that, as far as we know, the word nursery was first used to describe a plantation for the bringing up of young plants. Throughout the medieval period it was the combined total areas of the parks of the bishops and of the abbots that led the rest of the country in recreational land. In Somerset was the one garden in England that received the personal care of the Father of English Botany. In the centuries of the grand estates, Somerset may have lagged behind, perhaps with a just avoidance of their un-English exaggeration. Within our own times the county has provided models of what can be achieved by individual brilliance combined with hard work in the modest limits of Tintinhull and East Lambrook. It is to be hoped, and indeed confidently expected, that the Somerset of generations to come will continue to cultivate a Golden Mean *(Note 16)*.

APPENDIX

The visit of Cosmo III, Grand Duke of Tuscany, to Hinton St George on 9 April 1669.

> *The mansion of mylord Pawlet is an ancient building, irregular and the whole externally incrusted with tufa (tutta esteriormente incrostata di tufo). Yet the dwelling rooms are noble, fine and spacious, and there are also gardens both for utility and pleasure. On the one hand they contain all those sorts of plants and fruits which the climate will allow, and on the other a parterre, very different from the common usage of the gardens in England. For, where these have sanded walks perfectly levelled by rolling them with a stone roller (threaded through the centre with an iron rod, whose ends are joined together in a triangle by which it is pulled to and fro), and between the walks several flat spaces covered with very green turf and without other adornment, this garden of mylord Pawlett is a meadow with different beds having borders of bricks on end (?—in piedi), filled with flowers. Around the house is the park, of three miles in circumference, shut in by a thick plantation of trees . . .*

(translated from **Un Principe di Toscana in Inghilterra e in Irlanda nel 1669,** edited by Anna Maria Crinò; Rome, Edizioni di Storia e Letteratura, 1968, p 32).

This chapter is largely based on the collection of materials for the Register of Gardens of Britain being compiled by the Garden History Society. The work on Somerset was begun by the late Edward Malins and has been continued under the general direction of Mrs M. Batey.

Official Registers have now been issued for the counties of Avon and Somerset: see English Heritage, Register of Parks and Gardens of Special Historic Interest in England, Part 1: Avon; Part 36: Somerset, 1985.

In connection with the translation of the Appendix from the original Italian, I am most grateful for assistance from Dr I. Bulmer-Thomas.

Note 1   Though the Bishop of Coutances held a few manors elsewhere, almost all of his vast Domesday estate lay in Somerset (Thorn and Thorn 1980).

Note 2   The word pleasance here means 'a pleasure-ground, usually attached to a mansion' (Oxford English Dictionary), as its medieval French source, Plaisans, was used expressly to denote such western counterparts of the oriental inclosed 'paradise'. It was the earlier form of the landscape-park or 'grounds', forming an extension of the (pleasure) garden.

Note 3   Recueil des Historiens de France, t. xiv (1877), p 76–80. I am indebted to Professor R. H. C. Davis, for referring me to the account of this text by the late Professor J. Le Patourel (English Historical Review LIX, 1944, p 129–61), which shows that it is a sound and early source.

Note 4   These concepts derive from the walled paradise of Iran and the Near East, where it had been an important feature of courtly life for many centuries (Thacker 1979 p 15–17, p 27–41). Some medieval orchards were undoubtedly pleasure-grounds, and in Somerset the place-names Orchard Portman, Orchard Wyndham, and Orchardleigh all appear significant.

Note 5   It is necessary to insist on this, because very recent authorities have endorsed the older view, notably O. Rackham (Arboricultural Journal III No. 3, 1977, p 176; Rackham 1980, 3, where only one possible exception near Colchester, perhaps of c.1240, is admitted). The explicit evidence, both of account rolls and of chronicles, proves that woodland (especially oak, but including also ash, beech, elm, poplar and willow) was deliberately sown and planted in many parts of England from 1260 continuously until the 16th century (Harvey 1981 p 13–17). Perhaps the most striking case is that of the Northamptonshire squire, Henry de Bray, who recorded his sowing of acorns in an inclosure of four acres in 1305–06 (Willis 1916 p 9, p 50).

Note 6   Wells Cathedral Muniments, Liber Albus, f. 64v; HMC 1907 p 73–4.

Note 7   Dictionary of National Biography, s.v. FitzJocelin, Reginald; Rotuli Litterarum Clausarum, II (1844), p 173, p 176; Church 1894, p 138–9; cf. Rot. Litterarum Patentium (1835), I, p 77.

Note 8   Maxwell-Lyte and Dawes 1934, p xl; British Museum Quarterly, X (1935), p 70.

Note 9   Calendar of Close Rolls 1374–7, p 263–5.

Note 10   Chatsworth. Devonshire Collections, Lismore Papers, vol. 21, letters nos. 79, 80, from photocopies kindly supplied by the late T. S. Wragg, (the printed version in Lismore Papers ed. A. B. Grosart, 1st Series, V (1886), p 64, is inaccurate). Edmond Figgins of Westbury, gardener, died in 1671, when an inventory of his goods (but not of his garden) was taken on 15 December (Wiltshire Record Office, Salisbury Chantor's Court, Bundle 11/9, Admon. 11 February 1678/9). I am greatly obliged to Mr K. H. Rogers, for this reference.

Note 11   Turner refers to the Deanery garden in his New Herball completed in 1568.

Note 12   Bates 1900, p 105. Brympton as it was in 1707 appears in an engraving by Kip, conveniently reproduced in Harris 1982, 140–1.

Note 13   Two stone figures survive at Porch House, Wedmore, which was undoubtedly the home of Dr John Westover junior (1643–1706), who died two years before the reported date of the demolition at East Brent. John Strachey, F.R.S., in April 1730 wrote to Thomas Hearne (Chronicle of Walter Hemingford, 2 vols., 1731, II, p 657) that East Brent manor house 'was taken down 1708. . . Doctor Westover of Blackford in Wedmore bought some of them (monuments, etc.). . . for statues in his gardens'. Nothing is known of Westover having another property in the hamlet of Blackford, nor of substantial gardens at Porch House. I am indebted to Mrs F. Neale for this information, as well as to Mr M. McGarvie, who tells me that Strachey's note to the same effect is among the Egmont Papers in the British Library (see also F. Neale, 'A 17th Century Country Doctor: John Westover of Wedmore', The Practitioner, November 1969, vol. 203, p 699–704).

Note 14   I am grateful to Mrs S. W. Rawlins, for information on Newton Surmaville and its Victorian planting.

Note 15   The modern gardens of Somerset have been recently described by Mr J. Sales (1980, p 129–87).

Note 16   Information on Somerset gardens has been gathered from many sources, notably J. Collinson, The History and Antiquities of the County of Somerset (3 vols., 1791); W. Phelps, The History and Antiquities of Somersetshire (2 vols., 1836–39); Dunning 1974, 1978); and Hugh Prince, Parks in England (1967). I have particularly to thank Mr L. S. Colchester for much information on the present state of historic gardens and parks throughout the county.

Chapter 7
CONSERVING *the* HISTORIC LANDSCAPE
Kenneth Brown, Robert Croft and Russell Lillford

*I*t has often been said that one of the beauties of
Britain is its immensely varied landscape. To most
people the very mention of a County name produces a
mental picture of its predominant landscape. Norfolk or
Devon or Cornwall for example are immediately called to
mind as having very strong and memorable landscape
forms. And so it is with Somerset, ranging from the watery
expanses of the Levels and Moors to upland grandeur of
Exmoor, Quantock and Mendip.

Landscapes are the product of subtle interactions upon
the fundamental geology of the region by both the climate
and man's activities. Somerset displays these interactions
particularly well, having a landscape that is both rich and
varied. Today we must realise that we have been handed
down a landscape which reflects centuries of man's
sometimes unequal struggle with the elements to sustain a
predominantly rural economy. In recent years however the
pace of change has accelerated. The built environment of
towns, villages and roads has extended into a countryside
which was already undergoing dramatic changes as
agriculture adjusted to the demands of the modern age.
Seen in the historical perspective this may be only another
period of transition but the scale of change is such that
there must be fears that a heritage could be lost before it
has either been understood or interpreted adequately.

This chapter examines the mechanisms and initiatives
being pursued to achieve the protection of this heritage so
that the many roles that our landscape plays—that of an
endless source of pleasure and leisure, together with its
contribution to the economy of the county—can be
balanced. The historic landscape can be viewed in a

variety of ways, but for the purposes of this discussion, it
refers to any man-made features from earliest times up to
the present century.

What are the characteristics of an historic landscape and
how and where should efforts be made to conserve them?
It has been stated that "The Somerset landscape is one of
the most varied and beautiful in England, and it is this
variety which presents the most intriguing problems for
anyone trying to explain its history" *(Havinden 1981 p 29)*.

An understanding of what we mean by the historic
landscape is an essential pre-requisite to its successful
conservation. It is only by having an accurate picture of
what survives and what it represents that informed
decisions can be taken to ensure that important features of
such landscapes are protected and conserved for future
generations.

No single body is responsible for the historic
environment, its conservation requires the goodwill and
careful stewardship of a large number of private and
public owners as well as the integration of the work of a
range of different disciplines such as the archaeologist, the
landscape architect, the estates surveyor, the forester and
those with particular specialist conservation skills. The
long-term responsibility for the heritage, its management
and conservation, can only be met by increased financial
support from private and public funds.

THE MECHANISMS OF CONSERVATION
It is generally agreed that one of the primary aims of
historic landscape conservation policies must be to protect
such areas from damaging development or at least to
control or influence the form that development might take.
This is achieved in several ways.

In a county of relative economic prosperity the
overriding consideration in strategic planning terms has

7.1 *A general view of the Somerset landscape from West
Bagborough hill*

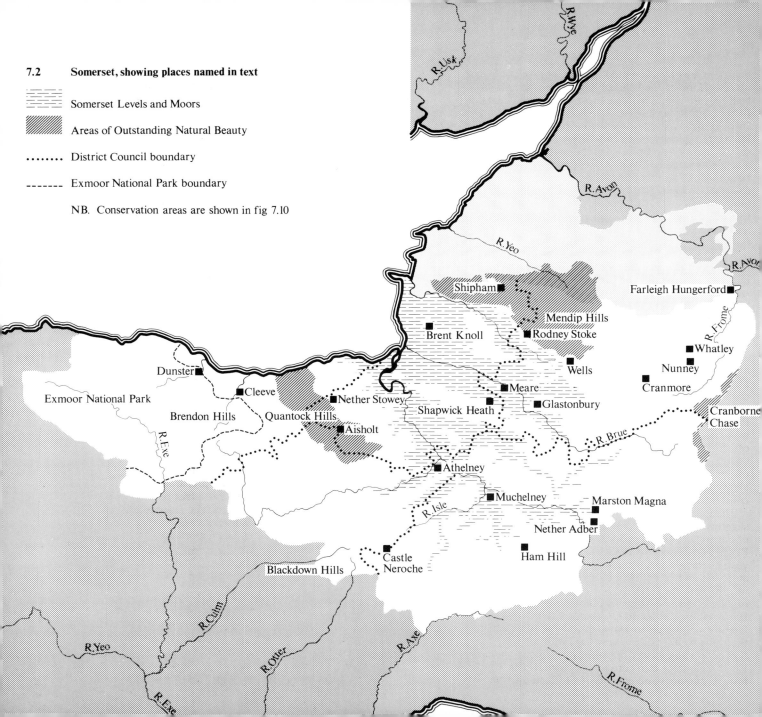

7.2 **Somerset, showing places named in text**

Somerset Levels and Moors

Areas of Outstanding Natural Beauty

District Council boundary

Exmoor National Park boundary

NB. Conservation areas are shown in fig 7.10

R. Wye

R. Usk

R. Avon

R. Yeo

Shipham

Farleigh Hungerford

Mendip Hills

Brent Knoll

Rodney Stoke

Whatley

Wells

Nunney

Dunster

Cranmore

Meare

Cleeve

Exmoor National Park

Nether Stowey

Cranborne Chase

Brendon Hills

Shapwick Heath

Glastonbury

Quantock Hills

R. Brue

Aisholt

R. Exe

Athelney

R. Isle

Muchelney

Marston Magna

Nether Adber

Ham Hill

Castle Neroche

Blackdown Hills

R. Culm

R. Otter

R. Yeo

R. Axe

R. Exe

R. Frome

R. Avon

R. Frome

been the need to accommodate increasing pressures for new development and change, whilst ensuring that the historic and natural heritage is preserved and maintained. In many instances this overall objective has been successfully achieved, but all too often badly designed or ill-conceived development has marred a cherished local scene, damaged an historic building or destroyed an archaeological site. The man-made heritage has frequently been regarded as an obstacle to progress rather than a challenge requiring a positive response combining imaginative change with preservation. The underlying theme of all local authority policies directed at the care and protection of the historic heritage is the requirement for a sensitive, practical and balanced approach.

Numerous local authorities have stated through the medium of **Structure Plans** and **Local Plans** their intention to conserve and protect the historic environment *(Hampshire 1984; Berkshire 1986)*. The Somerset County Structure Plan similarly contains several policies for the protection of the countryside *(Somerset County Council 1983)*. The County Structure Plan policy for archaeology states that "The Local Planning Authorities will seek to ensure that historical/archaeological sites, features and areas deemed to be of National or County importance, are protected from development". This, and the complementary policy dealing with natural sites, represent examples of fairly strongly-stated policies by Structure Plan standards, which are designed to create a context within which many other policies are interpreted. The constraints of the structure planning process, which have been justly criticized, and have led to proposals for a review of the whole system, have nevertheless in Somerset allowed appropriate emphasis to be given to the conservation of the natural and man-made heritage.

The main policy used to protect historic buildings is slightly different, but confirms similar aims and objectives of the archaeological policy above. The County Structure Plan was published in 1983 and in the subsequent five years there have been a number of changes in Government attitude towards the 'Historic Environment', most notably in 1983 with the National Heritage Act and the formation of the Historic Buildings and Monuments Commission for England (English Heritage) as an advisory body to the Department of the Environment. The positive effects of the new organisation are now beginning to be felt in Somerset and a variety of projects have been funded by English Heritage to record archaeological sites, repair historic buildings and enhance the historic environment.

PROTECTIVE DESIGNATIONS

The conventional system used in Britain for protecting landscape is the designation of certain areas and applying within them restrictive policies to control land use change. The range and extent of these designations has increased markedly over the years since the original proposals were put forward in the Dower Report on National Parks in England and Wales in 1945, and their subsequent endorsement by the National Parks Committee under the chairmanship of Sir Arthur Hobhouse *(HMSO 1947)*. The Hobhouse Report proposed 52 so called "Conservation Areas" covering about 26,000 square miles of different landscape types from all parts of England and Wales.

The creation of 10 **National Parks** in England and Wales was followed in 1956 by the commencement of a programme of designation of **Areas of Outstanding Natural Beauty** (AONBs), a process which is still continuing. There are now 38 AONBs covering some 12 per cent of England and Wales. AONB landscapes are considered no less important than those of the National Parks, but such areas are generally considered to be less suitable for recreational purposes.

Somerset has the larger part of the Exmoor National Park within its boundaries, together with the Quantock Hills and Mendip Hills AONBs. A small part of the Cranborne Chase and West Wiltshire Downs AONB also extends into the county on its eastern edge. A further area, the Blackdown Hills, is currently under consideration as a possible future AONB. The designation of this area is a firm policy proposal of the Countryside Commission *(Countryside Commission 1983a)*.

A Local Plan was adopted in 1987 for the Mendip Hills, and a Management Plan is under preparation for the Quantock Hills. Both areas have advisory committees of local authority members who co-ordinate the views of a range of interested bodies, local societies and other organisations. The importance of conserving the historic landscape is always given due priority in the work of these groups. On Exmoor similar arrangements ensure that due regard is given to the historic environment.

The designation of National Parks and AONBs is directly related to their landscape and amenity value, but within the designated areas there is a wide variety of archaeological sites, of all periods. Inclusion within these areas does not guarantee protection of these sites.

Other statutory designations include **National and Local Nature Reserves, Sites of Special Scientific**

Interest (SSSIs) and, most recently, an **Environmentally Sensitive Area** which covers more than 66,000 acres of the Somerset Levels and Moors. Whilst these designations are not specifically designed to protect historic landscapes, due regard is given to this aspect and generally the conservation objectives afford equal protection to natural and man-made features. On some sites protective designations may overlie one another, such as at Shapwick Heath, a fact which increases the protective powers available.

Non-statutory designations under the policies of the County Structure Plan or Local Plans include **Special Landscape Areas**, where the emphasis lies upon the preservation of the landscape character of the area: such plans also include and designate sites of ecological, archaeological or nature conservation importance.

The majority of forestry and agricultural operations are usually outside normal planning controls exercised by local authorities. Protection of the historic environment involves cooperation and agreements with agencies such as the Forestry Commission, the Ministry of Agriculture, individual farmers, and liaison with bodies such as the Country Landowners Association, the National Farmers Union and the Farming and Wildlife Advisory Group. In 1983 the County Council designated 27 areas of the Somerset Levels and Moors as being of special

7.3 *Common land on the Quantocks*

archaeological interest and details of these **Areas of High Archaeological Potential** (AHAPs) were circulated to individual landowners. The primary objective of this exercise was to identify these important sites and to ask private landowners to inform the County Planning Officer of any works they intend to carry out which might destroy or damage an area of archaeological interest. This system requires voluntary cooperation from farmers and has to date proved to be reasonably successful.

COMMON LAND

Commons today are a remnant of the manorial system which controlled the country's economic life in the Middle Ages. Somerset's registered common land lies principally in the uplands of Exmoor and the Quantocks but is also scattered in fragments throughout the county. Some commons are actively managed with grazing, small wood cutting or turbary rights exercised by registered holders of those rights; others are neglected and function principally as publicly accessible open space.

The main effect of the existence of common rights over a piece of land is that neither the owner nor holders of rights have ultimate authority to carry out works to the common. Public authorities and others cannot easily acquire, develop or improve such land. Therefore commons tend to remain undisturbed and as a result often contain extensive undisturbed archaeological remains. A variety of features such as old boundaries, enclosures, and occasionally settlement sites usually remain intact. Most Somerset commons are typically in permanent rough grazing, heathland or heather moor, or are wooded, with scrub woodland predominating, though a few areas carry ancient high forest.

As relics of ancient systems of land tenure and management, commons are important components of the historic landscape. The sizeable area of upland common on the Quantock Hills, for example, has probably been the single most important factor in retaining the special character of that area. However, the management of common land is becoming an increasingly acute problem as old traditions of grazing gradually die out and, because the land is essentially open and unfenced, public recreational pressures become more intense. Contrary to popular belief the public does not have the right to roam at will on common land with the exception of the areas with specific provisions for this purpose. Nevertheless there is *de facto* access to many commons which remain unchallenged by owners and commoners; however some activities, especially those involving vehicles, have given rise to concern.

Following the report of the Common Land Forum in 1986 the Government has promised early legislation to further protect commons by new management arrangements which will include free public access on foot to all such land. Subject to appropriate safeguards the passage of such legislation is to be welcomed as it will guarantee the safeguarding of an otherwise threatened landscape and amenity resource.

WOODLANDS

Woodlands, like churches and ancient roads, are amongst the most enduring features of our landscape and they can contain a rich treasure of ecological and historical interest and evidence. Only 5 per cent of Somerset is wooded, rather less than the national figure of 8 per cent, and the cover is very uneven in distribution. Large parts of the Levels and Moors are almost devoid of tree cover whilst the uplands, especially parts of the Brendons, Exmoor, Quantocks and Mendips, are by comparison well-wooded.

Almost half of Somerset's woods are known to be ancient in origin; that is to say there is evidence of woodland cover on the site dating back to at least 1600 AD. Of these, a little over half contains semi-natural woodland whilst the remainder is replanted, sometimes with predominantly alien species. Ancient woods have been generally carefully husbanded at least since Romano-British times to provide fuel, fodder and timber for construction. Few can be said to be truly 'primary' woodlands, ie relics of the natural 'wildwood' forest cover of the county, but many others, called 'secondary' woods *(Rackham 1976)*, have grown up again on land farmed by our prehistoric ancestors—the Neolithic and Bronze Age farmers who were originally responsible for the destruction of the original wildwood tracts of 5000 or more years ago.

Woodlands are significant landscape features. Ancient woodlands, in particular, contain a wealth of wildlife and historical interest and their conservation is considered to be a priority. Trees and shrubs, woodland flowers and ferns, mosses, lichens, animals and insects all occur in great profusion. When these are combined with the evidence of earlier management techniques and land tenure boundaries, they provide ample justification for stricter control policies.

Recent shifts in national policy have enhanced the protection afforded to broadleaved woodland and ancient woods in particular. Whilst the principle local authority power, the Tree Preservation Order, remains at most an imperfect tool for woodland conservation, the new emphasis given by the Forestry Commission to broadleaved woodland management schemes provides for positive long-term improvement. Felling control is another welcome and vital part of the protective powers. The acquisition of ancient woodland by bodies such as the Somerset Trust for Nature Conservation and the Woodland Trust has been strongly supported in recent years and many such woods have now come under sympathetic management eg Kings Castle Wood at Wells and Aisholt Wood on the Quantocks. Others have been notified as SSSIs and receive protection through those powers, whilst prime sites such as Rodney Stoke and Ebbor Gorge are National Nature Reserves. The 1980's has seen an immense improvement in the conservation status of these fragile, sensitive and threatened components of our historic landscape.

7.4 *Early lead working remains at Charterhouse on Mendip*

AGRICULTURE

Even more notable in the recent past has been the shift of attitudes and policies affecting agriculture and the countryside. The financial and moral embarassment of ever-increasing surpluses of certain commodities and the complexities of support mechanisms of the Common Agricultural Policy within the European Economic Community have lead to the belated realisation that the continued expansionist policies of agricultural growth could not, in the light of the resultant environmental destruction, continue to be justified *(Shoard 1980)*.

This re-think, perhaps more than any other factor, has brought home the truth that environmental protection, whether of natural or man-made features, is an issue with strong popular support and the growth of the 'Green Movement' is closely reflected in the policies of all political parties today.

The Wildlife and Countryside Act set the pattern as early as 1981 and the events of 1986–7, as the Ministers of the various departments with environmental responsibilities struggled to co-ordinate policies to accommodate the changing scene, demonstrated the shift which had taken place. For the first time in recent history, land, perhaps as much as 4.5 million hectares nationwide, was found to be surplus to the nation's food production needs.

The implications of these changes for the historic landscape remain to be seen. The introduction of milk quotas, the designation of Environmentally Sensitive Areas, the encouragement of new woodland planting on farmland and the most recently proposed "extensification" scheme will all bring landscape changes, some subtle, some more obvious. The need for diligence in monitoring new proposals and their effects will become paramount and the close co-operation of all the agencies involved is essential.

MINERAL EXTRACTION

At first sight, Somerset would not appear to be a county which is threatened by mineral extraction but its varied geology provides a wealth of different mineral resources which have been exploited at various times during the past 2000 years. The scale of quarrying varies across the county with the earliest evidence of large-scale working occurring at Charterhouse on Mendip where valuable lead and silver deposits were first exploited during Roman times and then again during the Middle Ages and the nineteenth century. This landscape is characterised by its humps and hollows. The County Council owns and manages an important site at Blackmoor where an interpretative board explaining some of the history of this area has recently been erected.

Mineral extraction in its various forms is perhaps the most devastating form of development in the countryside today because it often leads to major transformation of the landscape. The scale of such operations varies from peat diggings in the Somerset Levels to the extensive removal of parts of the Mendip limestone in such areas as Cranmore and Whatley. The introduction of the **Mineral Operators Code of Conduct** endorsed by the Confederation for British Industry has gone some way towards the archaeological monitoring of extraction but has yet to tackle the subject of preservation and conservation on any large scale *(CBI 1982)*.

Such works affect all aspects of the natural, physical and historic environment and there is often a direct conflict between the conservationist and the commercial pressures of the mineral companies . The archaeological resource is often totally destroyed, whereas the landscape and natural history interest within former quarry areas can be encouraged and nurtured after is has been disturbed. In several parts of the county, such as Ham Hill, old limestone workings have now become havens for wildlife and a popular amenity attraction. Ham Hill is now a Country Park.

In some parts of the county the archaeological and natural history interest of a particular site are inter-related. The extraction of peat on the Somerset Levels has often revealed evidence of ancient pieces of timber and the discovery and excavation of many prehistoric trackways by the Somerset Levels Project shows that these complexes are up to 6000 years old. Part of one of these trackways, the Sweet Track, is now a scheduled Ancient Monument and is situated beneath the Shapwick Heath National Nature Reserve. This part of the Reserve has a pumped irrigation scheme to maintain a high water table and in order to preserve the timber trackway it is essential that the water levels are maintained and regularly checked. This work is carried out in conjunction with the Nature Conservancy Council who are responsbile for the management of the flora and fauna in the reserve which is also dependant upon a high water table. The irrigation scheme was installed by the NCC with grant aid from the HBMC.

The publication of the **Draft Peat Local Plan** by the County Council *(Somerset County Council 1986)* outlines proposals for this part of Somerset as far as the end of the century. The needs of both archaeology and the natural

7.5 *Shapwick Heath National Nature Reserve*

environment contribute a substantial section of the plan's proposals which emphasise the need for appropriate conservation measures to protect this non-renewable landscape resource. A future vision of the peat-working area becoming a series of interconnected lakes and pools would perhaps be similar to its medieval appearance before it was drained, the significant difference being that most of the peat deposits and everything within them will have been removed in the intervening 5000 years.

In 1986 the levelling of an area of "gruffy ground" in Shipham parish marked the destruction of one of the last surviving areas of post-medieval calamine mining.

ANCIENT MONUMENTS

It is generally accepted that the historic environment is an important part of the character of this county and this country. The publication of the report of the House of Commons Environment Committee on Historic Buildings and Ancient Monuments *(HMSO 1986)* and the Department of the Environment Circular No. 8/87 have confirmed this and public opinion is now overwhelmingly in favour of conservation. How this conservation of the historic landscape is to be achieved is not so readily explained. The idea of conserving the historic landscape has been the subject of an increasing number of publications in recent years, and numerous conferences and seminars have been held to discuss landscape conservation and the management and presentation of field monuments *(Haynes 1983; Evans 1985; Hughes and Rowley 1986)*. Somerset can provide a number of examples where attempts have been made at conserving sites, monuments and buildings of archaeological and historic importance.

The statutory protection of sites considered to be of national importance is provided by the various Ancient Monuments Acts. The Ancient Monuments and Archaeological Areas Act 1979 supersedes all earlier legislation, but as yet no government circular has been issued giving guidance on the implementation of the new legislation. The Secretary of State for the Environment is required to publish a list of monuments of archaeological, architectural, historic and traditional interest which are considered to be of national importance; such sites are referred to as **scheduled ancient monuments.**

There were in 1986, 609 scheduled ancient monuments in Somerset with less than 20 per cent (116) of the total being medieval sites. Since 1974 the County Planning Department has identified more than 11,000 sites of archaeological interest in the county with medieval and post-medieval sites forming an increasingly important part of the archaeological resource with only approximately 1 per cent of the known medieval sites protected by scheduling. There is an urgent need for an accurate reassessment of the record.

In 1986 English Heritage announced their intention to enhance the list of scheduled ancient monument sites of all periods throughout England. Somerset County Council has been invited to cooperate with this proposed revision and it is expected that the total number and variety of medieval scheduled sites will be considerably increased in the next few years. The effect of this revision will be to provide a more accurate database from which informed planning decisions can be made regarding the protection of particular types of sites.

The single most important part of the 1979 Act which prevents development or destruction is Part 1.2 "which makes it an offence for any person to execute, cause or permit works to an ancient monument which may result in its demolition or damage, or cause it to be altered, flooded or tipped upon."

Works are allowed on ancient monuments, but only if the owner applies for **Scheduled Monument Consent** (SMC). The granting of SMC is not allowed without some form of archaeological recording by photographs, excavation or survey, whichever is most appropriate. Throughout the county an increasing number of SMC applications have been permitted by the Department of the Environment since 1983 and eighteen of these have affected medieval sites, the majority being bridges and standing buildings. As a proportion of these protected sites the number of archaeological field monuments affected by development has continued to be quite small, largely because of their rural nature.

7.6 *Air view of Nether Stowey Castle*

The majority of scheduled medieval sites occupy substantial areas, for example Ramspits near Westbury-sub-Mendip. The medieval motte and bailey castles at Nether Stowey and Castle Neroche and the deserted settlements of Marston Magna and Nether Adber (Mudford parish) are all good examples of medieval earthwork sites. It is often difficult for the public imagination to see such sites as anything more than a few grassy bumps and the occasional wet ditch. In contrast to this the image of the later stone-built castles at Nunney (1373 onwards) and Farleigh Hungerford (c.1370's) represents a much more romantic and more easily understood survivor of the medieval landscape.

There is a clear need for interpretation facilities to be provided at appropriate sites to enable the public to understand and appreciate the features which make up our historic landscapes. Interpretive boards have now been provided at a number of sites, such as Athelney, and there are plans for other more comprehensive facilities to be provided at selected sites in the County Council's ownership.

The Ancient Monuments and Archaeological Areas Act enables the Secretary of State to compulsorily purchase an Ancient Monument if the owner can be shown to be neglecting it. This power does not extend to local authorities but there are powers which enable them to acquire sites by agreement. The Department of the Environment can accept a monument site as a gift or contribute towards the acquisition of a site by any person including local authorities. Public ownership of important ancient monument sites can help to ensure their protection, management and interpretation. The acquisition of sites of historic importance is an important strand of County Council policy. In 1986 the County Council with grant-aid from English Heritage and the Parish Council acquired the extensive remains of an impressive medieval moated site at Marston Magna. The deserted farmstead site of Ramspits on land known as Deer Leap in Westbury sub Mendip parish contains the remains of house platforms, hollow ways and boundary banks stretching for more than 300 metres along the southern edge of the Mendip Hills. This site is in the process of being acquired by the County Council with support from the Countryside Commission and English Heritage. A programme of monument management and landscape conservation is being formulated for both sites.

The future protection of a variety of sites could be secured by similar local authority action both at County

7.7 *Moat and fishpond earthworks at Marston Magna*

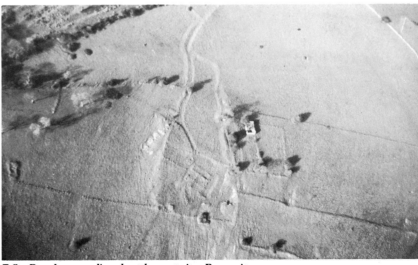

7.8 *Deerleap medieval settlement site, Ramspits, Westbury-sub-Mendip*

and District level. South Somerset District Council are attempting to formulate a management plan for the country park at Ham Hill near Stoke sub Hamdon. The County Council is directly responsible for several important archaeological sites and monuments and increased public awareness of the historic heritage has been actively pursued.

In Somerset the majority of scheduled ancient monuments are in private ownership, and the responsibility for their maintenance is usually vested with individual owners. The Secretary of State for the Environment is only responsible for maintaining sites which are in his care. These are termed **Guardianship Monuments** and there are nine examples in the county at Cleeve Abbey, Glastonbury Tribunal, Farleigh Hungerford Castle, Meare Fish House, Nunney Castle, Mulchelney Abbey, Dunster Butter Cross, Dunster Packhorse Bridge and Dunster Yarn Market.

The National Trust owns a wide variety of important archaeological sites, buildings and historic landscapes, such as Glastonbury Tor and Dunster Castle, and the management and protection of these nationally important sites is their direct responsibility. Of the English Heritage Guardianship sites in the county only Cleeve Abbey, Glastonbury Tribunal and Farleigh Hungerford are staffed and have a bookshop and sales counter providing interpretative literature. Access to and interpretation of these sites is geared to visits from a variety of interested persons, but in spite of this the long-term conservation of their historic landscapes is not always secured. The vast majority of archaeological and historically important sites are not scheduled or identified in any way on the ground or on Ordnance Survey maps. Visitors are frequently confused and unclear as to what they are looking at when they have "discovered" an historic site for the first time. The publication of academic and popular reports in conjunction with increased use of interpretative material will hopefully ensure the conservation of a large part of the historic landscape of Somerset.

On many sites the historic interest may be viewed in conjunction with other important features such as wildlife interest or public recreation opportunities. In such cases local authorities and others may obtain grant aid (to a maximum of 50 per cent) from a range of bodies including the Countryside Commission and the Nature Conservancy Council.

There are a number of areas within the county, notably within the Exmoor National Park and on the Mendip and Quantock Hills where the interpretation and the enhancement of a site should be encouraged but due care and attention to its existing condition and long term monitoring will be necessary. This will help to ensure that the important character of the landscape is preserved enabling the county to retain some of its special qualities for present and future generations to enjoy. One effect of more interpretation will be to increase the number of visitors to field monument sites and the long term effects of this need to be considered to prevent visitor erosion occurring and monuments being damaged. Some ancient monument sites such as Glastonbury Tor receive thousands of visitors every year and visitor erosion has been a real problem tackled in this case by the National Trust.

Sympathetic site ownership and management can also be achieved through acquisition by bodies such as the National Trust and the Somerset Trust for Nature Conservation. Although the latter body would always have wildlife conservation as its prime objective for the acquisition of a site, other interests can be similarly protected. Both County and District Councils are able to grant-aid such purchases by voluntary bodies, and notable recent examples are seen at Brent Knoll (NT) and Kings Castle Wood, Wells (STNC).

Project-funding by English Heritage has enabled new archaeological surveys to be carried out in several parts of the county. Detailed surveys and evaluations of the Quantock Hills AONB *(McDonnell forthcoming)*, Mendip Hills AONB (including parts of Avon) *(Ellis forthcoming)*; Somerset Claylands *(McDonnell 1985a, 1986 and forthcoming)* and parts of Exmoor *(McDonnell 1985)* have been undertaken in the last five years. The forthcoming publication by the County Council of the Quantock Hills and the Mendip Hills surveys will provide a more accurate assessment of the current state of the archaeological resource in these areas and will include some suggestions regarding its future management which can be incorporated into wider management proposals for these areas. Both Peter Ellis and Richard McDonnell have located a large number of medieval landscape features including deserted farmsteads and field systems, many of which are of countywide, if not national importance.

CONSERVATION AREAS

As has been seen many elaborate and often confusing arrangements for the evaluation and classification of the countryside have been created. These embrace National

7.9 *Brent Knoll*

Parks, Areas of Outstanding Natural Beauty, Nature Reserves, Sites of Special Scientific Interest and most recently Environmentally Sensitive Areas. Each designation is clearly defined and enjoys varying degrees of protection. Up until the late 1960's nothing comparable had been devised for safeguarding our historic towns and villages, notwithstanding the fact that the pressures for change are much greater in the urban areas than in the countryside.

The towns and villages of Somerset are as varied, interesting and in many instances as attractive in character and appearance as its countryside. They have been subject to continual change especially in the town centres. In the

recent past change has been gradual and piecemeal. In some instances planned or regular street patterns and property boundaries were consciously laid out as at Bruton, Castle Cary, Chard, Langport, Somerton and Wellington. Most of these towns were probably added to existing settlements *(Aston & Leech 1977)*. Simple linear settlements can still be seen clearly at Puckington, Barrington and most notably at Martock with Hurst and Bower Hinton *(Ellison 1983)*. Villages with open spaces still survive at for example Long Sutton, Tintinhull, Rode and North Curry.

We owe much to the slow, incremental process of renewal of the past, but today it is very different and the

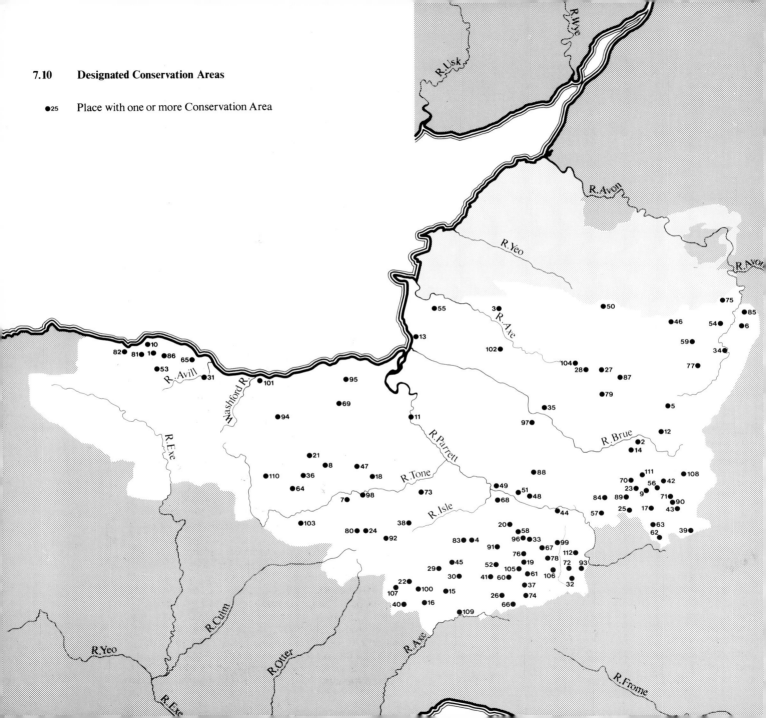

7.10 Designated Conservation Areas

● 25   Place with one or more Conservation Area

Designated Conservation Areas

1	Allerford	58	Martock & Bower Hinton
2	Ansford	59	Mells
3	Axbridge	60	Merriott
4	Barrington	61	Middle Chinnock
5	Batcombe	62	Milborne Port
6	Beckington	63	Milborne Wick
7	Bishop's Hull	64	Milverton
8	Bishop's Lydeard	65	Minehead
9	Blackford	66	Misterton
10	Bossington & West Lynch	67	Montacute
11	Bridgwater	68	Muchelney
12	Bruton	69	Nether Stowey
13	Burnham on Sea	70	North Cadbury
14	Castle Cary	71	North Cheriton
15	Chaffcombe	72	North Coker
16	Chard	73	North Curry
17	Charlton Horethorne	74	North Perrott
18	Cheddon Fitzpaine	75	Norton St Philip
19	Chiselborough	76	Norton sub Hamdon
20	Coat	77	Nunney
21	Combe Florey	78	Odcombe
22	Combe St Nicholas	79	Pilton
23	Compton Pauncefoot	80	Pitminster
24	Corfe	81	Porlock
25	Corton Denham	82	Porlock Weir
26	Crewkerne	83	Puckington
27	Croscombe	84	Queen Camel
28	Dinder	85	Rode
29	Donyatt	86	Selworthy
30	Dowlish Wake	87	Shepton Mallet
31	Dunster	88	Somerton
32	East Coker	89	South Cadbury & Cadbury Castle
33	East Stoke	90	South Cheriton
34	Frome	91	South Petherton
35	Glastonbury	92	Staple Fitzpaine
36	Halse	93	Stoford
37	Haselbury Plucknett	94	Stogumber
38	Hatch Beauchamp	95	Stogursey
39	Henstridge	96	Stoke sub Hamdon
40	Higher Wambrook	97	Street
41	Hinton St George	98	Taunton
42	Holton	99	Thorne Coffin
43	Horsington	100	Wadeford
44	Ilchester	101	Watchet
45	Ilminster	102	Wedmore
46	Kilmersdon	103	Wellington
47	Kingston St Mary	104	Wells
48	Knole	105	West Chinnock
49	Langport & Huish Episcopi	106	West Coker
50	Litton	107	Whitestaunton
51	Long Sutton	108	Wincanton
52	Lopen	109	Winsham
53	Luccombe	110	Wiveliscombe
54	Lullington	111	Woolston
55	Lympsham	112	Yeovil
56	Maperton		
57	Marston Magna		

tempo of development has quickened. Towns and villages are changing more rapidly than ever before in response to the need for more housing, better shopping facilities, light industrial estates, and the impact of motor traffic. The pattern is all too familiar with towns and villages expanding onto surrounding green field sites. The new development rarely blends into the landscape; more often than not it stands out with excessively wide roads and visibility splays being the focus of the estate and the apparently random arrangement of buildings having little regard for their established neighbours. In the past houses, farms, businesses and shops were built piecemeal one against another; the new estates of today are rigidly zoned for particular uses. Whereas the traditional character and appearance of the settlement may find feint echos in the choice of brickwork or the pitched roofs of the houses, in every other sense the new estates pay scant regard to the surrounding historic environment.

In recognition of this situation the concept of **conservation areas** was introduced by the Civic Amenities Act, 1967. This Act, which has now been incorporated and expanded in a number of subsequent Planning Acts, shifted the emphasis from merely preservation, often regarded as too restrictive, to conservation—a blend of preservation and enhancement. Conservation area policies therefore involve both protection and control of change, encouraging and sometimes actually initiating change in order to create opportunities for improvement.

Since 1969 some 134 Conservation Areas have been designated in Somerset by the County and District Councils (Fig. 7.10). The statutory definition of a conservation area is an "...area of special architectural or historic interest the character or appearance of which it is desirable to preserve or enhance" *(section 277, Town and Country Planning Act, 1971).* There is no standard specification for what constitutes a conservation area and they are of many different kinds, both large and small. In forming a judgement all factors which give the area its unique character and appearance, such as groups of historic buildings, walls, trees, archaeological sites and monuments, and so on are taken into account. An easily distinguishable physical boundary is selected which has regard to the settlement's topography including the historic alignment of streets, breaks of slopes and property boundaries—especially burgage plots and water courses.

Conservation areas in the county vary from the historic centres of Bridgwater, Taunton, Wells and Frome to the smaller towns or villages such as Axbridge, Somerton and

North

Wiveliscombe. In other places the conservation areas enclose the entire settlement including their immediate landscape setting as at Dunster and Montacute.

In the past the existence of a conservation area has been used as a control on development but in recent years a more positive approach has been adopted in the county and a programme of enhancement schemes has been implemented. Such schemes are directed at making lasting improvements and range from individual historic building repairs to landscaping open areas, tree planting, amenity lighting and traffic management. The initiative and much of the funding for enhancement schemes has primarily come from the local authorities, but as an important follow-up private individuals and companies have shown a marked increase in the level of investment in their own properties. Already the impact of enhancement works can be seen at, for example, Bridgwater, Wells, Somerton, Bruton and Wiveliscombe.

The protection and conservation of individual historic buildings is beyond the scope of this discussion but in passing it should be recorded that in 1986 the resurvey of most of the county's historic buildings was completed. As a result of this exercise the number of **listed buildings** of special architectural or historic interest has risen sharply from some 7000 to about 11,500. For the first time the true picture of the quality and quantity of historic architecture and buildings in Somerset can be appreciated, especially in the rural areas. Dr Harvey elsewhere in this volume draws attention to the many interesting follies, towers and garden architecture that survive in the county— these unique and irreplacable reminders of the past are now protected by the listed building legislation and attention is turning to the ways and means of ensuring their future. Current cases include Halswell House at Goathurst with its extraordinary ensemble of 18th century buildings and structures, and the Tuscan column at Burton Pynsent designed in 1765 by Capability Brown for William Pitt the Elder.

7.11 *Dunster conservation area*
   a. water meadows
   b. Castle and mound
   c. Deer Park
   d. village
   e. Folly
   f. Conygar Wood
   g. River Avill

7.12 *Market Cross, Somerton*

7.13 *Temple of Harmony, Halswell*

The conversion and change of use of many agricultural buildings is having a marked impact on the rural scene. Originally included in the County Structure Plan as a concession to help with preserving and maintaining historic buildings, the policy has in practice had quite the opposite effect. The relaxation of the normally strict controls on development in the countryside has been exploited to such an extent that remaining barns, stables, and other agricultural buildings, many of which are of architectural and historic interest, are now in danger from such conversions. Invariably the proposed new use is residential, being the most profitable for the owner, but it is not necessarily the most appropriate for either the building or its environment. There are residential conversions which have been sympathetically handled, but often, during the course of conversion, the structure has to be extensively altered, or, even in some cases, virtually rebuilt, to accommodate modern living requirements. This process inevitably damages the fragile architectural and historic integrity of the building. Unfortunately the financial incentive of residential conversion now normally rules out other uses, such as craft workshops or small-scale light industrial activities, which might otherwise have been able to occupy the building, with less need for alterations and change of character. In addition, all too frequently there is a danger that the appearance of the existing

7.14 *Redundant farmbuildings at Yeabridge with planning permission for conversion to residential development*

buildings and their landscape setting will be further affected by new buildings erected close by to replace those deemed 'redundant'.

THE FUTURE

The future of the countryside, as the factory floor of the farming industry, the refuge for our wildlife and plants, the resort for the recreation of an increasingly urban-based population, and as the main resource of our historic environment is in the balance. Major shifts in government policy during the 1980's have seen increasing emphasis being given to conservation in its many forms. The expansionist policies of post-war agriculture are clearly now out of place in a Britain beset by the cost of sustaining the production of surpluses of a range of commodities. The introduction of quotas on milk production seems likely to be merely the precurser for further more drastic measures to curtail over-production.

This does not necessarily bode well for the conservation of historic landscapes. For every farmer who has damaged the reputation of his industry by the destruction of features of interest or importance, there are many others, especially on family-run farms, whose stewardship, perhaps for generations, has ensured that there are still features left to be seen and interpreted. A new agricultural depression could see a major shift in land tenure, with institutional investors, anxious to maximise the profitability of their properties, taking the place of long-standing traditional family ownerships. The need to shift production to alternative crops could see ancient undisturbed pastures put to the plough, whilst to cut the costs of processed feedstuffs, livestock farmers must increasingly look to their own land to produce fodder.

New initiatives are under consideration to encourage extensive tree planting programmes on farmland. Welcome though the prospect might be of more trees of the right species and in the right place, adequate safeguards will be essential if the character and features of historic landscapes are not to be damaged or lost by unsympathetic tree planting.

Yet more radical and disturbing is the prospect of the dilution of policies which have safeguarded agricultural land from built development, but which may be seen to have less relevance at at time of over-production. Built development imposes a change which to all intents is permanent. Historic landscapes will be but part of the casualty list as more of our countryside is allowed to succumb to urban sprawl.

7.15 *The Somerset Levels near Burrow Mump*

Within this broad context of possible change other new initiatives offer more hope for effective future conservation of the historic landscape. Parts of the Somerset Levels and Moors have recently been designated as an Environmentally Sensitive Area by the Ministry of Agriculture Fisheries and Food *(MAFF 1986)*, one of the first six of such sites in England and Wales. The main objective of this designation is to ensure that traditional farming methods are employed within its boundaries and that the character of the landscape remains much the same. Individual farmers can decide for themselves if they wish to enter into an agreement with MAFF to continue to farm in traditional methods; once they have been accepted as part of the scheme they receive a subsidy payment to ensure that they help to conserve the existing landscape. This should help to protect a number of archaeological sites from damaging agricultural operations, but the

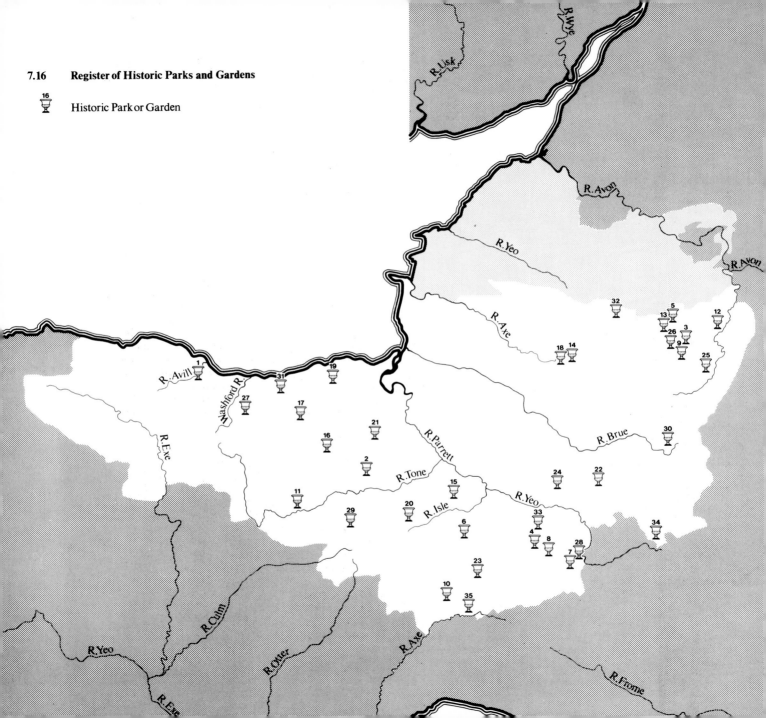

7.16   Register of Historic Parks and Gardens

16   Historic Park or Garden

Register of Historic Parks and Gardens

Grade I
1 Dunster Castle, Dunster
2 Hestercombe House, Cheddon Fitzpaine
3 Mells Manor House, Mells
4 Montacute House, Montacute

Grade II*
5 Ammerdown House, Kilmersdon
6 Barrington Court, Barrington
7 Barwick Park, Barwick
8 Brympton D'Evercy, Brympton
9 The Chantry, Whatley
10 Cricket House, Cricket St Thomas
11 Nynehead Court, Nynehead
12 Orchardleigh, Lullington

Grade II
13 Babington House, Kilmersdon
14 Bishop's Palace, Wells
15 Burton Pynsent, Curry Rivel
16 Cothelstone Manor, Cothelstone
17 Crowcombe Court, Crowcombe
18 The Deanery, Wells
19 Fairfield, Stogursey
20 Hatch Court, Hatch Beauchamp
21 Halswell Park, Goathurst
22 Hazelgrove House, Queen Camel
23 Hinton House, Hinton St George
24 Lytes Cary, Charlton Mackrell
25 Marston House, Trudoxhill
26 Mells Park, Mells
27 Nettlecombe Court, Nettlecombe
28 Newton Surmaville, Barwick
29 Poundisford Park, Pitminster
30 Redlynch Park, Bruton
31 St. Audries, West Quantoxhead
32 Ston Easton Park, Ston Easton
33 Tintinhull House, Tintinhull
34 Ven House, Milborne Port
35 Wayford Manor, Wayford

scheme will have to be monitored. It is early days to assess the possible value of these arrangements, which will depend upon a substantial entry into the scheme by individual farmers, but it is heartening that due regard is being given to archaeological and landscape conservation matters.

Historic parks and gardens often provide the setting for historic buildings. The setting is not, however, an incidental adjunct. Together a building or a monument and its surroundings are often equally important, one dependant upon the other. Visitor interest in historic gardens has risen dramatically over the past few years and the importance of this aspect of the historic heritage was recognised in the National Heritage Act 1983. In 1984 English Heritage issued the first **Register of Historic Parks and Gardens** of special interest. Whilst the present Register carries no statutory controls, it lists and grades gardens created before 1939, which still retain their special interest. The aim of the Register is to record the existence of parks and gardens so that local authorities and developers know that they should avoid them when planning road schemes and new developments generally. These first tentative steps can be seen as mirroring the advent of the Conservation Area concept in 1967, and it is to be expected that in time both financial assistance and protective legislation will eventually be introduced. Somerset has some 35 gardens and parks on the Register to be taken into account as part of the overall package of policies for safeguarding the historic landscape of the County *(see Harvey in this volume)*.

This chapter has outlined some of the measures and initiatives which contribute to the conservation of Somerset's historic landscape. The available legislation does not provide powers to guarantee adequate and comprehensive conservation. The vast majority of land in Britain is privately owned and it is to those private landowners that we must look if our heritage is to be conserved. It is therefore of paramount importance that the educational process of identifying, interpreting, and clearly explaining what we have and why it is so special must go on. The publication of this work is but part of that vital process so necessary to ensure an adequate resource for future generations.

"We cannot prevent change, but we can look very suspiciously at proposals which might involve permanent damage to the landscape." Havinden (1981 p 255)

BIBLIOGRAPHY

ADDYMAN ... South Avon Vernacular Building Research Angus ... Together ... second ... and its ... 17 pp ...

ALLAN M, 1970 *Fisons guide to gardens in England, Scotland, Ireland and Wales* Frewin, London

ALLEN D I P ... The National Heritage Act 1980 ... Development ... District of North Yorkshire ... *Geographers Transactions* ...

AND ... *Studies* 3 Oxford pp 1–33 ... before ... N90 which ... their special ... and correction factors for ... pollen spectra Danmarks Geologiske Undersogelse, Copenhagen

ASSER *De ... Alfred* ... ways of ...

ASTON ... Parish, Yeovil, Somerset *... Archaeology and Natural History* ...

ASTON ... Hardington ... 122 pp 11–18

ASTON M A, 1982 The medieval pattern 1000–2000 Wessex ...

ASTON M A, 1983 'Deserted Farmsteads on Exmoor and the Lay Subsidy of 1327 in West Somerset' *Somerset Archaeology and Natural History* 127, pp ...

ASTON M A ... Batsford ...

ASTON M A, 1985 ... 'Rural Settlement in Somerset: some preliminary thoughts ...' Hooke pp 81–100

ASTON M ... in Som ... Aston ... Sheffield pp 49–77

ASTON M A and BURROW I G, 1982 ...

ASTON M A and LEECH R H, 1977 *Historic Towns in Somerset—Archaeology and Planning* ...

ATTHILL R, 1976 ed *Mendip* ... David and Charles, Newton Abbot

AUSTIN C, BROWN M, DALLIMORE J T, HEELEY A, TAYLOR M (=Somerset and

... Sutton: their houses, ... settlement and people ...

BAKER A R H and BUTLIN R A, 1973 eds ... *Field Systems in the British Isles* Cambridge University Press

BARKER K, 1984 'Sherborne in Dorset: an Early Ecclesiastical Settlement and its Estates' ... Hawkes, J Campbell and D Brown ...

HARPER-BILL C, 1985 ... eds *The Church* ... Pre-Reformation Society Bowdell Press, London

BATES E H, 1899 ed 'Two Cartularies of The ... of Muchelney and ... county of Somerset' *Somerset* ...

BATES E H, 1900 'Gerards Survey of Somerset 1633' *Somerset Record Society* 15 ... *Ecclesiastical History of the* ... with an introduction by D ...

BERESFORD M W, 1954 *The Lost Villages of England* Lutterworth, London ... 1967 *New Towns of the* ...

BERESFORD M W and HURST J G, 1971 eds *Deserted Medieval Villages* Lutterworth, London

... 1979 'Three deserted ... settlements on Dartmoor: a report on ... Minter's excavations' *Medieval Archaeology* 23 pp 98–158

... County Council, 1986 *Review of ... Structure Plan*

... *Rural Life in Wessex 1500–1900* Moonraker, Bradford on Avon

BETTEY J H, 1983 *Church and Community in ... the Sixteenth Century* Bristol

... *The English Church and the Local Community* The Historical Association

BETTEY J H, 1986 *Wessex from AD 1000* ... London

... 1794 *General view of the ... agriculture of the county of Somerset* London

BIRCH W de G, 1885–93 *Cartularium Saxonicum* London

BLAIR J, 1985 'Secular Minster Churches in Domesday Book' in P Sawyer *Domesday Book, a reassessment* pp 104–42

BOWENS J and CHESHIRE ... *Agriculture, the Countryside and Land Use* Methuen

BOYD W E, 1984 'Prehistoric Hedges; Roman Iron Age hedges from Bar Hill' *Scottish Archaeol Rev* 3 pp 32–4

BURROW I C G, 198... 1000BC–1000AD' in Aston and Burrow pp 83–97

BUSH R J E, 1974 'Charlton Adam' pp 81–94 and 'Charlton Mackrell' pp 95–110 in Dunning 1974

BUSH R J E, 1978 'Chaffcombe pp 121–8, 'Cricket St Thomas' ..., 'Combe ... Beauchamp, pp 210–22, 'Martock, pp 78–109, 'Dowlish Wake' pp ..., 'Wayford pp 68–75 in Dunning 1978

BUSH R J E, 1985 'Clatworthy' ... 'Crowcombe' pp 54–64 in Dunning ...

CADMAN C E, 1983 'Raunds 1977–83: An Excavation Summary' *Medieval Archaeology* 27 pp 107–22

CADMAN G E and FOARD G, 1984 ... Manorial and Village Origins ... 100

CAMPBELL I and CLAXDON N, 1980 *The Law of Commons and Village Greens*, Open Spaces and Footpaths Society, Henley on Thames

CANTOR L, 198... *The medieval parks of England: a gazetteer* Loughborough

CARLEY J P, 1978 ed *John of Glastonbury's Cronica* British Archaeological Reports 47 Oxford

CARTER G, GOODE P, LAURIE K, 1982 *Humphrey Repton, Landscape Gardener 1752–1818* Sainsbury Centre for Visual Arts, Norwich

CHURCH C M, 1894 *Chapters in the Early History of the Church of Wells* Elliot Stock, London

CLAPHAM A R and GODWIN H, 1948 'Studies in the post-glacial history of British vegetation. VIII Swamping surfaces in peats of the Somerset Levels. IX Prehistoric trackways in the Somerset Levels' *Phil Trans Roy Soc London B* 233 pp 233–73

COGGINS D, FAIRLESS K J, BATEY C E,

1983 'Simy Folds: An Early Medieval Settlement Site in Upper Teasdale' *Medieval Archaeology* 27 pp 1–26

COLES J, 1982 'Prehistory in the Somerset Levels 4000–100BC' in Aston and Burrow pp 29–41

COLES J M and ORME B J, 1977 'Neolithic hurdles from Walton Heath, Somerset' and 'Rowlands's hurdle trackway' *Somerset Levels Papers* 3 pp 6–29 and 39–51

Confederation of British Industry 1982 *Archaeological Investigation—Code of Practice for Mineral Operators* London

CORCOS N J, 1982 'Shapwick: the enclosure of a Somerset parish 1515–1839' Leicester Department of English Local History unpublished MA thesis

CORCOS N J, 1983 'Early estates on the Poldens and the origin of settlement at Shapwick' *Somerset Archaeology and Natural History* 127 pp 47–53

COSTEN M, 1983 'Stantonbury and District in the Tenth Century' *Bristol and Avon Archaeology* 2 pp 25–34

COSTEN M, 1985 'Rimpton in Somerset' *Southern History* 7 pp 13–74

COSTEN M, 1988 'Huish and Worth: Old English Survivals in a Later Landscape' in eds S C Hawkes, J Campbell and D Brown *Anglo-Saxon Studies in Archaeology and History*

Countryside Commission, 1983 *Areas of Outstanding Natural Beauty—A Policy Statement* Cheltenham

Countryside Commission, 1983b *What Future for the Uplands* Cheltenham

Countryside Commission, 1983 *Small Woods on Farms* Cheltenham

Countryside Commission, 1986 *Common Land The report of the Common Land Forum* Cheltenham

Countryside Review Committee, 1976 *The Countryside, problems and policies* HMSO

Countryside Review Committee, 1979 *Conservation and the Countryside Heritage* Topic Paper no 4 HMSO

COWLEY P, 1970 *The Church Houses* London

COX J C and GRESWELL W H P, 'Forestry' *Victoria County History Somerset* 2 pp 547–72

CRITTALL E, 1953 ed *Victoria County History of Wiltshire* 7

CROSSMAN C D, 1894 'Adrian Schaell's Memoir of High Ham Church and Rectory' *Proceedings of the Somerset Archaeological and Natural History Society* 20 pp 17–22

DARVILL T, 1986 *The Archaeology of the Uplands* Council for British Archaeology London

DARVILL T, 1986 *Upland Archaeology and the future of the past* Council for British Archaeology

DILKS T B, 1933 ed 'Bridgwater Borough Archives 1200–1377' *Somerset Record Society* 48

DOWER J, 1945 *National Parks in England and Wales* HMSO

DUNNING R W, 1974 ed *Victoria County History of Somerset* 3

DUNNING R W, 1975 'The Interpretation and continuity' *Somerset Archaeology and Natural History* 119

DUNNING R W, 1976 ed *Christianity in Somerset* Somerset County Council

DUNNING R W, 1976a 'The Minster at Crewkerne' *Somerset Archaeology and Natural History* 120 pp 63–8

DUNNING R W, 1978 'Ilchester, a study in continuity' *Somerset Archaeology and Natural History* 122

DUNNING R W, 1978 'Ilchester' and 'Barrington', 'Curry Rivel', 'South Petherton' pp 130–48, 153–72 in Dunning

DUNNING R W, 1980 *Somerset and Avon* Bartholomew, Edinburgh

DUNNING R W, 1983 ed *Victoria County History of Somerset* 4 Somerset County Council, Bridgwater

DUNNING R W, 1985 *Victoria County History of Somerset* 4

DUNNING R W, 1985 'Halse' and 'Chipstable' pp... 'Huish Champflower', 'Kilve', 'West Quantoxhead', 'Quantoxhead', 'West Quantoxhead', 'Raddington' 'Dunning' in Dunning

DUNNING R W, 1985 'Old Cleeve' 'Cleeve Abbey' in Barron and Harper-Bill pp...

DUNNING R W and STAMP L D, 1978 'Crewkerne' pp 4–38 in Dunning 1978

DYER C C, 1982 'Deserted Medieval Villages in the West Midlands' *Economic History Review* 2nd Series Vol 35 No 1 Feb 1982 pp...

EDWARDS A C, 1886 'The Medieval Churchwardens Accounts of St Michael's Church, Yatton' *Somerset and Dorset Notes and Queries* 2

EKWALL E, 1960 *The Concise Oxford Dictionary of English Place Names* 4th ed

ELLIS P, forthcoming *An Archaeological Evaluation of the Mendip Hills AONB* Somerset County Council

ELLISON A, 1983 *Medieval Villages in South East Somerset* Committee for Rescue Archaeology in Avon Gloucestershire Somerset, Bristol

EVANS D MORGAN, 1985 'The Management

of Historic Landscapes' in Lambrick

GRAY H St G, 1906 'The Saxon Church at Winford' *Somerset Archaeology and Natural History*

EVERETT S, 1968 'The Domesday Geography of Three Exmoor Parishes' *Somerset Archaeology and Natural History* 112 pp 54–69

FARMER D H, 1985 *The Saints of Lincoln*

FAULL M L, 1984 ed *Studies in Late Anglo-Saxon Settlement* Department for External Studies, Oxford University

FINBERG H P R, 1964 *The Early Charters of Wessex* Leicester University Press

FINBERG H P R, 1972 *The Agrarian History of England and Wales* Cambridge

FOARD G, 1978 'Systematic fieldwalking and the investigation of Saxon settlement in Northamptonshire' *World Archaeology* 9 pp 357–74

FORESTRY COMMISSION, 1984 *Broadleaves in Britain* Edinburgh

FOX H S A, 1981 'Approaches to the adoption of the Midland system' in Rowley

FOX H S A, 1986 'The Alleged Transformation from Two-Field to Three-Field Systems in Medieval England' *The Economic History Review* Second Series Vol 39 No 4 November 1986 pp 526–548

FOWLER P J, 1975 'Archaeology and M4 and M5' *Archaeological Journal* 136 pp...

GARMONSWAY G N, 1953 *The Anglo-Saxon Chronicle* Dent, London

GERRARD C M, 1987 *Trade and Settlement in Medieval Somerset* Unpublished PhD thesis, University of Bristol

GIRLING M A, 1985 'An old forest beetle fauna from a Neolithic and Bronze Age deposit at Stileway, Somerset Levels' *The Somerset Levels Papers* pp 80–4

GODWIN H, 1956 *Studies in the history of British vegetation XIII The Meare Pool region of the Somerset Levels' *Philosophical Transactions of the Royal Society B* 239 pp 161–190

GODWIN H, 1960 'Prehistoric wooden trackways of the Somerset Levels: The constructional and chronological significance' *Proceedings of the Prehistoric Society* 26 pp 1–53

GRAY M, 1974 'The Saxon Settlement at New Wintles, Eynsham, Oxon' in ed T Rowley *Anglo-Saxon Settlement and Landscape* British Archaeological Reports 6 pp 51–55

GREEN B H, 1981 *Countryside Conservation* Allen and Unwin, London

GREEN E, 1902 *Bibliotheca Somersetensis* 3 vols Barnicott and Pearce, Taunton

GROVE R, 1983 *The Future for Forestry* British Association of Nature Conservationists

GRUNDY G B, 1927–34 'The Saxon Charters of Somerset' *Proceedings of the Somersetshire Archaeological and Natural History Society* 73–80 appendices

HADFIELD M, 1967 *Landscape with the Trees* Country Life, London

HADFIELD M, 1969 *History of British Gardening* John Murray, London

HALL D, 1981 'The Origins of Open Field Agriculture—Archaeological Fieldwork' in Rowley pp 22–38

Hampshire County Council, 1983 *Hampshire's Countryside Heritage—Ancient Woodland* Winchester

Hampshire County Council, 1984 *Hampshire's Heritage and a Policy for its future* Winchester

HARDWICK J, 1978 'Strip Lynchets: the case study of South Cadbury' *Somerset Archaeology and Natural History* 122 pp 29–35

HARRIS J, 1982 *Die Hauser der Lords und Gentlemen* Dortmund Harenburg

HARVEY J H, 1969 ed *William Worcestre: Itineraries* Oxford Medieval Texts

HARVEY J H, 1972 *The Medieval Architect* Wayland, London

HARVEY J H, 1974 *Early Nurserymen* Phillimore, Chichester

HARVEY J H, 1981 *Medieval Gardens* Batsford, London

HARVEY J H, 1982 'The Church Towers of Somerset' *Transactions of the Ancient Monuments Society* 26 pp 157–83

HASLAM J, 1984 ed *Anglo-Saxon Towns in Southern England* Phillimore, Chichester

HAVERFIELD F J, 1906 'Romano-British Somerset' in ed W. Page *Victoria County History of Somerset* 1 pp 207–371

HAVINDEN M, 1981 *The Somerset Landscape* Hodder and Stoughton, London

HAYNES J, 1983 *Historic Landscape Conservation* Gloucester

HELM P J, 1949 'The Somerset Levels in the Middle Ages' *Journal of the British Archaeological Association* 3rd Series 12 pp 37–52

HENDRY G, BANNISTER N, TOMS J, 1984 'The earthworks of an ancient woodland' *Bristol and Avon Archaeol* 3 pp 47–53

HICKS M, 1985 'Chantries, Obits and Almshouses: The Hungerford Foundations 1325–1478' in Barron and Harper-Bill pp 123–33

HILL D, 1981 *An Atlas of Anglo-Saxon England* Oxford

Historic Buildings and Monuments Commission for England, 1985 *Register of Parks and Gardens of Special Interest in England—part 36 Somerset*

HMC 1907 and 1914 Historical Manuscripts Commission *Calendar of the Manuscripts of the Dean and Chapter of Wells* 1 1907, 2 1914

HMSO, 1947 *National Parks (England and Wales)* Report of the Committee (The Hobhouse Report)

HMSO, 1986 Report of the Environment Committee

HOBHOUSE E, 1887 ed 'The Register of John of Drokensford' *Somerset Record Society* 1

HOBHOUSE E, 1890 ed 'Somerset Pre-Reformation Churchwardens' Accounts' *Somerset Record Society* 4

HODGES R, 1982 *Dark Age Economics—the origins of towns and trade A D 600–1000* Duckworth, London

HOOKE D, 1981 'Open Field Agriculture—the evidence from Pre-Conquest Charters of the West Midlands' in Rowley pp 39–63

HOOKE D, 1981a *Anglo-Saxon Landscapes of the West Midlands* British Archaeological Reports British Series Oxford 95

HOOKE D, 1985 ed *Medieval Villages: A Review of Current Work* Oxford University Committee for Archaeology, Oxford

HORNE E, 1941 'The Falconry, Farleigh Hungerford' *Proceedings of the Somerset Archaeological and Natural History Society* 87 pp 106–7

HOSKINS W G and STAMP L D, 1963 *The Common Lands of England and Wales* Collins, London

HUGHES M and ROWLEY L, eds 1986 *The Management and Preservation of Field Monuments* Department of External Studies, University of Oxford, Oxford

HUNT W, 1893 ed 'Two Chartularies of Bath Abbey' *Somerset Record Society* 7

HURST J, 1983 'The Topography of Wharram Percy Village' in eds B K Roberts and R E Glasscock *Villages, Fields and Frontiers* British Archaeological Reports International Series 185 pp 3–20

HURST J, 1984 'The Wharram Research Project Results to 1983' *Medieval Archaeology* 28 pp 77–111

JACKSON, J E, 1872 'Rowley alias Wittenham' *Wiltshire Archaeological Magazine* 13 pp 227–51

JOHN E, 1966 'Folklore Reconsidered' in E John *Orbis Britanniae* Leicester University Press

JONES B, 1974 *Follies and Grottoes* Constable, London

JONES G R J, 1979 'Multiple Estates and Early Settlement' in Sawyer pp 9–34

KELLOR J D D, 1924 *Buckland Dinham* Somerset Standard, Frome

KELLY E R, 1875 ed *County Topographies: Somerset* from the Post Office Guide

KEMBLE J M, 1839–48 *Codex Diplomaticus Aevi Saxonicum* London

KEYNES S and LAPIDGE M, 1983 eds *Alfred the Great: Asser's Life of King Alfred and other contemporary sources* Penguin, Harmonsworth

KEIL I, 1964 'The Estates of the Abbey and Glastonbury in the Later Middle Ages' Unpublished PhD Thesis, University of Bristol

KEIL I, 1965 'Farming on the Estates of Glastonbury Abbey' *Dorset Natural History and Archaeological Society* 87 pp 234–50

KING A, 1978 'Gauber High Pasture, Ribblehead—An Interim Report' in ed R A Hall *Viking Age York and the North* Council for British Archaeology Research Report 27 pp 21–25

KNOWLES D, 1963 *The Monastic Order in England* 2nd Edition Cambridge

LEACH P J, 1982 'A Deserted Farm in the Brendon Hills' *Somerset Archaeology and Natural History* 126 pp 43–60

LEECH R H, 1977 'Romano-British Rural Settlement in South Somerset and North Dorset' Unpublished PhD thesis University of Bristol

LEECH R H, 1978 'Air Reconnaissance over Somerset: some Recent Results' *Somerset Archaeology and Natural History* 122 pp 57–78

LEECH R H, 1982 *Excavations at Catsgore 1970–73: A Romano-British Village* Western Archaeological Trust Excavation Monograph 2, Bristol

LEECH R H, 1986 The Excavation of a Romano-Celtic Temple and a Later Cemetery on Lamyatt Beacon, Somerset' *Britannia* 17 pp 259–328

MACEWEN M and SINCLAIR G, 1983 *New Life for the Hills* Council for National Parks, London

MAFF, 1986 *Volume of Maps of Somerset Levels and Moors Environmentally Sensitive Areas*, London

MAXWELL-LYTE H C and DAWES M C B, 1934 eds 'The Register of Thomas Bekynton'

Somerset Record Society 49

MCDERMOTT E C, 1911 *The History of the Forest of Exmoor*

MCDONNELL R, 1985 *Recommendations for the Management of Archaeological Sites in the Exmoor National Park at Warren, Pinfold, Tom's Hill and Hayne's Allotment* Western Archaeological Trust, Bristol

MCDONNELL R, 1985a *Archaeological Survey of the Somerset Claylands: Report on Survey Work 1984–5* Somerset County Council, Taunton

MCDONNELL R, 1986 *Archaeological Survey of the Somerset Claylands: Report of Survey Work 1985–6* Somerset County Council, Taunton

MCDONNELL R, forthcoming *An Archaeological Survey of the Quantock Hills AONB* Somerset County Council, Taunton

MCGARVIE M, 1974 'Marston House' *Somerset Archaeology and Natural History* 118 pp 15–24, revised edition Foster Yeoman 1985

MCGARVIE M, 1981 *Witham Friary* Frome Society for Local Study, Frome

MCGARVIE M, 1983 'The Duckworths and the Building of Orchardleigh House' *Trans of the Ancient Monuments Society*, New Series 27 pp 119–45

MCGARVIE M, 1987 *Gardening at Marston House, 1660–1905* Frome Society for Local Study

MCGARVIE M and HARVEY J, 1980 'The Keepers Lodge in Hardington Park' *Trans of the Ancient Monuments Society* 24 pp 143–52

MILLET M and JAMES J, 1983 'Excavations at Cowdery's Down, Basingstoke, Hampshire 1978-81 *Archaeological Journal* 140 pp 151–279

MORLAND S C, 1938 'The Making of the Field System of Somerset' in T Stuart-Menteath *The Land of Britain. . . .part 86: Somerset* pp 131–7

MORRIS R, 1983 *The Church in British Archaeology* Council for British Archaeology Research report 47

MOSS C E, 1907 'Geographical Distribution of Vegetation in Somerset: Bath and Bridgwater district' *Royal Geographical Society*

MURRAY, 1882 *Handbook for travellers in Wiltshire, Dorsetshire and Somersetshire* John Murray, London

National Trust, (current) *Properties of the National Trust*

Nature Conservancy Council, 1977 *Rodney Stoke* Bishops Hull, Taunton, Somerset.

Nature Conservancy Council, 1986 *Ancient Woodlands Inventory—Somerset* Peterborough

NEALE F A, 1976 'Saxon and Medieval Landscapes' in Atthill pp 75–101

ORME B J and COLES J M, 1985 'Prehistoric woodworking from the Somerset Levels 2 Species selection and prehistoric woodlands 3 Roundwood' *Somerset Levels Papers* 11 pp 7–50

PEARCE S, 1982 ed *The Early Church in Western Britain and Ireland, Essays in Honour of C A Ralegh Radford* British Archaeological Reports British Series Oxford 102

PEARCE S, 1982a 'Estates and Church Sites in Dorset and Gloucestershire: The emergence of a Christian Society' in Pearce pp 117–138

PETERKEN G F, 1974 'A method of assessing woodland flora for conservation using indicator species' *Biol Cons* 6 pp 239–45

PETERKEN G F, 1981 *Woodland conservation and management* Chapman and Hall, London

POLLARD E, HOOPER M D, MOORE N W, 1974 *Hedges* Collins, London

RACKHAM O, 1976 *Trees and Woodland in the British Landscape* Dent, London

RACKHAM O, 1977 'Neolithic woodland management in the Somerset Levels: Garvin's, Walton Heath and Rowland's tracks' *Somerset Levels Papers* 3 pp 65–71

RACKHAM O, 1980 *Ancient woodland: its history, vegetation and uses in England* Edward Arnold, London

RACKHAM O, 1982 'The Avon Gorge and Leigh Woods' in eds M Bell and S Limbrey *Archaeological Aspects of Woodland Ecology* British Archaeological Reports International Series 146 pp 171–6

RACKHAM O, 1986 *The History of the Countryside* Dent, London

RACKHAM O, 1986a 'The ancient woods of Norfolk' *Trans Norfolk Norwich Nat Soc* 27 pp 161–77

RACKHAM O, forthcoming 'The forest of Neroche and the fuel supply of the Donyatt kilns' in eds R Coleman-Smith and T Pearson *Excavations at Donyatt, Somerset*

RAHTZ P A, 1982 'The Dark Ages 400–700AD' in Aston and Burrow pp 99–107

ROBERTS B K, 1977 *Rural Settlement in Britain* Dawson, Folkestone

ROBERTS B K, 1982 *Village Plans* Shire Archaeology, Aylesbury 27

ROBINSON M, 1978 'The problem of hedges enclosing Iron Age and Roman fields' in eds H C Bowen and P J Fowler *Early Land Allotment* British Archaeological Reports British Series 48 pp 155–8

RODWELL W J, 1982 'From Mausoleum to Minster: The Early Development of Wells Cathedral' in Pearce pp 49–59

ROWLEY T, 1981 ed *The Origins of Open-Field Agriculture* Croom Helm London

SALES J, 1980 *West Country Gardens* Alan Sutton, Gloucester

SALZMAN L F, 1952 *Building in England down to 1540: a documentary history* Clarendon Press, Oxford

SAVAGE J, 1830 *History of the Hundred of Carhampton* William Strong, Bristol

SAWYER P, 1968, ed *Anglo-Saxon Charters—An Annotated List and Bibliography*

SAWYER P, 1979 ed *English Medieval Settlement* Edward Arnold, London

SCOTT HOLMES T, 1895 and 1896 ed 'The Register of Ralph of Shrewsbury' *Somerset Record Society* 9 and 10

SCOTT HOLMES T, 1913 and 1914 ed 'The Register of Bishop Bubwith' *Somerset Record Society* 29 and 30

SHEPPARD J, 1974 'Metrological Analysis of Regular Village Plans in Yorkshire' *Agricultural History Review* 22 pp 118–35

SHEPPARD J, 1976 'Medieval Village Planning in Northern England: Some Evidence from Yorkshire' *Journal of Historical Geography* 2 pp 3–20

SHOARD M, 1980 *The Theft of the Countryside* London

SHORROCKS D M M, 1974 ed 'Medieval Deeds of Bath and District' *Somerset Record Society* 73

SIRAUT M C, 1985 'Bicknoller' pp 13–19, 'Elworthy' pp 69–73, 'Monksilver' 'Nettlecombe' pp 107–120, 'Sampford Brett' 'Stogumber' 'Nether Stowey' pp 171–200 in Dunning 1985

SIXSMITH R A, 1957 *A History of Thurlbear* privately published, Taunton

SIXSMITH R A, 1958 *Staple Fitzpaine and the Forest of Neroche* privately published, Taunton

SMIRKE E, 1866 'Early historical documents among the muniments of the town of Axbridge' *Archaeological Journal* 23 pp 224–30

SMITH A H, 1970 'English Place Name Elements' *English Place Name Society* 25 and 26

Somerset County Council, 1974 *The Quantock Hills AONB* Taunton

Somerset County Council, 1983 *Somerset County Structure Plan, Written Statement* Taunton

Somerset County Council, 1983 *Somerset Levels and Moors Plan* Taunton

Somerset County Council, 1985 *Buildings of Special Architectural or Historic Interest* Taunton

Somerset County Council, 1985 *Conservation Areas* Taunton

Somerset County Council, 1986 *Peat Local Plan—Draft for Public Consultation* Taunton

Somerset County Council and Avon County

Council, 1980 ... Written Statement Taunton ...

STRATTON J M ... William, Oxford ... Pembroke Roxburghe Club

STRONG R, 1979 *The Renaissance Garden in England* Thames and Hudson, London

STROUD D, 1975 *Capability Brown* Faber, London

STUBBS W, 1874 *Memorials of Saint Dunstan Archbishop of Canterbury* Longman and Trübner, London

TATE W E, 1948 *Somerset Enclosure Acts and Awards* Somerset Archaeological and Natural History Society

TAWNEY R H and POWER E, 1924 *Tudor Economic Documents* Volume 1 Longman, London

TAYLOR C C, 1966 ...

TAYLOR C, 1977 'Polyfocal Settlement and the English Village' *Medieval Archaeology* 21 pp 189-93

TAYLOR C C, 1983 *Village and Farmstead: A History of Rural Settlement in England* George Philip, London

THACKER C, 1979 *History of Gardens* Croom Helm, London

THIRSK J, 1976 'The Common Fields and The Origin of the Common Field' in ... *Peasants, Knights and Heretics: Studies in Medieval Social History* Cambridge University Press

THORN C and THORN F, 1980 ed *Domesday Book 8 Somerset* Phillimore, Chichester

THORPE H, 1964 'Rural Settlement' in Watson and Sissons *The British Isles: A Systematic Geography* Nelson, London pp 358-379

TOULMIN SMITH L, 1906-08 *Leland's Itinerary* George Bell and Sons, London

TURNER T H, 1851 *Notes ... Elements*, ...

WADE-MARTINS P, 1980 'Fieldwork and Excavation on Village Sites in Launditch Hundred Norfolk' *East Anglian Archaeology* 10

WATKIN A, 1947-56 ed 'The Great Chartulary of Glastonbury' *Somerset Record Society* 59, 63 and 64

WEAVER F W, 1981 ...

WEAVER F W, 1903 ed 'Somerset Wills' 1383-1500 *Somerset Record Society* 19

WEAVER F W, 1905 ed 'Somerset Wills' Area ... *Somerset Record Society*

WEAVER ... 1909 ed *Cartulary of Buckland Priory* *Somerset Record Society* 25

WEDMORE 1883 'Trees in the grounds of the Bishops Palace Wells' pamphlet

WEST S, 1985 'West Stow, The Anglo-Saxon Village' *East Anglian Archaeology* 24

WHITELOCK D, 1955 ed *English Historical Documents Vol 1 c 500-1042* Cambridge

WHITFELD M, 1974 *In Praise of Bratton St Maur* Bratton, Edinburgh

WHITFELD M, 1981 'The Fields of South-East Somerset' *Somerset Archaeology and Natural History* 125 pp 17-29

WICKHAM A K, 1965 *Churches of Somerset* David and Charles, Dawlish

WILLIAMS M, 1970 *The Draining of the Somerset Levels* Cambridge University Press

WILLIAMS M, 1970a 'The Enclosure and Reclamation of waste land in England and Wales in the 18th and 19th centuries' *Transactions of the Institute of British Geographers* 51 pp 55-69

WILLIAMS M, 1971 'The Enclosure and Reclamation of the Mendip Hills 1770-1870' *Agricultural History Review* 19 part 1 pp 65-81

WILLIAMS M, 1972 'The Enclosure of Waste Land in Somerset 1700-1900' *Transactions of the Institute of British Geographers* 57 pp 99-123

WILLIAMS M, 1976 'Mendip Farming: the last three centuries' in Atthill pp 102-25

WILLIAMSON T, 1985 'Sites in the Landscape: Approaches to the Post-Roman Settlement of South-Eastern England' *Archaeological Review from Cambridge* 4, 1 Spring 1985 pp 51-64

WILLIS D, 1916 ed *The Estate Book of Henry de Bray* Royal Historical Society Camden 3rd Series 27

WILLSON E J, 1961 *James Lee and the Vineyard Nursery Hammersmith* Hammersmith Local History Group

WOODWARD G, 1982 'Chantry Grants' *Somerset Record Society* 77

INDEX

Aisholt 114
Aldhelm bishop 41
Alford 45, 59, 85, 91
Alfred, king 41
Alfreds Tower 105
Alham river 46
Alhampton 46
almshouses 59
Almsworthy 43
Alston Sutton 53, 79
Ammerdown 104, 105
Ancient Monuments 116
Ansford 44
Areas of High Archaeological Potential 113
Areas of Outstanding Natural Beauty 111, 118
Ash 84, 93
Ashill 28, 29
Ashwick 58
assart 25, 42, 89
Asser 41
Athelney 45, 55, 63, 117
Axbridge 20, 23, 25, 28, 30, 44, 62, 121
Axe river 64

Babington 59
Badgworth 43, 53
Bagley 70
Baltonsborough 33
Baneworth 43
Banwell 45, 50, 61, 64, 101, 105
Barrington 39, 93, 104, 119
Barlinch 55
Barrow 37
Barwick 104
Batcombe 41, 42, 44, 62
Bath 37, 44, 45, 49, 55, 61, 63, 64, 105
Bathampton 44
Bathwick 105
Bayford 45
Beaufort, Cardinal 101
Beckington 39
Bede 49
Bedminster 57
Beggearn Huish 43
Berkley 58
Bickenhall 21
Bicknoller 73, 92
bishops of Bath and Wells 23, 25, 30, 57, 58,
    63, 87, 101
bishops of Coutances 99, 101, 106
bishops of Winchester 45, 53, 64, 101

Bishops Lydeard 42, 76
Black Death 59, 80
Blackdown Hills 111
Blackford 45
Blackford (Selworthy) 63
Bleadon 19, 44
bookland 39, 51
boroughs 44, 53
boundaries 43–44, 69, 92
Bratton Seymour 91
Brean 79
Brendon Hills 37, 70, 83, 85, 91
Brent 33, 87, 118
Brewham 89
Bridgwater 62, 79, 121, 123
Brihtric Grim 72
Bristol 62, 63, 64
Broadway 59
Brockley 28
Brompton 37
Brompton Ralph 92
Brompton Regis 70, 71, 72
Brown, Lancelot 103
Brue river 37, 46
Bruton 20, 28, 37, 41, 44, 55, 59, 83, 89, 101,
    119, 123
Brympton d'Evercy 102–103, 107
Buckland 58
Buckland Dinham 103
Burnham-on-Sea 43
Burrow Mump 105
Burton Pynsent 103, 105, 123
Butcombe 28, 29, 101
Butleigh 28, 35, 105–106

Cameley 59
Cannington 37, 79
Carhampton 37, 79
Castle Cary 119
castles 59, 117
Catcott 39
cathedral 51, 53
Catsgore 68
Chaffcombe 93
chantries 59
chapel 53, 57, 58
Chapel Allerton 53
Chard 64, 119
Charlcombe 44
Charles I 25
Charlton Adam 94

Charlton Horethorne 76
Charlton Mackrell 94
Charterhouse 23, 25, 63, 114
charters 19, 33–35, 42, 43
Chaucer 27
Cheddar 20, 21, 23, 25, 28, 29, 30,
    42, 50
Chedzoy 59
Chew Magna 37, 58, 64, 65, 101
Chew river 37, 58
Chew Stoke 58
Chewton Keynsham 58
Chewton Mendip 37, 62
Chilton Polden 39
Chipstable 43, 91, 92
churches 33, 49, 51–53, 55–65, 79, 113
Clatworthy 43, 91, 92
Claverham 61
Claverton 101
Cleeve 55, 64, 118
Clevedon 102, 104
Clifton (Bath) 44
Closworth 43
Codsend 94
colleges 59
Combe Hay 102
Combe St Nicholas 29, 76
common 15, 23, 25, 27, 59, 83, 92, 113
Compton Bishop 20, 41, 45
Compton Dundon 16, 73
Compton Martin 56
Congresbury 64
Conservation Areas 118–123
coppice 13, 18, 21, 23, 28, 29
Corfe 44
Corston 19, 42
Cossington 39, 73
Cothelstone 105, 106
Country Park 115, 118
Court de Wyck 61
Cranmore 105, 115
Crewkerne 37, 43, 44, 58, 62, 94
Cricket St Thomas 93
Cromwell, Thomas 64
Croscombe 61
Crowcombe 65, 91, 92, 93, 103
Cudworth 93
Culbone 56
Curry Rivel 41, 80
Cutcombe 94
Cynegils, king 49

deer 15, 20, 22, 23, 25, 89, 99
deserted settlements 23, 43, 58–59, 80–81
Dillington 39
Dinnington 39
Ditcheat 44, 46–47, 63
Dodington 92
Domesday Book 20–21, 35, 37, 39, 41, 44, 50–51, 53, 56, 63, 70–71, 99
Dommett 31
Doniford 92
Donyatt 27, 30
Doulting 63, 64
Dowlish Wake 94
Downhead 28, 29
drainage 55, 63, 64
Dundry 58, 61, 64, 105
Dunkery 87
Dulverton 72
Dunstan 20, 50
Dunster 61–62, 63, 103, 105, 118, 123

Eadmer 20
East Brent 59, 101, 102, 107
East Coker 102, 104
East Harptree 65
East Lambrook 104, 106
East Pennard 33, 41, 44, 46, 57
East Quantoxhead 92
Ebbor 43, 114
Edgar, king 51, 53
Edington 73
Edmund, king 19–20, 30, 50
Edstock 79
Egford 39
Elm Decline 17, 29
Elm Disease 17, 27
Elworthy 43, 92, 105
enclosure 23, 25, 31, 64, 80, 85, 89, 91, 97
Englishcombe 56
Enmore 43
Environmentally Sensitive Areas 112, 125
estates 35–39, 43–44, 50, 62–64, 76, 94, 101
Evercreech 46, 64, 101
Exford 43, 72
Exmoor 21, 22–23, 31, 70, 83, 111, 118

Fairfield 102
Fairoak 58
fairs 55, 65
Farleigh Hungerford 59, 105, 117, 118
Faulkland 80
Fideok 37, 42
field names 35, 43, 72, 97
Filwood 27
Flax Bourton 57
folkland 39
fords 45
Forest 15, 20, 21–27
forestry 28, 112
Fosse Way 44, 45, 46–47

Frome 37, 39, 41, 45, 83, 121
Frome river 59

gardens 59, 81, 127
Gerard, Thomas 102
Glastonbury 16, 20, 23, 33, 39, 45, 49–50, 55, 63–64, 65, 68, 76, 105, 118
Goathurst 123
Green Ore 64
Greinton 73
Guardianship Monuments 118
Gupworthy 85

Hadspen 104
Halse 92
Halsway 101
Halswell 106, 123
Ham 35
Ham Hill 115, 118
Hamp 33
Hardington 39, 59, 102, 103, 105
Hazelgrove 68, 103, 106
hedges 15, 19, 30–31, 44, 87, 89, 97
Hemington 39, 80
Henry III 23, 25
Henstridge 44, 45
Hestercombe 104
High Ham 42, 44, 59, 80
Hinton 72
Hinton Chaterhouse 55, 63–64, 65
Hinton St George 73, 93, 102, 106
Holcombe 59
Holford 91, 92
Honeywick 37
Hornblotton 37, 46–47
Horsey 79
Huish Barton 43
Huish Champflower 43, 91, 92
Huish Episcopi 42, 43
Hurscombe 70
Hutton 102

Ilchester 41, 44–45, 50
Ile 33
Ile Abbots 42
Ilminster 19, 20, 35, 39, 62
Ilton 43
infield–outfield 42, 85, 87, 91–94
iron blooms 21

Jekyll, Gertrude 104
John, king 23

Kelston 63, 103
Keynsham 50, 55, 58, 63
Kilmersdon 58
Kilton 92
Kingsbury Episcopi 72
Kingsdon 43
Kingweston 106

Knapp 73
Knight, John 23
Knights Templars 63

Lambrook 77
Lamyett 44, 46, 77
landscaping 81, 101, 127
Langport 119
Lansdown 105
Lattiford 45
lay subsidy 70–71
Leigh Court 104
Leigh on Mendip 57–58, 62, 105
Leigh Woods 27, 28
Leland, John 30–31, 58, 62
Levels 15–17, 63, 70, 83, 87, 112, 115, 118, 125
Lexworthy 43
Lilstock 92
limekiln 23
Limington 73, 77
Listed Buildings 123
Littleton 77
Little Marston 80
Litton 63
Local Plan 111, 115
Locking 57
Long Ashton 65, 99, 101, 102, 103
Long Load 43, 73
Long Sutton 76, 119
Lopen 76, 93
Lottisham 44, 46, 80
Lovington 43
Low Ham 102–103
Luccombe 70
lug 31
Lullington 39, 56–57
Lutyens, Sir Edward 104
Lyng 41
Lytes Cary 104

Manworthy 42
markets 43, 44, 55, 73, 83, 94
Marksbury 41, 42, 44
Marston Bigot 103
Marston Magna 77, 117
Martock 20, 64, 72, 73, 76, 93–94, 119
meadow 84
Meare 63, 68, 101, 118
Mells 44, 57–58, 62, 73, 101
Mendips 19, 23, 25, 28, 29, 31, 63, 70, 111, 115, 118
Merriott 76, 101
Mesolithic 29
Middlezoy 35
Midelney 103
Milborne Port 37, 44, 105
Milton Clevedon 41
Milton Mead 84
Milton Podimore 76, 84, 94

134

Milverton 42, 44
Minehead 85
mining 25, 55, 64, 116
minsters 49–53, 79
mints 44
Misterton 58
monasteries 33, 43, 49–50, 55, 58
Monksilver 92
Montacute 55, 64, 102, 105, 123
Mousehanger 71
Muchelney 33, 45, 49, 50, 55, 63, 64, 118
Mudford 45, 72, 73, 80, 94, 117
Mudgley 102

Nailsbourne 101
National Nature Reserve 28, 111, 114, 115
National Parks 111
National Trust 118
Naturalist Trust 28, 30, 114
Nature Conservancy Council 28, 115
Neolithic 17–18, 29–30
Neroche 20–21, 25, 28, 29, 30, 31, 41, 87, 89,
  117
Nether Adber 72, 117
Nether Stowey 92, 117
Nettlecombe 43, 59, 91, 92, 106
Newton 73
Newton St Loe 99, 103
Newton Surmaville 104
Northover 79
North Brewham 80
North Cadbury 41, 59
North Curry 73, 119
North Newton 73
North Petherton 25, 27, 37, 73
North Stoke 35
Norton 58
Norton St Philip 65
Norwood 101
Nunney 117, 118
nursery 31, 101–102, 106

Old Cleeve 92
open fields 19, 42–43, 84–87, 92–94
Orchardleigh 99, 104, 107
Orchard Portman 102, 107
Orchard Wyndham 103, 107
Othery 59
Otterford 44
Otterhampton 103

park 15, 25, 27, 59, 64, 87, 99, 101, 106, 127
Parret river 37
Pennard 33, 35
Pilton 19, 35, 44, 61, 63, 64, 101
Pitminster 27, 41, 42, 44
placenames 33–39, 72, 107
planned villages 43, 68, 73–76
Poelt 33, 39
Polden Hills 39, 50, 70

pollard 15
pollen 15, 17, 18
Porlock 72
pottery 27, 30, 68
Poundisford 27, 101, 102
Priddy 80
Prior Park 101, 103, 105
Priston 44
Puckington 39, 119

Quantocks 19, 25, 28, 37, 41, 70, 91, 111, 113,
  118
Quantoxhead 72
quarries 64, 114–115
Queen Camel 68, 72, 103, 106

Rackley 64
Raddington 37, 91, 92
Radstock 43
Ramspits 117
Redlynch 102, 104
Repton, Humphrey 103
Richard I 22, 101
Richard II 27
ridge and furrow 85
Rimpton 41, 42, 43, 44, 45, 72, 76
Road 70
roads 44–45, 58, 64, 101, 113
Rode 119
Rodhuish 43
Rodney Stoke 28, 29, 114
Rowdon 91
Ruishton 84
Rowley 59

St Catherine 101
St Cuthbert Out 43, 55
St Decumans 51, 92
St Mary Redcliffe 57
Sampford Brett 92
Sandford Orcas 45
Sandhill 103
Scheduled Monument Consent 116
Seaborough 58
Sedgeborough 91
Selwood 20, 21, 25, 41, 89
Selworthy 63
Shapwick 39, 43, 50, 72, 73–76, 101, 112, 115
Sharpham 101
Shepton Beauchamp 91, 93
Shepton Mallet 43
Shepton Montague 37
Shipham 80, 116
Simonsbath 72
Sites of Special Scientific Interest 111
Somerton 21, 27, 37, 43, 50, 68, 94, 119, 121,
  123
South Brent 43
South Cadbury 77, 87, 91
South Petherton 37, 50, 72, 76, 93

South Stoke 44
Spangate 70
Sparkford 45
Special Landscape Areas 112
Speckington 80
Standerwick 59, 102
Stanton Prior 44
Staple Fitzpaine 27
Staplegrove 49
Stocklinch Ottersey 59
Stogumber 92, 93
Stogursey 57, 63, 102
Stoke sub Hamdon 56–57, 63, 65, 91, 118
Ston Easton 103
Stone Allerton 53
Stowey 58
strip lynchets 87
Structure Plan 111, 124
Sutton Bingham 56
Sweet Track 16–17, 115
Sweetworthy 70
Swell 56

Taunton 19, 28, 30, 37, 41, 42, 44, 45, 49,
  52–53, 62, 83, 121
Tedbury Camp 44
Thornfalcon 43
Thurlbear 28, 29
Thynne, Sir John 101
timber 13, 19, 23
Tintinhull 61, 104, 106, 119
Tone river 37
towns 44, 55, 64, 73, 119
trackways 16–18, 115
Tree Preservation Order 114
Trent 64, 105
Tytherington 39

underwood 13, 21, 29
Upper Weare 53, 79

Valor Ecclesiasticus 59
Ven House 105
village greens 79–80
village origins 70–73

Wansdyke 44
Watchet 64, 92
Wayford 58, 94, 104
Wearne 42, 73
Weathergrove 72
Wedmore 53, 101, 102, 107
Wellington 41, 44, 45, 105, 119
Wellow 33, 43, 45, 59
Wells 23, 37, 41, 50–51, 55, 63, 64, 101, 102,
  104, 106, 114, 118, 121, 123
West Buckland 45
West Camel 80
West Coker 72
West Harptree 63

West Hatch   43
West Lydford   41
West Monkton   19
West Newton   73
West Quantoxhead   92
Westbury sub Mendip   87, 117
Westhay   16
Weston   101
Weston (Bath)   41, 42, 44
Westonzoyland   59
Whatley   115
Wheddon Cross   72
Whitelackington   39
wildwood   13, 15–17
Willet river   37
Williton   37, 50, 92
Winsford   70, 71, 85
Winscombe   18
Winsham   73
Witham Friary   55, 58, 73, 101, 103
Withiel   33
Withiel Florey   35, 83
Withycombe   85
Wittenham   59
Wiveliscombe   64, 101, 123
wood   13, 19, 23
woodbank   15, 28–29
Woodhouse   72
woodland   13, 19, 25, 27, 39–41, 44, 83, 93,
   113
Woodland Trust   114
woodmanship   13, 17–18
woodpasture   15, 27
Woodspring   55, 63
Woodworthy   43
Wookey   23, 64
Woolavington   39, 73
Woolston   73
Wootton Courtenay   70, 87
Wraxall   99

Yarlington   87
Yatton   43, 60–61, 65
Yeovil   43, 61, 62
Yeovilton   80